ANIMAL SPIRITS WITH CHINESE CHARACTERISTICS

ANIMAL SPIRITS WITH CHINESE CHARACTERISTICS

INVESTMENT BOOMS AND BUSTS IN THE WORLD'S EMERGING ECONOMIC GIANT

By Mark A. DeWeaver

First published in 2012 by
PALGRAVE MACMILLAN®
in the United States—a division of St. Martin's Press LLC,
175 Fifth Avenue, New York, NY 10010.

Where this book is distributed in the UK, Europe and the rest of the
World, this is by Palgrave Macmillan, a division of Macmillan Publishers
Limited, registered in England, company number 785998, of Houndmills,
Basingstoke, Hampshire RG21 6XS.

Palgrave Macmillan is the global academic imprint of the above
companies and has companies and representatives throughout the world.

Palgrave® and Macmillan® are registered trademarks in the United
States, the United Kingdom, Europe and other countries.

ISBN: 978–0–230–11569–9

Library of Congress Cataloging-in-Publication Data

DeWeaver, Mark A., 1962–
    Animal spirits with Chinese characteristics : investment booms and busts
    in the world's emerging economic giant / Mark A. DeWeaver.
       p.   cm.
    ISBN 978–0–230–11569–9 (hardback)
    1. Investments—China.   2. Business cycles—China.   I. Title.
    HG5782.D49 2012
    338.5′420951—dc23   2012020325

A catalogue record of the book is available from the British Library.

Design by Integra Software Services

First edition: December 2012

10 9 8 7 6 5 4 3 2 1

For my parents

Yi fang jiu luan, yi luan jiu shou, yi shou jiu jiao, yi jiao jiu fang, yi fang jiu luan.

[When policy is relaxed there is chaos; when there is chaos policy is tightened; when it is tightened people complain; when they complain policy is relaxed; when it is relaxed there is chaos.]

—Chinese saying

Contents

Figures and Tables

ACKNOWLEDGMENTS

Many people have contributed to this book. In particular, I would especially like to thank my father, Norman DeWeaver, for proofreading the entire draft. His efforts have resulted in significant improvements in both the clarity of the reasoning and the quality of the writing.

I also thank my wife, Angela See, for designing a great cover on a pro bono basis, and my mother, Mary Feeherry, who also helped proofread the draft. I am grateful for helpful comments and suggestions from Daniel Cloud of Princeton University; Tara Sinclair of George Washington University; Tim Swanson, formerly of the Anhui University of Finance and Economics; my brother, Eric DeWeaver, of the National Science Foundation; Andrew Yarrow of the Institute for American Values; seminar participants from the National Economists Club in Washington, DC; and participants in the Spring 2010 SUNY Buffalo Law School New York City Program in Finance and Law. I am also indebted to Zhang Jianjing of the Library of Congress for his invaluable assistance in navigating the library's Chinese economic statistics databases.

This book also owes a lot to my dissertation advisor, James Roumasset, of the University of Hawaii at Manoa. Many of my arguments draw heavily on ideas from welfare economics and the theory of institutions that I originally learned from him.

Finally, I'll always be grateful to my uncle, Thomas Feeherry, who was the first to put the idea of learning to read Chinese into my head. May he rest in peace.

PREFACE

A Chinese investment boom was in full swing in 1988. As a new student at Sun Yatsen University in Guangzhou, a few hours up the Pearl River from Hong Kong, the signs were all around me. Food prices were soaring at the local farmers' markets just outside the walls of our bauhinia-shaded campus. So were the black market foreign exchange rates available at the small dry-goods stores opposite the main gate or from the touts that hung around in front of all the big hotels.

Several years later I realized that these symptoms of excess demand had been the result of overinvestment. But this realization gave rise to another question: How could the economy of China—a socialist country—experience such wild gyrations? Following the start of the "reform and opening" policy in 1978, the state had relaxed its grip somewhat. But it was obviously still calling the shots.

I had not imagined that dramatic fluctuations in investment could occur under socialism. The state's firm hand, guided by the wisdom of its central planners, was supposed to keep economic activity on an even keel. Investment booms and busts were for capitalist countries.

Back then it seemed unlikely that anyone in the twenty-first century would still be analyzing trends in socialist economies. Socialism was on its way out. The successes of the Solidarity Movement in Poland and the progress of glasnost in the Soviet Union suggested that Leninist dictatorships would soon be a thing of the past. Enterprise reform and democratization were the wave of the future.

This impression was only confirmed by the student protests that began in Beijing in the spring of 1989 and quickly spread to Guangzhou and various other big cities. The Chinese Communist Party seemed destined to join its Polish counterpart in the dustbin of history.

As it turned out, of course, no transition took place. The students were crushed by the People's Liberation Army, which did not "love the people" as much as had been hoped. The Party remained very much in control.

Since then "socialism with Chinese characteristics" has kept analysts as busy as ever. Far from fading into irrelevance, the topic is becoming increasingly important as China's role in the world economy continues to expand.

I began to pay more attention to the cyclical character of Chinese investment during the early 1990s. At that point I was writing research for Peregrine Brokerage, a rising star in the Hong Kong financial firmament during the go-go years before the 1997 Asian financial crisis. As Hong Kong–listed companies began making big bets across the border, China's investment swings became a topic of considerable interest to Peregrine's foreign institutional clients.

There was plenty to write about. Following Deng Xiaoping's famous "Tour of the South" in January 1992, investment took off—as did China's nascent stock and property markets—only to come crashing back to earth in the middle of the following year. As had been the case in 1989, rapidly rising inflation left the government with no choice but to impose draconian austerity measures.

Ten years later, I watched yet another cycle unfold—this time as a fund manager. Once again the asset markets soared as an investment mania took shape. In this case, the inflationary effects were less severe and the currency was strengthening. Yet for all the dramatic changes that had taken place in China since my student days, the 2003 boom actually had more in common with the 1958 Great Leap Forward than with those of 1988 and 1992. Local government-sponsored investment in heavy industry was now the driving factor, just as it had been in Chairman Mao's time. The policy of "reform and opening" that had seemed so exciting in the 1980s had somehow taken the country back to square one.

One of my favorite books during my time at Sun Yatsen University was a 1980s Chinese bestseller titled *Sun Tzu's Art of War and Enterprise Management*. Like many modern-day applications of Sun Tzu's 2,000-year-old classic to nonmilitary fields, it began with the famous admonition to "know the other, know yourself" (often inaccurately translated as "know the enemy and know yourself"). Enterprise managers seeking the path to success in China's post-command-economy era of market competition were advised to begin by making a thorough analysis of business rivals, customers, and their own organizations.

Today, China itself is often the "other" that competitors in the global marketplace need to understand. To those with such a purely practical motive, the importance of the Chinese investment cycle will be obvious. But the average reader can find the subject equally rewarding.

China's socialist system reminds us of the foundations of prosperity in free market economies—private ownership of the means of production, free contracting, and an impartial legal system. The dynamics of Chinese booms and busts, which result from an absence of these features, make it easy to appreciate why a strong private sector, accompanied by the checks and balances of democratic political institutions, is desirable.

Knowing the other may be worthwhile for the sake of winning wars and making money. But it also contributes to knowing yourself. I hope that this book will help non-Chinese readers gain a better understanding not only of China but of their own countries as well.

CHAPTER 1

INTRODUCTION AND OVERVIEW

> Seek truth from facts.
>
> —The Book of Han

THE CHINESE ECONOMY is a large and still-expanding part of an increasingly global system. What happens in the "Middle Kingdom" now affects us all. A booming China creates opportunities and jobs all over the world. A bust would be felt from Silicon Valley to sub-Saharan Africa.

In China, as elsewhere, investment fluctuations are the primary driver of the business cycle. When investment is growing rapidly, it not only contributes directly to GDP growth but also boosts consumption via the multiplier effect. During investment slowdowns, the reverse is the case. Projects are put on hold or canceled, workers lose their jobs, and demand for both industrial products and consumer goods slows down.

This book looks closely at investment cycles in China and what we might call the "animal spirits" that drive them. It addresses two basic questions. First, what causes these cycles and how do they differ from those observed in other countries? Second, what tools does Beijing have in its economic management "toolbox" and how well do they work? The answers reveal significant differences between the Chinese economy and economies based on private enterprise. They also remind us of the limitations to any government's power to bring about economically optimal outcomes.

The analysis combines economic theory, economic history, and empirical evidence from a variety of sectors. Conventional macroeconomic models, which are built on a Western template, are inappropriate for China because of the dominant role of the state in the Chinese economy. I draw instead on the contributions of socialist theoreticians, who described how socialism is supposed to work; Austrian economists, who explained why it generally fails to live up to its promises; and on the Hungarian economist Janos Kornai's account of investment cycles in real world command economy systems. Economic history lessons are drawn both from China's own experience and from that of the former Soviet Union. Boom–bust dynamics are examined in the specific contexts of heavy industry, infrastructure, property development, and banking.

The basic premise is that contemporary Chinese investment cycles are part of the continuum of booms and busts that occurred under the old command economy (from 1949 to 1977). While new types of investment projects and financing methods have been introduced, soft budget constraints and perverse incentives at the local government level continue to be the underlying drivers. Neither extinct nor even endangered, the animal spirits of the Maoist era are still thriving more than thirty years after the introduction of China's "reform and opening" policy in 1978.

Beijing's approach to macroeconomic policy is also a holdover from the command economy. Standard monetary and fiscal policy measures are relatively ineffective. These methods of influencing private sector investment decisions do not work well in China, where most investment is undertaken by entities that are at least partially state owned, particularly by local governments. China's leaders must rely instead primarily on ad hoc administrative interventions, much as their predecessors did during the early decades of the People's Republic.

The book draws two main conclusions. First, the Chinese economic system is still far from being free-market driven. The persistence of command economy investment cycles indicates that the state, not the private sector, plays the leading role in investment decision making. There is thus considerably more continuity between the "reform and opening" period and the Maoist era than is commonly imagined. Second, Beijing's ability to control the economy is relatively weak, much as it has always been. Booms are mainly the result of local government initiatives, which often directly violate central government policy. Busts result from the reimposition of the central government's authority. This requires strict austerity measures and harsh crackdowns on violations. The central government has relatively little scope for macroeconomic "fine tuning."

1. CHINESE INVESTMENT CYCLES AND THE WORLD ECONOMY

Chinese investment cycles are an important source of economic volatility, not only for China but for the rest of the world as well. In addition to their direct effects on demand for industrial raw materials, capital equipment, and trade- and investment-related services, they also move world prices for a wide range of consumer staples. China's booms and busts have become an international phenomenon.

China is similar to most other industrialized economies in that investment is both highly cyclical and more volatile than overall GDP. The most extreme swings occurred during the command economy period, when booms in 1958, 1964, and 1969–1970 were followed by severe contractions. Since the early 1970s, the fluctuations have been more muted, with the peaks in 1978, 1984, 1993, and 2003 followed by slowdowns rather than periods of negative growth. (See Figure 1.1.)

At the same time, the investment share of GDP has been trending steadily upward for most of the past fifty years. After falling to only 15 percent in 1962 (in the aftermath of the Great Leap Forward), this metric reached 46 percent in 2010. This upward trend occurred mainly at the expense of household consumption, which fell from 71 percent to only 34 percent of GDP during the same period. (See Figure 1.2.)

Until fairly recently, Chinese investment cycles were of little more than academic interest to outsiders. Today their effects are felt on every

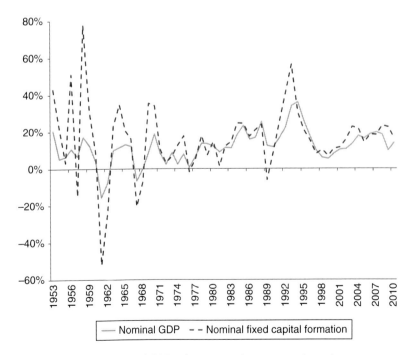

Figure 1.1   Chinese nominal GDP and investment (year-on-year changes)
Source: Bloomberg, author's calculations.

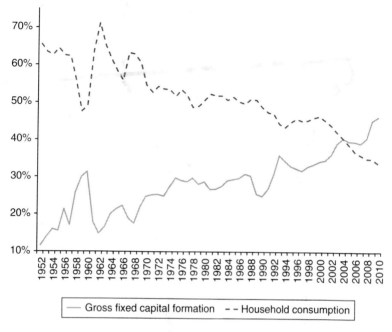

Figure 1.2   Investment and consumption as percentages of nominal GDP
Source: Bloomberg, author's calculations.

inhabited continent. Investment booms attract imports of raw materials such as coal, iron ore, and copper from as far away as Australia, Brazil, and Canada. They are good news for equipment suppliers in Japan, the European Union, the United States, and South Korea. Other beneficiaries include freight forwarders, shipping companies, port operators, engineering firms, and investment banks.

Chinese investment also has important effects on global agricultural prices. Investment draws farm labor into industry and construction and results in the large-scale conversion of farmland to industrial and residential uses. Under the old command economy, such reallocations of the factors of production led to food shortages. In the 1980s they generated trade deficits and pushed up domestic inflation. Since the 1990s, their inflationary impact has been felt throughout the world, resulting in higher prices for everything from Thai rice to Brazilian soybeans.

Chinese investment booms are no longer limited by domestic resource constraints. They draw upon the resources of the entire planet. China has become both a "locomotive" for the world economy and a source of global instability.

The fall 2010 issue of the quarterly magazine *The International Economy* contained a survey of economists and business leaders that asked, "Who globally would be the most affected if the Chinese bubble bursts?" The answers ranged from North Korea, which depends on China for over half of its external trade, to African commodity exporters such as Zambia, where copper mining is a key sector, to neighboring countries such as South Korea and Japan, which are highly dependent on exports to China for their own economic growth.

A separate article in the same issue pointed out that Germany would be hit particularly hard in the bursting bubble scenario. It is the most export-dependent of the world's major economies (exports account for about half of GDP) and now relies heavily on China because of the effect of the Eurozone sovereign debt crisis on its traditional trading partners. The author points out that Chinese markets for capital goods such as "manufacturing equipment, power generating turbines, tunnel drilling machines, chemical plants, construction equipment, green energy technology, and magnetic levitation trains" have become indispensible to German GDP growth.[1] The next downturn in China's investment cycle might well push Europe's largest economy into recession.

2. MODELS OF CHINA

Despite the increasing global importance of Chinese investment cycles, little has been written on them outside of China. Foreign observers tend to focus on the sources and sustainability of China's high GDP growth, while largely ignoring the reasons for its variability. They are primarily interested in "big picture" questions: What accounts for China's remarkable transformation into an economic superpower? Will China soon "rule the world"? Is the country on the verge of a "coming collapse"?

While ups and downs in investment growth also attract considerable attention, they are rarely seen as part of a cycle. Instead, analysts typically fit them into long-term bullish or bearish narratives. These often have as much to do with the analysts' own preconceptions as with Chinese realities.

The bulls tend to think of China as a highly organized society run according to rational principles. This idea has a long history. It can be traced back to early modern authors such as the Jesuit polymath Athanasius Kircher, whose 1677 book *China Illustrata* described the country as a realization of Plato's republic. In the modern version of this tradition, China is said to "do capitalism" better than Western countries. It is supposed to have a unique "model" that tempers the "anarchy" of the market with the rationality of the state.

Investment booms should not really be possible under such a system. Overbuilding is therefore seen as a sign of the leadership's long planning horizon rather than of inefficiency or irrationality. High vacancy rates for residential and office property, for example, are not evidence of a property bubble, as they would be elsewhere. China's long-term trend toward urbanization is instead taken to imply that excess supply in the real estate sector can always be justified on the basis of the "fundamentals."

At the same time, the bulls also typically believe Beijing's claim that China is in the midst of a transition to a more sustainable "mode of growth." Even if boom–bust investment cycles may have existed in the past, they are unlikely to occur in the future. Once Beijing has "rebalanced" the economy, consumption will be the primary source of aggregate demand. Fluctuations in investment will no longer be an issue.

For the bears, on the other hand, the Communist Party's right to rule is based on its ability to deliver economic prosperity. If GDP growth slips below some critical level, typically believed to be 8 percent, the long-suffering masses will revolt and the country will descend into chaos. In this view, China is a bit like the bus in the movie *Speed*. It will blow up as soon as it slows down. The cyclicality of investment, like the location of the next bus stop, is moot.

Neither of these extreme views is supported by the facts. The bullish view is based on an exaggerated idea of the power of the central government and its ability to impose economic rationality. In fact, investment booms in China result in excess capacity and wasted resources just as they do in other countries. During the command economy era, these problems were even more severe than they are today, despite the state's much larger role in the economy. The alleged stabilizing role of the state is nowhere to be seen in the data.

There is also no evidence for a change in the mode of growth. The decades-long trend shown in Figure 1.2 remains unbroken. Claims that a rebalancing toward household consumption is taking place ignore the fact that its share of GDP continues to shrink. It would clearly be premature to claim that investment cycles have ceased to be relevant.

The idea that the Communist Party cannot survive economic growth rates below 8 percent is also inconsistent with the facts. Even the severe contractions of the 1960s did not weaken the Party's hold on power. More recently, full-year real GDP growth rates for 1981, 1989, and 1990 fell to 5.2 percent, 4.1 percent, and 3.8 percent, respectively. By one estimate, year-on-year quarterly real growth remained below 6 percent in every quarter from the third quarter of 1989 to the first quarter of 1991, falling as low as −0.3 percent in the fourth quarter of 1989 in the aftermath of the Tiananmen "incident."[2]

Official annual growth rates for 1998 and 1999 of 7.8 percent and 7.6 percent, respectively, were not only below the 8 percent level, but are also widely believed to have been exaggerated by local government misreporting. The economist Thomas Rawski has estimated that real growth could not have exceeded 2 percent in either of these two years and may even have been negative in at least one of them.[3] If 8 percent were China's minimum speed limit, the social unrest bomb should have detonated ten years ago.

Chinese commentators do not think of investment cycles as nonexistent or irrelevant. They expect neither an imminent transformation in the mode of growth nor a catastrophic collapse. Their main concerns are with the risk of "overheating" and the prospects for countercyclical government intervention. Compared to their peers in the United States, China's mainstream media pundits have relatively little to say about the "China model." They have much more to say about excess investment, inflation, and "macroeconomic adjustment."

Indeed, one Chinese author has shown that the idea of a distinct "China model" originated in the Western media.[4] The idea of a "model," he points out, is a Western social science concept. Even for the Chinese themselves it is not possible to describe their country's supposedly unique way of doing things without using English-derived neologisms!

The "Beijing consensus" is also a foreign invention. In Beijing itself many views are advocated—some calling for reinvigorating the reform process, others for "building socialism." The only point about which there is a clear consensus among the leadership is that the Party must remain in power.

3. TRUTH FROM FACTS

Until fairly recently, China was still a far-off land onto which foreigners were free to project their own fantasies, much as it had been in the time of Athanasius Kircher. Getting the China story wrong had few practical consequences for people in other countries.

Now that China has become a "locomotive" for the world economy, this is no longer the case. The source of their train's forward motion cannot be a matter of indifference to the passengers. It has become necessary—as Deng Xiaoping liked to say, quoting the second-century chronicle *The Book of Han*—to "seek truth from facts."

The facts about China's investment cycle show that much of what has been claimed about the Chinese "model" is wrong. The country is not following a flawless master plan. Its progress is erratic. Investment decision making is no more rational in China than it is on Wall Street. Nor does the central government have any more effective means of smoothing fluctuations than do its counterparts in other countries.

The Chinese investment cycle also teaches us an important lesson about the effects of government involvement in the economy. Contrary to what many have imagined, socialism can produce booms and busts as extreme as anything generated by economies based on private enterprise. There can be no presumption that a heavier government hand at the economic tiller leads to smoother sailing.

4. AN OVERVIEW OF THE BOOK

This book argues that Chinese investment cycles are a different phenomenon from those observed in capitalist countries. The analysis shows how the country's socialist economic institutions lead to booms and why these are inevitably followed by busts resulting from central government interventions. The argument begins with some theoretical and historical preliminaries, then describes the state sector weaknesses that lead to overinvestment, and finally examines the central government's countercyclical policy options and the prospects for system reform.

Chapter 2 outlines the distinctive features of China's economic institutions. The most important of these are state ownership and local government control. The majority of China's investors are at least partially owned by the state, which also controls the banking sector and is the de facto owner of most of the country's land. China does not "do capitalism" better than other countries. The basis of its economic system, as the Chinese constitution tells us, is "socialist public ownership."

State ownership does not imply central government control. Most of China's state-owned/controlled assets are in the hands of local governments. This means that booms are led neither by Beijing nor by the private sector, but by local government officials motivated by interests all their own.

Chapter 3 begins with a review of business cycle theory, which generally blames investment booms on private sector mistakes. The implication seems to be that in the absence of a private sector there would be no cycles. This is incorrect. State ownership does not reduce volatility. Central authorities generally lack both the information necessary for detailed economic planning and the power to ensure that their plans are carried out. Lower-level officials inevitably end up controlling investment decisions and their activities are often poorly coordinated.

Some of the most extreme investment booms and busts on record occurred in China in the 1950s and 1960s. Like today's cycles, these episodes involved overinvestment by local governments followed by central government-imposed contractions.

Chapter 4 covers the history of the Chinese investment cycle from 1978 to 2009. During this period, China moved from the chronic trade deficits, exchange rate weakness, and excess demand of the 1980s and early 1990s to widening trade surpluses, currency appreciation, and excess supply. This change in the country's external position has made the investment cycle more manageable by making it possible to supplement insufficient domestic resources with imports.

The cycle's essential character has remained unchanged, however. Ironically, the very efficiency gains that made it possible for Chinese industry to expand into world markets have given the old command economy boom–bust cycle a new lease on life.

Chapter 5 analyzes the incentives facing local government officials and shows how these lead to overinvestment by both state-owned and private sector entities. The basic problem is that officials tend to be evaluated primarily on the basis of GDP growth within their jurisdictions. This provides strong incentives to maximize investment at the expense of economic rationality.

At the same time, state enterprises and investors in local-government-promoted projects can afford to bet on long shots. The former can count on bailouts when things go wrong. The latter enjoy significant cost savings, which reduce their need for financial leverage and thereby allow them to survive bigger downturns than they otherwise could. As a result, even privately owned companies overinvest.

Chapter 6 shows why the state-owned banking sector continues to finance investment booms. State ownership and Party control mean that lending is still often policy driven while prudential supervision is viewed primarily as a form of countercyclical policy.

When supervision is lax, financing becomes readily available for local-government-promoted schemes and all manner of speculative investment. Later, when Beijing wants to tighten, supervision becomes stronger. Once the risk of economic overheating has abated, this stricter stance will inevitably be abandoned. Under these conditions, technical changes to the banks' internal control systems can have only a limited impact. Ultimately, it is the Party, not the bankers, that controls credit allocation.

Chapter 7 turns to the central government's countercyclical monetary policy options. These include open market operations, changes to the required reserve ratio and administratively controlled interest rates, and credit controls targeting particular sectors and types of financing.

Soft budget constraints and China's exchange rate peg make conventional interest rate policy relatively ineffective. The central bank must rely instead mainly on administrative measures that impose or remove artificial restrictions on borrowers and lenders. This approach is undesirable because it does not allow market forces to operate. It is, however, the only effective option for an economy that is not primarily based on private enterprise.

Chapter 8 looks at nonmonetary approaches to restricting new investment and eliminating excess capacity. These include measures targeting inefficient industrial production and high-end property projects for which there is little end-user demand.

In theory, Beijing should be able to restructure the economy by administrative fiat, replacing the "creative destruction" brought about by market forces with centrally directed rationalization programs. In practice, this is only possible when special interests are unable to intervene. Excess investment must be eliminated through competition in the political rather than the economic arena. There is no guarantee that this process will result in efficient outcomes.

Chapter 9 considers Beijing's plans to transition to a more rational "mode of growth" through "scientific development." The transition is supposed to involve a shift to productivity-based development driven by technological innovation. This is to be accompanied by an increase in the share of consumption in national expenditure and a redistribution of income in favor of lower-income households.

Scientific development would make Chinese investment more rational and less volatile. So far, however, no significant reforms to China's economic institutions have been implemented. Nor have there been any real challenges to the economic power of the local governments that control much of the investment-decision-making process. The central government has failed to put its rhetoric into practice.

Chapter 10 concludes with a brief discussion of the political changes that would be required for China to change its mode of growth. These would have to include democratization and the privatization of most state-owned assets.

Such changes would require a wide-ranging reform of the state sector and entail the loss of many of the privileges that the beneficiaries of the current system now enjoy. As long as the "leadership of the Party" cannot be challenged, such a transformation is highly unlikely.

CHAPTER 2

INVESTMENT
WITH CHINESE
CHARACTERISTICS

> The basis of the socialist economic system of the People's Republic of
> China is socialist public ownership of the means of production.
>   —The Constitution of the People's Republic
>   of China, Chapter I, Article 6

AN ANALYSIS OF INVESTMENT CYCLES must begin with the underlying
economic system that gives rise to them. In China, the system is essentially socialist. The main players are state-owned enterprises and local
governments; the rules of the game are primarily a consequence of public ownership. This chapter focuses on these "Chinese characteristics,"
describing the nature and extent of the state's role in investment.

Economists define investment as current-period output set aside for
future use. This includes not only assets such as factory machinery, roads,
and intellectual property but also inventories of inputs and finished goods.
Investment cycles are thus fluctuations in the aggregate value of all such
expenditures, defined in terms of changes either in the absolute level of
investment or in its rate of growth.

In the case of China, where the level of investment has risen continuously since 1990, the growth-rate-based definition is the most appropriate. To keep things simple, it is also useful to limit consideration to
fixed capital formation (FCF) and fixed asset investment (FAI), measures that exclude inventories. The cycle considered in this book is thus a
FCF/FAI growth cycle.

There is no obvious reason why investment should necessarily be cyclical, with growth rising for several years, then peaking and declining for

several more years before rising again. One might equally well imagine a world where there was no relationship between one year and the next, so that the growth-rate series did not exhibit any obvious serial correlation. This might be the case, for example, if weather conditions were the main driving factor or if adjustments to randomly occurring technological changes could be made instantaneously.

In fact, investment cycles are observed in all industrialized countries. While not really cycles—they do not have fixed amplitudes and durations—they are easily recognizable as multiyear wave-like patterns in charts of time-series data. They are generally the most volatile contributor to the economic expansions and contractions commonly known as business cycles.

In China, the state is the country's biggest investor and dominates investment in strategic sectors. It enjoys monopoly control over land and credit. It is also free to expropriate public goods such as clean air and water for the benefit of polluting industries. Nor can there be any presumption that the country is gradually making a transition toward a Western-style private enterprise system. In recent years, some industries have even experienced a trend in the other direction, with the "state advancing and the private sector retreating (*guo jin min tui*)."

The Chinese investment cycle differs from those observed in most other countries primarily as a result of this institutional context. Chapter I, Article 1, of China's constitution sets out this context in unmistakable terms: "The socialist system is the basic system of the People's Republic of China." Article 7 goes on to state that "the state-owned economy, that is, the socialist economy with ownership by the whole people, is the leading force in the national economy." Similarly, according to Article 6, "the state upholds the basic economic system with public ownership remaining dominant and diverse forms of ownership developing side by side."

State ownership is not a straightforward phenomenon, however. Most of the state's assets are controlled by local governments rather than by the central authorities. The situation mirrors that of dynastic times, when local-level officials were responsible for all but the largest of the state's economic interventions. Misconceptions of China common among foreigners today also mirror mistaken understandings of the imperial system. In practice it never really bore much resemblance to the "oriental despotism" imagined by nineteenth- and early-twentieth-century Western authors.

This chapter opens with a look at the Chinese state's traditional role as investor, then turns to how it continues to play this role under the current system. Section 1 reaches back to China's first recorded investment boom, led by Yu the Great more than four millennia ago. Section 2 examines the nature of public ownership, a key concept for understanding how investment happens today. Section 3 explores the state's monopoly over key factors of production, while Section 4 analyzes various statistical measures of the state share of fixed asset investment (FAI). Beijing's strategy of occupying the "commanding heights" is described in Section 5. Section 6 reviews recent trends in the FAI shares of the state and private sectors, addressing the possibility that the former may now be gaining ground at the expense of the latter. Finally, Section 7 concludes by identifying two essential differences between China and private enterprise economies.

1. INVESTMENT IN THE CHINESE ECONOMY: A LONG LOOK BACK AT THEORY AND PRACTICE

The history of investment in China can be traced back to the reign of the Emperor Shun in the twenty-third century BCE. The *History Classic* tells us that in that semilegendary period, the country was once inundated by a great flood. Yu the Great, the minister of works, solved the problem by building a network of canals to drain away the floodwaters.

In recognition of his services, Shun later named the minister as his successor. On Shun's death, Yu became the founder of China's first dynasty, the Xia.

Four thousand years later, the state continues to be China's biggest investor. It still plays its traditional role, carrying out irrigation and flood-control schemes along with transport and other construction projects. Since the founding of the People's Republic in 1949, state investment has expanded into virtually every modern economic sector.

Today, the legacy of Yu the Great lives on in Hu Jintao, general secretary of the Chinese Communist Party from 2004 to 2012. Like Yu, he is a hydraulic engineer. More recent priorities are reflected in the resumes of the other eight members of the Politburo's Central Committee during Hu's term. Seven of them also had engineering backgrounds. Their specialties included electronics, chemistry, and geology.

Precedents for Chinese-style state investment are quite common. They can be found not only throughout the country's five millennia of recorded history but also in the former Soviet bloc countries and even in the "miracle" Asian economies of the 1960s, 1970s, and 1980s. However, since the fall of the iron curtain there has been no other country of comparable economic size where the state has played such a large role, both as investor and as investment promoter.

The story of Yu the Great may be contrasted with John Locke's account of the origin of investment. In the second of his *Two Treatises of Government,* Locke's hero was not a wise ruler but rather the all-too-fallible progenitor of the human race—Adam himself. Following his expulsion from paradise, it was necessary for him to improve the postlapsarian world to make it suitable for farming. He became the first investor by obeying God's commandment "to subdue the earth."[1] Locke interprets this as meaning to "improve it for the benefit of life."[2]

Yu and Adam both invested in improvements to the land. But the social consequences of their activities were quite different. Yu's success gave him the right to rule and led to the establishment of the dynastic system. For Adam and his posterity, on the other hand, Locke argues that investment gave rise to private property rights. Anyone who "subdued, tilled, and sowed" any part of the earth, "annexed to it something that was his property"[3]—his own labor—and thereby made the land he had improved his own property as well.

Whether or not we accept these stories as literally true, they provide valuable insights into the differences between the traditional Chinese conception of the role of the state and that of the modern West. In China, the state's dominant role in investment is not simply a consequence of Communist Party rule. It is entirely consistent with the country's traditional political ideology, just as the dominance of the private sector in the West reflects the spirit of Locke's *Second Treatise.*

In the Chinese story, investment gives rise to the first dynasty. It is an essential means for the state to carry out its duty to "nourish the people"—a maxim the *History Classic* attributes to Yu. Or, as the motto of the People's Republic has it nowadays, to "serve the people." For Locke, investment gives rise to private property rights.

It does not follow that state management of water-control projects historically resulted in all power being centralized in the person of the emperor, as Wittfogel claimed in his famous account of the "Asiatic mode of production."[4] Most such projects are necessarily local and fall within the purview of local governments. Furthermore, as the environmental historian Mark Elvin has pointed out, "the majority of hydraulic schemes in imperial times were relatively small-scale ... the state's main role in their regards was only arbitrating disputes between the participants, or re-establishing a local hydraulic organization that had decayed."[5] The resulting system was not Wittfogel's "Oriental despotism" but rather what Elvin calls "consultative oligarchy under central legitimation."[6] Most of the actual investing was carried out by localities and wealthy families.

Wittfogel's claim that managing hydraulic works "involves an organizational web which covers either the whole or at least the dynamic core, of the country's population"[7] is only really true for very large projects. It would be true of the 1,776-km Grand Canal, built during dynastic times to link Hangzhou and Beijing. Its modern-day counterpart, the North–South Water Transfer Project, designed to divert water from the Han River (a tributary of the Yangtze) to Northern China along a route following part of the Canal's original course, is another case in point.

Most water-management projects are not this big. Polders are a more typical example. These are fields surrounded by a dike with irrigation channels sloping down to a drainage ditch at the lowest level. From that point water can be removed when necessary using a pedaled pump.[8] In places where the land was high, an alternative was to set up small dams. These could raise the water level sufficiently to allow for irrigation using sluice gates or water wheels.[9]

Projects like these require organization at the local, not the national, level. While "hydraulic leadership" could conceivably give rise to "political leadership," as Wittfogel argued, it seems an unlikely basis for what he called "supreme political power."[10] Such leadership is not necessarily even political. In the Pearl River Delta, Marks finds that "most of the smaller irrigation projects were private affairs," while "large flood control projects" were "organized and perhaps even financed by the state." In other cases "ownership and control is not explicit."[11]

Yu the Great is more plausible as the head of a district than as the emperor of "all under heaven." To the extent that water management was the basis for political authority, it would have been the basis for strong local, rather than central, governments. Yu's legend, while ostensibly an account of the origins of imperial absolutism, actually makes more sense as a story about the emergence of powerful lower-level officials.

The fact that the dominant role of the state—or more specifically of local governments—is traditional does not necessarily mean that it is desirable under all circumstances. One problem with the "Yu the Great" model is that it requires incorruptible officials. The Han dynasty historian Sima Qian tells us that Yu dressed and ate poorly and traveled simply, traversing bogs on a sledge and crossing hills with the aid of handheld spikes. His modern-day successors prefer designer suits, lobster tails, and motorcades of German cars.

When corruption is widespread, investments that are supposed to "nourish the people" can easily become a burden rather than a benefit. Farms are confiscated without adequate compensation, untreated industrial waste poisons the air and water, and assets that are supposed to be collectively owned are expropriated by the powerful.

The legacy of Yu the Great is then turned on its head. Investment "nourishes" the state and its officials rather than the "people" while government land grabs and pollution replace the natural disasters of earlier times as threats to public well-being.

2. THE MEANING OF PUBLIC OWNERSHIP

In today's China, the majority of investment is carried out by entities that are at least partly state owned. Essential inputs such as land are also the property of the state. Understanding how Chinese investment cycles differ from those observed in capitalist economies therefore requires an analysis of the differences between public and private ownership.

For economists, ownership implies de facto property rights. These include (1) a claim to the residual surplus produced by an asset, (2) control over the asset, (3) the right to exclude others from using it, and (4) the right to sell it. This is very different from the de jure ownership evidenced by a registration document. From an economic point of view, legal title is of little relevance.

Under this definition, ownership implies risk. The residual referred to in (1) is the surplus remaining after all prior obligations have been satisfied. This residual may be either positive or negative. The owner, as residual claimant, not only receives the profits associated with the property but also bears the losses, if any.

Any classification of investment by ownership on the basis of these economic criteria is problematic when the investors are state entities. State assets typically have no clear residual claimants. The citizens to whom they ostensibly belong do not have meaningful residual claims. In contrast, the state's managers, to a much greater extent than their private sector counterparts, tend to act as residual claimants in good times, though not in bad. Officials and managers also frequently appear to be owners on the basis of (2) and (3) but not (4).

In the case of China, this kind of ambiguity is amplified. Entities are often deliberately set up in a manner that disguises the identity of their real owners. Companies registered as wholly or partly state owned are in many cases run as though they were the personal property of their managers. Managers may also set up subsidiaries, private companies, or public–private enterprises for the sole purpose of siphoning off assets from the state-owned firms that are their employers.

X. L. Ding has described a variety of schemes that have been used to "alter the ownership status of a state firm's assets by obscuring its corporate identity." He classifies these into three categories: "organizational proliferation," "consortium building," and "one manager, two businesses."[12]

The first generally involves setting up new entities that are independent in principle, but in practice have a parasitical relationship with a state firm. For example, their operations might consist entirely of buying the firm's products at a discount and selling them at market prices.

Managers using the second strategy will transfer assets to new entities that are difficult for authorities to monitor. For example, they may establish joint ventures with collective or private firms in rural areas or special economic zones. Profits are then retained in these new businesses and eventually distributed to the management through various channels.

Finally, in a "one manager, two businesses" situation, the manager simply sets up a private business, often in the name of a relative. The new business then takes advantage of the manager's dual role to obtain free access to the state firm's assets and possibly also to borrow from it on favorable terms.

The existence of such arrangements, apparently quite common, makes it impossible to draw a clear line between state and private ownership. A project classified as belonging to a limited liability company (LLC), for example, might have been undertaken by the wholly owned subsidiary of a state enterprise, in which case it would logically be thought of as a state sector investment. But if such an LLC were actually part of one of Ding's "consortia," it might make more sense to classify its projects as private.

The essential feature of the Chinese system is not simply that the majority of investment is wholly or partially state owned. Ownership itself is also much less well defined. The state cannot really be an owner in the same sense as an individual. Because its assets belong to everyone, there is also a sense in which they belong to no one.

The same could be said of state-owned assets in other countries. The vague ownership status of Chinese investment is not a characteristic of China per se. It is simply an unavoidable consequence of the large size of China's state sector.

Chinese state-owned entities are not really comparable to widely held stock-exchange-listed companies in a market economy, despite the fact that ownership is diffuse in both cases. Citizens of a country, as Alchian has noted, cannot be thought of as having voting rights proportional to their shares in national wealth. Nor can they "shift wealth among governments, as one can among different corporations."[13]

Indeed it is hard to see what criteria of ownership individual citizens' putative stakes in state property really satisfy. They are not residual claimants. They also do not own something from which others can be excluded or that they can sell. Nor does the right to vote usually give the citizen a say in how state-owned assets are used. Elections are not a satisfactory mechanism for the exercise of control rights even in a multiparty democracy, let alone in a one-party state such as China.

At the same time, as Barzel observes,[14] state-owned assets are also not in the public domain. If that were the case, there would be no one with an incentive to maintain them. Sooner or later they would cease to function. "The distinction between the private and public sectors," he finds, is therefore "not to be equated with that between the presence and absence of private property rights."[15] While such rights may be only informal, they must exist In any setting where it is necessary to incentivize performance.

In Barzel's view, the managers, officials, and workers who run the public sector are its true owners. This would not be true if they simply earned a fixed wage regardless of their performance. But, like any other employees, they inevitably share to some extent in the surplus generated by their own actions. They may be rewarded for diligence with better working conditions, promotions, or bonuses. If they do not work at all they can be fired. They are thus partial residual claimants.

This is, of course, also true of the staffs of private firms. The difference is simply one of degree. The primary residual claim to a private firm's returns is not usually in the hands of its employees. But in the case of state assets, the citizens' lack of real ownership rights means that individuals working for the state enjoy the only such rights that exist.

3. STATE-OWNED INPUTS: LAND, CREDIT, AND PUBLIC GOODS

The state's role in investment activity is not limited to its participation as full or part owner. Even wholly private projects rely on the state for land and bank credit. Investors are also often highly dependent on the lax enforcement of environmental regulations by local officials.

Article 10 of the Chinese constitution specifies that "land in the cities belongs to the state," while rural and suburban land, with a few exceptions, belongs to agricultural collectives. Collectively owned land must, in most cases, be converted to state ownership before it can be developed for nonagricultural uses. There is no private land ownership. Since 1987, however, it has been legal to buy and sell land-use rights for state-owned land covering periods of up to seventy years.

Strangely, neither the constitution nor any of the relevant laws precisely identify the agricultural collectives to which they refer. Under the administrative system established during the 1958 Great Leap Forward, rural areas were organized into communes, production brigades, and production teams. Land was collectively owned at the production team level. In the early 1980s townships replaced communes, administrative villages replaced production brigades, and natural villages/villager's groups replaced production teams. In principle, the natural villages/villager's groups should have taken over as collective landowners. But this was never made explicit.[16]

Control at this lowest level of the rural government hierarchy would give farmers the final say over how their land is used. In practice, township and administrative village leaders typically exercise the ownership rights instead. In many cases, they do so illegally, turning over collectively owned fields to developers without first going through the required conversion from collective to state ownership.[17]

Farmers thus find themselves with only a tenuous hold on their supposed collective property. With little warning, they may be forced off farms their families have worked for generations. Their compensation may be only a fraction of the market price. In one case in suburban Beijing farmers got 117 yuan per square meter for sites worth 6,750 yuan.[18] Once evicted, they often face a grim future with no way to make a living, no social safety net, and sometimes not even a place to live.

The property rights of city dwellers are no more secure. In older areas, residents typically do not have title to either the units they occupy or the associated land-use rights.[19] In the event the authorities decide to evict them, they have few legal protections and little choice but to accept whatever compensation is offered. Those refusing to move face sometimes fatal violence "at the hands of hired thugs and local police."[20] Holdouts have even been buried alive with bulldozers.[21] Municipalities effectively have a free hand to level entire neighborhoods.

The legalization of land-use rights trading made possible the large-scale expropriation of farmland and residences that had, under the old system, effectively been owned by their tenants. In the absence of a real estate market the legal ownership status of this property was relatively unimportant. Once trading in land was allowed, however, assigning all the previously existing de facto land-use rights to the state or to the higher levels of township administrations effectively transferred control to local governments.

This development has been likened to the so-called tragedy of the commons that occurred in late fifteenth- and early-sixteenth-century England.[22] In that episode, powerful landlords deprived villagers of land they had formerly owned communally. Fields that had been available to anyone for uses such as farming, grazing, and gathering firewood were enclosed and taken over by a single owner. Most commonly such enclosures were used to raise sheep, leading Thomas Moore (in *Utopia*) to speak of "sheep eating men." Marx devoted the entire twenty-seventh chapter of *Das Kapital* to this example of what he called "primitive capital accumulation."

In today's China the tragedy is being restaged, with factories, property developments, and even Olympic Games facilities replacing sheep farms, Communist Party cadres acting the part of Renaissance nobles, and ordinary Chinese citizens playing British peasants. The main elements of the plot are the same. First, property is transferred from weak hands to strong through the introduction of new private ownership rights. Next, large-scale forced evictions are followed by the wholesale destruction of farms and residential areas. Finally, dispossessed farmers, like the "vagabonds" created by the enclosure movement, have no alternative but to migrate to the cities in search of work.

The state of China's natural environment is the result of a similar dynamic. Here the assets being expropriated are public goods. These are, by definition, (1) nonrival—one person's use does not reduce the total amount available—and (2) nonexcludable—no one's access can be blocked. (Note that the term "public good" does not mean "good provided by the government" as is sometimes imagined.)

Environmental amenities such as clean air and clean water are classic examples. Although these cannot literally be enclosed, they are similar to collectively owned land because of the diffuse nature of the associated property rights. While public goods expropriation involves the destruction of an asset rather than its use, the risk to politically powerless collective owners is essentially the same.

China does not lack environmental regulations, but their enforcement is left almost entirely at the discretion of local governments. In the absence of effective tort law, localities have become the willing accomplices of investors, both public and private, in the destruction of the natural environment. The theft of public goods has become commonplace, as manufacturers are routinely allowed to operate without required pollution-abatement equipment. Factories can emit dangerously high levels of poisonous chemicals into the air and dump untreated wastewater into rivers and streams with almost complete impunity.

This problem is common to many countries. The Chinese case is particularly severe, however, due to a combination of local government power, high economic growth, and a philosophy of "catching up" with the developed world at all costs.

Most fixed asset investment requires land and environmental approvals. Local governments have almost complete control over both, making their cooperation indispensable. As a result, outcomes are quite different from those that would occur if land ownership were mainly in private hands and laws protecting rights to public goods were effectively enforced. The composition of investment, whether public or private, will inevitably be skewed toward whatever sectors local officials consider to be priorities. Successful businesses will almost exclusively be those they decide to promote.

The state also monopolizes the banking system. The five largest banks—the Industrial and Commercial Bank of China, China Construction Bank, the Bank of China, the Agricultural Bank of China, and the Bank of Communications—accounted for 47 percent of total commercial bank assets as of March 2012. These are all centrally controlled enterprises under the Ministry of Finance. Joint stock commercial banks, some centrally controlled, others under local governments, accounted for 16 percent. Commercial banks set up by municipalities accounted for 9 percent, while a variety of other institutions including thousands of small rural commercial banks and rural cooperative banks accounted for the remaining 28 percent.[23]

With the exception of Minsheng Bank, a joint stock commercial bank in which non-state-owned enterprises own the controlling shares, private sector lenders are generally quite small. Typically they are family operated nonbank financial institutions.

Access to bank credit is thus concentrated almost entirely in state hands. Naturally this means that investment favored by the government is more likely to get financing. And even if the relationship between the banks and the state were entirely "arms length," bankers would still be biased in favor of government-backed projects. These not only have more land to use as collateral but are also perceived as having at least an implicit government guarantee. Such borrowers are simply better risks.

State dominance is thus not only a matter of the state being the largest investor. State control over land, public goods, and credit is equally important. In addition to controlling most of the players, governments at various levels also make up the rules, act as referee, and own the playing field, the goal posts, and the ball.

4. THE STATE AS INVESTOR

Chinese investment may be classified in two ways. First, there is the obvious distinction between the state and non-state sectors. Second, within the state sector there are central and local-level entities. These may be government departments—provincial transportation bureaus, for example—or state-owned enterprises. Most of the latter, while officially the property of the whole people, are controlled by local governments.

China's best-known investors can be found among the 120 firms directly administered by the State Council's State-owned Asset Supervision and Administration Commission (SASAC). (The State Council is the country's highest executive body.) Examples include the oil and gas giant China National Petroleum Corporation; China Three Gorges

Corporation, which built and operates the Three Gorges Dam; and China Aerospace Science and Technology Corporation, whose products include Long March rockets and the Shenzhou manned spacecraft.[24] Such "central enterprises" typically dominate sectors considered to be strategic—oil and gas, telecommunications, engineering and construction, and electric power, for example. Many rank among the top names in their industries worldwide.

The massive size of these enterprises might lead one to conclude that the central government directly controls most Chinese investment. Such a conclusion would be unwarranted. Centrally directed projects like the Grand Canal and the Great Wall of China are not proof of imperial absolutism. Neither are today's massive hydropower and high-speed rail schemes evidence for a modern-day "hydraulic despotism."

Just as most pre-modern hydraulic projects were local, most investment today comes under the jurisdiction of local governments. (See Chapter 5 for some examples.) While central government projects dominate the headlines, smaller-scale schemes under local control are of much greater economic significance. In 2010 only 9.4 percent of urban FAI by "construction units, enterprises, institutions, or administrative units" was regulated by the central government.[25] (Urban FAI accounted for 86.8 percent of that year's nationwide FAI total.) Beijing continues to be primarily a source of legitimacy rather than a manager.

The *China Statistical Yearbook* gives FAI totals for eleven types of investor based on legal status of registration. Table 2.1 gives the percentage of the 2010 nationwide total for each. These statistics include investment not only by enterprises but also by "government agencies,

Table 2.1   FAI by type of investor

Type of investor	FAI share (%)
(1) State owned	30.0
(2) Collectively owned	3.6
(3) Cooperative*	0.5
(4) Jointly owned	0.3
(5) Limited liability (LLCs)	25.3
(6) Shareholding	6.2
(7) Private	21.8
(8) Self-employed individuals	3.4
(9) Other domestic	2.8
(10) Funds from Hong Kong, Macao, and Taiwan	3.0
(11) Foreign funds	3.2

*Equivalent to Western-style private partnerships.
Source: China Statistical Yearbook 2011.

institutions, and social organizations which are not registered in industrial and commercial administration agencies." These are classified "mainly by their sources of funding and manner of management," which presumably means that most are in the state-owned category.

From a legal point of view, (1) and (2) are the only domestic categories that are unambiguously publicly owned. Only (3), (7), and (8) are clearly private. Note that "private enterprises" are defined as "profit-making economic units invested [in] and established by natural persons," including "private limited liability corporations, private shareholding corporations, private partnership enterprises, and private-funded enterprises."[26] This implies that the separate categories for LLCs (5) and shareholding corporations (6) do not include wholly privately owned entities.

Purely private domestic FAI thus accounts for only 27 percent of the domestic total (categories 1–9). Unambiguously publicly owned FAI has the largest share, 36 percent, while the LLC and shareholding company investment included in categories (5) and (6) contribute another 34 percent. (The "other" category accounts for the final 4 percent.)

Clearly the majority of investment involves some degree of state participation. The extent of this participation depends on the status of the category (5) and (6) investors. Huang Yasheng has made a convincing case that these are predominantly controlled by state-owned entities.[27] They include, he points out, companies like Daqing Oil Field, an LLC that is 100 percent owned by PetroChina. Or PetroChina itself, which is a listed subsidiary of China National Petroleum Corporation. Or SAIC Motor, a listed company that is 70 percent owned by the Shanghai city government.

While their legal form is different, from the point of view of ownership and control rights such companies do not differ in any significant way from other state-owned investors. They are a product of the state-owned enterprise reforms of the 1990s, which, Huang finds, "had nothing to do with actually changing the owners of the firms" but rather served to securitize the state's "previously implicit equity holdings."[28] These reforms, while copying the "superficial forms of a capitalistic market economy," were never intended to result in genuine privatization. Boards of directors were introduced, but the real power remained in the hands of companies' Party committees. State-owned enterprise equity was sold to the public, but the state almost always retained a controlling stake.

Including FAI by foreign investors and those from Hong Kong, Macao, and Taiwan raises the private percentage somewhat, but by less than these investors' combined 6.2 percent share. Much of this investment actually comes from domestic entities taking advantage of tax and other incentives by "round tripping" their funds through offshore companies.

→ private 30% ↷ —> public 70% ↷

Investment by Hong Kong's so-called red chips—Hong Kong–registered mainland companies listed on the Hong Kong Stock Exchange—would be included in this category. The red chips are practically all state controlled. They include names such as China Overseas Land and CITIC Pacific—both subsidiaries of central enterprises, Guangdong Investment—the listed flagship of the Guangdong provincial government, and Beijing Enterprises—an arm of the Beijing municipality. There is no reason not to classify them as state sector companies.

5. CONTROLLING THE COMMANDING HEIGHTS

The state's dominant role in investment is evidence of a desire to "occupy the commanding heights." This is a strategy originally described by Lenin in a 1922 address to the Fourth Congress of the Communist International on his New Economic Policy. The NEP, introduced in the previous year, was a retreat from earlier attempts to achieve a "direct transition to purely socialist forms," as Lenin put it. These attempts, combined with the disastrous effects of the Russian Civil War, resulted in an economic collapse. The Soviet government had no choice but to restore a measure of private participation in the economy.

The fact that command economy methods had failed was not taken as a sign that they were unworkable. For Lenin, the problem was simply that their time had not yet come. He decided that a preliminary period of "state capitalism" would be necessary before "full communism" could be realized.

Retaining state control over key sectors was necessary to prevent a return to the prerevolutionary status quo during this transitional period. In his address, Lenin advocated (1) keeping the land and the "vital branches of industry" in the hands of the state, (2) leasing out "only a certain number of small and medium plants," and (3) forming "mixed companies," in which "part of the capital belongs to private capitalists—and foreign capitalists at that—and the other part belongs to the state."[29]

Surprisingly, despite being considerably more advanced economically, today's China has much in common with the NEP-era Soviet Union. All land is state owned, as are many strategic sectors. The largest plants are almost all part of central government-controlled enterprises. Mixed companies, like those listed on the Hong Kong Stock Exchange, are quite common.

The extent to which the state controls the "commanding heights" is easy to see from the FAI data. Investors in the "state-holding" category accounted for over 60 percent of urban fixed asset investment in nine of the nineteen sectors for which statistics are included in the 2011 *China Statistical Yearbook*.[30] (See Table 2.2.)

Table 2.2   Sectors with the largest state investment shares

Sector	State share (%)
Production and supply of electricity, gas, and water	79
Transport, storage, and post	88
Information transmission, computer services, and software	92
Financial intermediation	72
Scientific research, technical services, and geologic prospecting	66
Management of water conservancy, environment, and public facilities	86
Education	84
Health, social security, and social welfare	83
Public management and social organization	78

Source: China Statistical Yearbook 2011.

The state would be the main investor in some of these areas in practically any country. It is not surprising to find large state shares in fields such as environmental management, education, and social organizations, for example. Yet the fact remains that there is still very little private investment even in sectors where there is no obvious reason for the state to intervene. In many countries, and indeed even in China's own Hong Kong Special Administrative Region, industries such as electricity, natural gas, information transmission, and finance are dominated by privately owned companies.

The sectors in Table 2.2 are of obvious economic importance. But the fact that an industry is important does not necessarily mean that the government should run it. In fact, given the inefficiencies associated with state management, it might make more sense to argue from an economic efficiency perspective that the "commanding heights" should be occupied by privately owned businesses.

It is also worth noting that there is little justification in Marxist theory for Lenin's commanding heights idea. According to Marx and Engels, communism was supposed to be the culminating phase of an evolutionary process beginning with the "primitive communism" of the tribe and progressing through "slave society," feudalism, and capitalism.[31] Each stage is supposed to emerge from the last as a result of changes in the "mode of production" (primarily brought about by technological innovation), which lead to "contradictions" between the existing social order and its material foundation.

Lenin's "state capitalism" does not fit into this schema at all. The transition to communism is supposed to occur spontaneously once capitalism is no longer viable. It is not supposed to be preceded by a period during which the state takes over key industries and continues to run them in the same way (though perhaps not as well) as their former owners, while the rest of the economy remains in private hands.

In hindsight, the main purpose of the NEP was to allow the private sector to accumulate a surplus that the state could expropriate for large-scale investment in heavy industry starting in the 1930s. The NEP was only a temporary retreat in the Soviet advance toward total state control of the economy.

The Chinese government's commanding heights policy is less easily explained as part of a long-range development strategy. While it also originated (in 1978) as a retreat from command economy methods, it has evolved into a permanent state of affairs rather than a transitional phenomenon. After over thirty years, it makes sense in economic terms as neither a temporary retreat nor part of a transition to a private enterprise system.

If the state's occupation of the commanding heights does not serve any real economic purpose, its true purpose can only be presumed to be political. It appears to be little more than a means of preserving Communist Party rule.

6. WITHER THE PRIVATE SECTOR?

The private sector has grown from where it was in 1980. However, its increased role in Chinese investment occurred primarily in the subsequent decade. It slumped in the 1990s and regained the lost ground only in the 2004 to 2007 period. Overall its percentage of total FAI has fluctuated during the last three decades, hitting a low of 11 percent in 1993 and a high of 26 percent in 2010. (See Figure 2.1. As in Section 4, the "private" share for each year is the sum of investment by domestic cooperatives, private investors, and self-employed individuals divided by total domestic urban FAI.)

The fact that the series does not exhibit a linear trend is evidence that China's high GDP growth over the period cannot be attributed to any consistent long-range policy on economic reform. The relatively liberal policies of the 1980s were replaced, following the 1989 Tiananmen student protests, with policies favoring the state sector in the 1990s.[32] The private FAI share returned to pre-Tiananmen levels only in 2006 and has since shown signs of leveling off.

Since 2008, Chinese commentators have noted that the policy environment has again shifted in favor of the state sector. This may in part be a result of the stimulus measures that the central government adopted in the wake of the global economic crisis. These were particularly supportive of local government and state enterprise projects. The apparent failure of

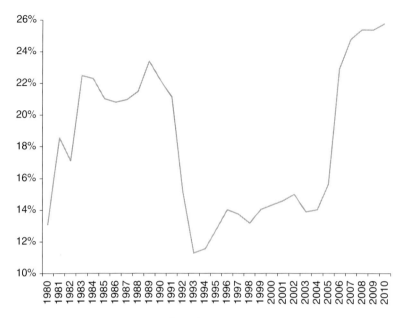

Figure 2.1   Private investment as a share of FAI

Source: China Statistical Yearbook, various years.

market economies around the world may also have convinced some factions within the leadership that "building" socialism might be preferable to reforming it.

The advance of the state is not yet obvious at the aggregate level. Figure 2.1 shows a leveling off of the private sector share rather than a decline. Proponents of the idea that "the state is advancing while the private sector is retreating" base their arguments mainly on trends in particular industries or on anecdotal information.

A report by Unirule, a Beijing-based think tank, cites a variety of industries in which state sector actors appear to have successfully muscled in on non-state competitors. For example, the state-owned enterprise share of gross industrial output value in the "electric power, steam, and hot water production and supply industries" rose from 90.5 percent in 2005 to 98.9 percent in 2008.[33] From 2008 to 2011, two-thirds of the private sector petroleum wholesalers closed as did one-third of the privately owned gas stations.[34]

In some cases private companies have simply been forced to merge with their state sector competitors. In 2009, Shandong Province forced Rizhao Steel, a private company with a net profit of 1.8 billion yuan in the first half of 2009, to merge with Shandong Steel, a loss-making state-owned enterprise controlled by the provincial government.[35] Similarly, in Shanxi Province, hundreds of private coal mine owners have been forced to sell to state-owned rivals. Compensation was set administratively at levels as low as a tenth of the prevailing market price for the private mines' reserves.[36]

The main justification for such policies is that they are efficiency enhancing. The Chinese economy, it is argued, needs larger companies to remain competitive. But if China's industrial structure is to be changed by administrative fiat, it seems inevitable under current conditions that the private sector will lose out.

Consolidation that leads to a larger role for the state is unlikely to be beneficial. The Unirule report found that the average return on equity (ROE) for the period from 2001 to 2009 was 8.16 percent for "state-owned and state-holding industrial enterprises." The figure for all industrial enterprises "above designated size" was 12.9 percent.[37]

The authors point out that these two ROEs are not comparable because the state sector return was inflated by a variety of direct and indirect subsidies. The largest of these was the savings in interest expense enjoyed by state enterprises, which borrowed at an average rate of 1.6 percent while the equivalent rate for other borrowers was 4.68 percent. Adjusting for this, and for fiscal subsidies and savings on rent and resource taxes, they calculate a 2001–2009 average return for state-owned and state-holding industrial enterprises of –1.47 percent.[38]

While the private sector may not yet be in "retreat," the near term outlook does not look promising for purely privately owned firms.

7. FREEWHEELING SOCIALISM

The nature of the Chinese economic system has important implications for an analysis of the investment cycle. If the system is a kind of "freewheeling capitalism," as is sometimes claimed, China is now socialist in name only. The cycle should then be driven by the same forces that operate in capitalist economies. If on the other hand, the system combines the best elements of both capitalism and socialism, as some imagine, perhaps there should be no cycle at all. Perhaps Beijing's mandarins have found a way to tame the animal spirits of the free market while at the same time still allowing them to work their optimizing magic.

In fact, China cannot really be said to have either capitalism or central planning. It can hardly be called capitalist when the state controls most investment either directly, as full or part owner of the investor, or indirectly, as a monopoly provider of land, credit, and public goods. At the same time, the fact that most investment comes under the jurisdiction of local governments implies that Beijing can have only a limited role as a planner. As was true in imperial times, it continues to be the case that "the sky is high and the emperor is far away."

Seen from this perspective, the investment cycle is a fundamentally different phenomenon from that generated by the private sectors of capitalist economies. There is also no reason to expect that the central government enjoys any special advantages in controlling it.

The most important features of the Chinese economy for purposes of understanding the investment cycle are (1) state ownership and (2) local government control. These are what give the system its "freewheeling" character. The first implies that the ownership status of most investment is murky. While state-owned assets are in theory the property of the whole people, in practice they cannot really be said to belong to anyone. Those in charge of them are thus less motivated to act with restraint. The second is a recipe for excess. China's local governments are typically constrained neither by the market nor by their constituents and only to a limited extent by Beijing.

None of these problems are unique to China. State property and economically powerful localities can be found in every country. The associated inefficiencies are also not unusual. What is characteristically Chinese is simply the extent to which they dominate economic life.

CHAPTER 3

SOCIALIST BOOMS AND BUSTS

> Grey, dear friend, is all theory
> And green the golden tree of life.
>
> —Goethe

ONE MIGHT THINK THAT CHINA WOULD BE IMMUNE TO BOOMS and busts. Under capitalism, the investment cycle appears to be primarily the result of mistakes by the private sector. In a country where the economy is dominated by the state, these should be relatively unimportant. Why should investment still be cyclical? This chapter begins by examining this question from a theoretical point of view, then traces the Maoist-era roots of today's investment cycle.

Evaluating claims for the superiority of socialism requires answers to two questions. First, why are there cycles in market economies? Second, can central planning work? Macroeconomic theory provides a variety of answers to the first question. Most of these support the idea that private sector outcomes are suboptimal. The answer to the second question is "no." Decentralized decision making is an essential precondition for economic rationality. Central planning cannot be an antidote for investment manias and crashes.

The founders of the Soviet system, which was later copied in China, believed that society can be understood "scientifically." Using the "objective laws" revealed by Marx, Engels, and Lenin, they claimed the economy could be analyzed as precisely as a clock mechanism. Bukharin, whom Lenin called a "major theorist" and the "favorite of the whole Party," even believed that Soviet social scientists would eventually be able to forecast events such as wars and economic crises. "We cannot predict the *time* of the appearance of any such phenomenon," Bukharin wrote, simply because "we do not yet possess sufficient information regarding the laws of social evolution to be able to express them in precise figures."[1]

"The laws of development of society," Stalin says in his *History of the Communist Party of the Soviet Union,* are "fully knowable."[2] To this Bukharin adds that under full communism "all the relations between men will be obvious to each."[3] While this perhaps might not be the case for everyone during the preliminary phase of the dictatorship of the proletariat, something of the sort would presumably be true of the vanguard Party and its members. Armed with a correct theoretical understanding of the economy and supposedly comprehensive knowledge of the interrelations among economic actors, the central planners would naturally be able to achieve more stable outcomes than the poorly informed profit-seeking businessmen busy "digging their own graves" in the capitalist West.

In practice, this was not the case. A real economy is simply too complex for any central authority to direct, Marxist pretensions to the contrary notwithstanding. In the Chinese case, central planning was not even carried out consistently. The argument for the superiority of socialism proves to be not only invalid but also often irrelevant.

There is no consensus among economists on the cause of investment cycles in market economies. In almost all models, however, cycles result from the limitations of private investors. These could easily be remedied by a planner with the advanced understanding of society that Marxism was supposed to provide.

Unfortunately, the planner faces two significant limitations. First, it is not really possible for all the relations between men to be obvious to each. Knowledge available to different individuals is often difficult to aggregate. While the planning authority may know more than any one person, it can never know as much as all the members of society collectively. Second, it will not generally be able to ensure that its plans are carried out. Practical considerations will invariably make it necessary for power to be shared. This opens the door to factional struggles within the leadership, which lead not only to poor decision making but to erratic policy implementation as well.

The actual record of the socialist economies makes it clear that these difficulties are insurmountable in practice. Planning never worked well enough to prevent constant discrepancies between targeted and actual output. Investment continued to be as volatile as ever, in many cases exhibiting even wider swings than those observed under capitalism.

In China the problems with central planning were exacerbated by the devolution of investment-decision-making authority to lower levels of government. This made economic coordination even more difficult and produced powerful incentives for overinvestment. Ironically, some of the very instabilities the revolution was supposed to eliminate became more extreme. Transferring ownership of the means of production to the state resulted not in a new age of rational resource allocation, but rather in an exaggerated version of the capitalist cycle.

This chapter provides a brief excursion into the realms of economic theory and economic history in order to put the origins of today's investment volatility in perspective. Section 1 offers an overview of some of the better-known investment-cycle theories in order to show why central planning might conceivably be desirable. Section 2 looks at why, even in theory, it is not possible for central planning to eliminate booms and busts. Sections 3 and 4 bring us to the real world, describing the fluctuations observed in the formerly socialist countries of Eastern Europe and in China under the old command economy. Finally, Section 5 draws some parallels between these fluctuations and those of a market economy.

1. MODELS OF THE CYCLE

The goal of most investment-cycle theories is to explain the cycles observed in market economies. As such fluctuations take place primarily in the private sector the explanations tend to focus on the limitations of private sector actors. They may be modeled as lacking information about each other, unable to understand the effects of government policy, capable of only "bounded rationality," or simply irrational.

While these accounts have little relevance to socialist countries, they often seem to imply that state ownership of the means of production would eliminate the investment cycle. If the problem is that investors tend to be poorly informed and irrational, surely a state that had mastered Stalin's "laws of development of society" could do better.

This conclusion could be drawn, for example, from any but the last of the following models:

1.1. KEYNES' ANIMAL SPIRITS MODEL

John Maynard Keynes believed that investment decisions are primarily based on what he called "animal spirits"—spontaneous impulses to act that are not derived from any rational calculation of expected returns.[4] During booms, he wrote, animal spirits give rise to "spontaneous optimism" about future returns, but as this has no underlying basis in reality it can give way to an equally spontaneous pessimism.[5] Then, "enterprise will fade and die;—though fears of loss may have a basis no more reasonable than hopes of profit had before."[6]

This suggests that if investors were more rational, or perhaps guided by perfectly informed state planners, booms and busts could be avoided. Keynes' position was that "the duty of ordering the current volume of investment cannot safely be left in private hands."[7] For Keynes, investor irrationality implied that the government should intervene to smooth investment fluctuations.

1.2. THE MARXIST MODEL

Keynes had a more positive view of capitalism than Marx, for whom the problem is essentially not one of investor psychology but rather one inherent in the very nature of production for exchange. Where production is primarily for the producer's personal use, coordination of production and consumption is assured; the producer and the consumer are the same person. With production for exchange, however, the two are separate individuals. There is no guarantee that the seller will spend her sales proceeds, and therefore no guarantee that Say's law—"Supply creates its own demand"—will hold.

While Keynes believed that Say's law does not generally hold, for him this was a matter of individuals failing to consume or invest all of their income. For Marx, the key issue is rather the exploitation of labor by capital, which he saw as a central feature of the capitalist system. Production and consumption are virtually guaranteed to be poorly coordinated because the workers do not earn enough in wages to purchase their own product. While the capitalists' desire to "enrich themselves and enlarge their capital" is "unlimited . . . the working people can only expand their consumption within very narrow limits."[8] As a result, excess capacity builds up and must inevitably precipitate crises of accumulation. These wipe out many of the producers and thus set the stage for the start of the next cycle.

Marx also believed that production under capitalism is inherently "anarchic" because the activities of producers are not well coordinated. Hilferding, a leading early-twentieth-century Marxist, developed this idea in a model where unanticipated consequences of technological innovation play the key role. Initially, new production technology raises profits in those sectors that can make use of it, resulting in an investment boom. Naturally, this spreads to other sectors as well via supply-chain networks. As the new capacity will not come on line immediately, margins continue to be high for some time and new projects continue to be started. Eventually production starts to rise, prices start to fall, and a crisis ensues as the extent of the overinvestment becomes apparent.[9]

While Hilferding does not make this point explicitly, the obvious problem is that his capitalists are making decisions on the basis of current rather than expected future prices. There is nothing in his story to explain why they cannot anticipate the eventual emergence of excess capacity. As Mises put it in his critique of nonmonetary explanations of the business cycle, the implication is that "all businessmen are short-sighted. They are too dull to avoid certain pitfalls, and thus blunder again and again in their conduct of affairs."[10] They are, in other words, irrational.

1.3. THE ACCELERATOR/MULTIPLIER MODEL

The same accusation might be leveled at the investors in accelerator/multiplier models.[11] They also exhibit "adaptive" rather than "rational" expectations—their choice of what to do in the current period is based on what would have been optimal in the previous one rather than on forecasts incorporating all available information. As in a common critique of military planners, they are fighting the last war.

In Samuelson's original version of the model, each period's consumption is a fraction of the previous period's GDP while investment is proportional to the previous period's change in consumption. Following some initial stimulus, consumption increases by less in each succeeding period because people do not consume the entire amount of the increase in output (their marginal propensity to consume is less than one). This causes investment to fall, which eventually pulls down GDP as well. At this point, however, the downtrend begins to reverse. Because people do not cut consumption by the entire amount of the output decline, subsequent period consumption declines become smaller, and investment and GDP eventually turn around.

Here the investors must be thought of as having only limited computational capabilities. Otherwise, they could easily use the model itself to determine how much to invest. After all, for any given initial conditions the modeler can correctly work out the values of all the variables for any point in the future. Why should the people she is modeling be limited to calculations based only on their observations of the previous period? Shouldn't they logically be assumed to know the model too?

1.4. THE AUSTRIAN MODEL

For Mises, Hayek, and other economists of the Austrian school, the investment cycle is driven by money supply increases. These may result from either central bank policy or fractional reserve banking. (In the latter case, bank lending increases the money supply because funds made available to borrowers take the form of either cash or new deposits.) Under either scenario, the interest rate will be lower than the equilibrium level at which investment is equal to savings.

The effect of this distortion will be greatest on projects that take longer to generate profits because net present value (NPV) is more sensitive to interest rates when the returns being discounted are farther in the future. Consider, for example, a project with a payout of $100 five years from now, compared to one with the same payout in one year. With an interest rate of 10 percent, the NPVs of the two payouts are $62 for the five-year payout and $91 for the one-year payout. If the interest rate falls to 5 percent, these NPVs rise to $78 for the five-year payout, a 26 percent increase, and $95 for the one-year payout, an increase of only 3 percent. [The NPV of $X, n years in the future, at an interest rate of i is given by $X/(1 + i)^n$.]

Resources will thus be misallocated into projects in the producer-goods sectors, which typically have longer payback periods, at the expense of consumer-goods production. This is unsustainable because the new projects will not be able to satisfy current consumer demand. To put it another way, consumers' aggregate savings are not sufficient to free up all of the resources required by investors. As a result, the prices of consumer goods are bid up. This leads to an increase in inflation, which in turn puts upward pressure on interest rates, either because lenders expect a decline in the real value of money or because the central bank is forced to tighten. The rising rates then trigger a crisis by pushing producer-goods firms into bankruptcy.

These investors are arguably a bit brighter than Hilferding's. Rather than failing to anticipate developments in their own industry, they are misled by monetary conditions into an incorrect assessment of the overall state of the economy. They might be faulted for not realizing that interest rates at the start of the cycle were artificially low, but perhaps there was no way they could have known this. As Hayek argued in his seminal 1945 article "The Use of Knowledge in Society," individuals must rely on prices to provide them with information about economic conditions that they cannot observe directly. If the interest rate—the price of loanable funds—ceases to be a reliable indicator, investors are left without much to go on.

1.5. The Lucas Imperfect Information Model

Investors in the Lucas imperfect information model[12] face a similar predicament. Unlike their counterparts in the models cited above, they exhibit rational expectations—their forecasts are consistent with those of the model itself—but they do not have complete information. As a result, cycles may also be driven by money supply increases. When these are unexpected, they lead to a rise in the general price level, which individual business owners initially mistake for product price increases in their own particular industries. This leads to an expansion in the short run, but no one is fooled for long. Once it becomes clear that all prices are rising, the economy returns to its initial equilibrium.

1.6. THE REAL BUSINESS-CYCLE MODEL

Few non-Marxian business-cycle theorists have been advocates of central planning. Yet in most of their models an all-wise central planner could improve upon the outcome. Any rational person could do better than investors driven only by animal spirits. Where expectations are adaptive, putting the modeler herself in charge would be an improvement. Incomplete information could conceivably be remedied by a government with superior information-gathering resources. And a planner could eliminate anarchy in production, while at the same time eliminating crises of accumulation by setting output levels corresponding to actual consumer demand.

There is, however, one class of models in which such enlightened planning would not result in any improvement. In real business-cycle theory, investment is driven by exogenously determined changes in productivity. The agents form expectations rationally and the market equilibrium, while varying, is optimal in every period. A planner would therefore find it desirable to schedule the same investment fluctuations that would occur in a market economy.[13]

This view of the investment cycle is appealing to economists because it does not require any ad hoc assumptions about investor limitations. For this very reason, however, it is inconsistent with most anecdotal evidence about how investors actually behave. It also leads to some surprisingly Panglossian conclusions. The breadlines, bankruptcies, and over 20 percent unemployment rates of the Great Depression, for example, must have been the optimal response to some mysterious slowdown in productivity growth and therefore for the best in the best of all possible worlds.

2. OBSTACLES TO CENTRAL PLANNING

It would be a mistake, however, to conclude that there would be no investment cycles in the absence of the economic institutions of capitalism. In claiming a role for the state on the grounds that the duty of ordering the current volume of investment cannot safely be left in private hands, Keynes is taking what Demsetz refers to as a "nirvana approach."[14] Keynes treats the outcomes that could theoretically be achieved by an ideal government as realistic alternatives to what can be achieved by actual investors. His argument for government intervention is that a system directed by angels would be preferable to one run by fallible human beings.

Keynes' claim in the conclusion of the *General Theory* that over the long term there should be a "somewhat comprehensive" socialization of investment is typical of this mode of thinking. While he did not believe that the state should eventually assume ownership of the "instruments of production," he wrote that it should "determine the aggregate amount of resources devoted to augmenting the instruments and the basic rate of reward to those who own them."[15] Exactly how this would be done is unclear. His answer to this question was simply that "public authority" may "cooperate with private initiative" using "all manner of devices."[16] It is also not clear in what sense there would still be private ownership if owners are not free to make use of their property as they choose and cease to be the residual claimants to the economic surplus it generates.

Similarly, few descriptions of real-world institutions can be found in Bukharin and Preobrazhensky's 1920 classic *The ABC of Communism,* one of the early twentieth century's most widely read popular accounts of the subject. The book was particularly influential in China. Mao Zedong told Edgar Snow it was the source of much of his early knowledge of Marxism.

According to Bukharin and Preobrazhensky, in the communist economy of the future "the factories, workshops, mines, and other productive institutions will all be subdivisions, as it were, of one vast people's workshop, which will embrace the entire national economy of production." Production will then cease to be anarchic. The state will "know in advance how much labor to assign to the various branches of industry; what products are required and how much of each it is necessary to produce; how and where machines must be provided."[17] Products will not be bought or sold but "simply stored in communal warehouses" and "subsequently delivered to those who need them."[18]

In the real world, however, it is practically impossible for there to be anything remotely resembling the all-knowing, superrational, all-powerful state imagined by authors who claim that central government control can reduce or eliminate economic fluctuations. One obvious problem is that absolute power corrupts absolutely. Those put in charge would be sorely tempted to maximize their own welfare rather than that of society as a whole.

A more fundamental objection can be raised on logical grounds. Even if incorruptible planners could be found, there would still be no way for them to make the necessary plans.

The first difficulty they would encounter is that there would be no satisfactory way to evaluate the relative costs and benefits of alternative methods to accomplish their objectives. Mises gives the example of a fully communist country trying to decide whether or not to build a new rail line.[19] In a market economy, the savings in transport costs that various possible routes would make possible could be added up and compared to the total costs involved. Without market-set prices, such a computation would be impossible. The necessary quantities of the various goods and services involved could be worked out on technical grounds but there would be no objective way to value them.

In the final analysis, comparing the values of two goods or services means determining how much of one could be exchanged for the other. But in the worker's paradise, such exchanges would not take place. There, as *The ABC of Communism* tells us, there will no longer be commodities (i.e., goods produced for exchange), only products, which "are not exchanged for one another." The problem of establishing relative valuations would become insoluble.

The socialist cure for anarchic production turns out to be considerably worse than the disease. In a world like that described by Bukharin and Preobrazhensky, the planners, as Mises put it, would have to "cross the whole ocean of possible and imaginable economic permutations without the compass of economic calculation."[20] Contrary to Bukharin and Preobrazhensky's claim that every detail of communist production would be "precisely calculated,"[21] Mises finds that their vision of socialism would amount to nothing less than "the renunciation of rational economy."[22]

The case for central planning also presupposes that a planner could identify all of society's economic problems and the available solutions. This would not generally be possible even if market prices were still available (e.g., if they could be observed in a neighboring capitalist country). Hayek makes this point in "The Use of Knowledge in Society," arguing that for central planning to work, the issues it is supposed to address must be identified in advance. For the steel industry to produce x tons of steel, for example, it will require y tons of iron ore and z tons of coking coal. In a real economy, things are seldom this straightforward. In practice, Hayek argues, "the continuous flow of goods and services is maintained by constant deliberate adjustments, by new dispositions made every day in the light of circumstances not known the day before, by B stepping in at once when A fails to deliver."[23]

Central planning requires knowing in advance what questions to ask. The planning authority must anticipate what facts will be relevant and how they should be reported. The planners' own cognitive limitations are not the only constraint. There will also be blind spots in any reporting system. Even the largest imaginable computer database will be of little use if it lacks the appropriate records or if the records do not include the right fields. When there are "circumstances not known the day before," the associated problems are likely to involve information that was not initially expected to matter and was therefore never reported. Inevitably much of the decision making will have to be left to the "man on the spot" (as Hayek puts it).

Hayek's examples generally involve what is known as declarative or propositional knowledge. This is knowledge of facts, knowledge that something is the case. A freight consolidator knows, for example, that a particular ship unexpectedly has a certain volume of space available in a particular configuration. Or an arbitrageur is aware that a certain commodity is temporarily in short supply. Such facts would be easy for a planning authority to miss due to their idiosyncratic character. It is at least conceivable, however, that someone might report them.

Much of society's economically useful knowledge does not even fall into this category. It is knowledge of how to do something—variously referred to as tacit knowledge,[24] metis,[25] or performative knowledge[26]—rather than factual information. Scott gives as an example the knowledge required to put out oil well fires. Since every fire is different, this is a task that requires "an inspired mixture of experience and improvisation."[27] The team must "begin with the unpredictable—an accident, a fire—and then devise the techniques and equipment" necessary to extinguish it. This is a job that defies routinization.[28]

Unlike declarative knowledge, performative knowledge is not amenable to any precise explication. The problem is not simply that, as Hayek notes, there is no way all the facts known to the man on the spot can be communicated to the planners. He might not even be able to tell the planners what he knew if he met with them in person.

Whether the planner is building a new rail line, as in Mises' example, putting out oil well fires, or overseeing practically any other aspect of economic life, the problem with central planning is that it is not possible to aggregate all the necessary information. Costs and benefits cannot be aggregated without prices. Centralized reporting systems cannot reliably cover what Hayek calls "the particular circumstances of time and place." Performative knowledge can not even be written down. In a market economy, these difficulties are resolved through disaggregated decision making and the price system. The socialist approach rules out these solutions but has nothing to offer in their place.

None of this would matter in a world free of uncertainty. In such a world it would be possible to plan everything down to the last detail. But even in a much less complex world than ours this would not really be possible. Moreover, modern economic growth is driven primarily by technological innovation, something that is unpredictable ipso facto.

In practice, decentralized decision making must occur in any real-world economic organization. Hayek's reasoning is just as relevant to the Ford Motor Company as it was to the Soviet government. Arguments for consolidating ownership of the means of production in the hands of the state assume that this must lead to a corresponding consolidation of information in the minds of the planners. But since not all information can be aggregated, this approach simply does not work. The fact that Ford's divisions are all part of a single company does not mean that their employees can effectively share everything they know with the head office. Nor would this be possible if the company were state owned. It is not really conceivable that all of its activities, let alone those of an entire economy, could be centrally planned.

Beyond the difficulty of formulating a satisfactory central plan, there is the further problem of how it would be implemented. Will people identify their own interests so completely with those of society as a whole that they will voluntarily do whatever is required of them, as Bukharin and Preobrazhensky optimistically predicted? There seems little reason to think so. If not, what will ensure that the planners' dictates will be carried out?

It is commonly imagined that in a command economy the state's orders are invariably obeyed without question—that the plan will be followed to the letter. Such claims rest on the assumption that political power can be entirely concentrated in a single individual. In practice this is impossible. No one person can control an entire country single-handedly. As a practical matter, power must always be shared among leaders at various levels. Their interests will invariably diverge.

Through the years Communist Party rule has always featured what Mao Zedong referred to as "contradictions among the people"—struggles among producers for plan allocations of raw materials, struggles among localities for investment funds, struggles among Party factions with differing economic agendas. Nor has it ever been possible for the planners to disregard public opinion entirely. Central plans invariably run into resistance from lower-level officials and managers and always have to be modified when their social costs become high enough to pose a threat to the regime.

For Mises, the central planner is demonic rather than angelic. Yet he makes a similar error to Marxist theorists in regarding investment cycles as being impossible under socialism. In his model, cycles result from incompatibilities among the plans of different economic actors. Producers' planned investment exceeds society's aggregate savings while production falls short of total consumer demand. Such incompatibilities, Mises believes, cannot arise in a socialist state. There, he imagines there can only be one plan—that of the all-powerful dictator. Producers will produce what the plan requires; consumers will do as they are told. "If the dictator invests more and thus curtails the means available for current consumption, the people must eat less and hold their tongues. No crisis emerges because the subjects have no opportunity to utter their dissatisfaction."[29]

While arguing that planning would be impossible in the absence of prices, Mises fails to realize that absolute power is equally impossible and for much the same reason. It is no more possible for the dictator to be omniscient than it is for the planner. Power must always be decentralized to some extent and there will then invariably be as many plans (or at least agendas) as there are powerful people.

Even in the Soviet Union, central planning never reached the level of scientific precision described in *The ABC of Communism*. While the planners went to great lengths to determine inputs and outputs for practically every sector of the economy, the system was plagued by chronic imbalances. As a result, allocations came to be based on political rather than economic considerations. As Alec Nove puts it in his *Economic History of the USSR*, "persistent shortages of goods inevitably led to intrigue and string-pullings designed to persuade the allocation authorities that this or that project or enterprise was deserving of official priority."[30]

Bukharin and Preobrazhensky believed that it would be possible for the economy to be directed entirely on the basis of centralized, declarative knowledge. "Just as in an orchestra all the performers watch the conductor's baton and act accordingly," they wrote, so under communism "all will consult the statistical reports and will direct their work accordingly."[31] In fact, however, the shortcomings of Soviet-style economic management meant that decentralized, performative knowledge had to play a key role as well. "In the everyday working of the system," Nove notes, "much depended on unofficial links between people at all levels, which helped to overcome many deficiencies and gaps in the plan . . . by improvisation of many kinds."[32]

3. BOOMS AND BUSTS UNDER SOCIALISM

Claims for the superiority of central planning turn out to be both logically flawed and inconsistent with the performance of actual centrally planned economies. There is, in fact, no reason why socialist countries should be free of investment cycles. Indeed, they sometimes have experienced fluctuations even more extreme than those observed under capitalism.

Comparing investment growth in a sample of socialist and capitalist countries for the period from 1960 to 1989, the Hungarian economist Janos Kornai finds that "while some socialist economies grow relatively smoothly," for example, East Germany and the Soviet Union, "others show wild fluctuations, even larger ones than many capitalist countries."[33] The most extreme cases in this latter category were Yugoslavia, Poland, and Hungary, where he finds coefficients of variation for the annual growth rate of investment of 278 percent, 187 percent, and 171 percent, respectively. The highest value for his sample capitalist countries was 159 percent, for Ireland. (The coefficient of variation is the ratio of the standard deviation to the mean.)

Socialist investment booms were driven by a very different set of animal spirits than those bedeviling the market economy. Kornai refers to the main culprits as "investment hunger" and "expansion drive." The former was an unavoidable consequence of soft budget constraints— administratively imposed constraints on credit, subsidies, taxation, and pricing that were binding on enterprises in theory but routinely relaxed in practice through negotiation with the relevant government departments. For example, managers might successfully lobby to have state-set input prices reduced or to reschedule their loans from the state-owned banks. Such opportunities to bend the rules resulted in overinvestment by artificially increasing returns and eliminating bankruptcy risk.

Expansion drive, an official obsession with high rates of investment growth, generally reflected both the leadership's belief that there was an urgent need to catch up with the developed countries and the eagerness of lower-level cadres for career advancement. It is also relevant that Marxist theory itself often stressed the importance of large-scale industry in building socialism.

Kautsky,[34] for example, held that the "will to socialism" would remain undeveloped in a society of small producers because, with the economy's productive assets dispersed among a large number of individual owners, there would be only a "will to uphold or to obtain private property." Industrialization would break down resistance to the socialization of economic life by making it impossible for most individuals to "obtain a share in the means of production unless they take on a social form."

Lenin shared this view, writing in "Left-wing Communism: An Infantile Disorder," that "small-scale production *engenders* capitalism and the bourgeoisie continuously, daily, hourly, spontaneously, and on a mass scale."[35] Similarly, in his report to the eighth All-Russia Congress of Soviets in 1920, he argued that only a modern industrial base could eliminate the institutions of Russia's smallholder economy. This was the basis for his famous claim that "Communism is Soviet power plus the electrification of the whole country."[36]

Unlike capitalist economies, where slowdowns in investment tend to be associated with insufficient aggregate demand, in the socialist countries Kornai finds that "the brake is applied by central control" when the leaders sense "an inadequacy of resources available to the accelerated process of growth."[37] This generally is the result of limits on imports and indebtedness, the emergence of widespread shortages of industrial raw materials, public discontent with the cuts in personal consumption necessitated by increased investment, or some combination of these factors.[38] Following a subsequent slowdown, the leadership eventually is "reassured that tension has fallen, or even a measure of slack, an apparent underuse of resources, has appeared." Expansion drive and investment hunger revive and the cycle begins anew.[39]

Thus, as Kornai concludes, "one thing can certainly be said: socialist planning has belied the hope that it would produce smooth growth free of the fluctuations, standstills, and setbacks of capitalism."[40] The elimination of the private sector put an end to Marx's crises of overproduction only to replace them with crises of overinvestment. Substituting Kornai's expansion drive for the profit motive meant that investment booms and busts continued as before, though as a product of government mismanagement rather than of manias and panics in the private sector. As a curb for speculative excess, administrative controls proved a poor substitute for the threat of bankruptcy.

4. INVESTMENT FLUCTUATIONS IN PRE-REFORM CHINA (1949–1977)

During the command economy period (1949–1977), China experienced a number of investment booms and busts of the type Kornai describes. Eckstein considers these cycles to be the result of "a confrontation between Mao's vision of development possibilities in the Chinese economy and society and the country's economic backwardness"[41] with fluctuations "generated by the interactions of a harvest cycle and a policy cycle." The former, he finds, was "in part weather induced and in part policy-induced" while the latter resulted from a "vision-induced pursuit of industrialization."[42]

Eckstein distinguishes four main phases of the cyclical process: (1) A good harvest makes it possible to extract a larger surplus from the agricultural sector to support increased fixed capital investment. (2) The investment upswing is brought to a halt due to a combination of limited resources, organizational problems, and the disincentive effects of "mobilization and accumulation policies" on the peasantry. (3) The strategy of supporting the drive for industrial expansion at the expense of agriculture leads to a poor harvest, which generates a "cumulative downswing or contraction." (4) Policy is adjusted to provide better incentives for crop and livestock production. A better harvest is forthcoming, and the cycle starts again.[43]

Eckstein found that for the period from the establishment of the People's Republic in 1949 until 1965 there were four to five short cycles, each peaking when it became necessary to reallocate resources (particularly manpower) from industry back to agriculture. This pattern continued in subsequent years, with peaks and troughs in year-on-year growth in gross fixed asset investment and gross agricultural output corresponding quite closely (Figure 3.1).

Eckstein's analysis is something of an oversimplification because it treats the state as a single monolithic entity. In fact, both intra-Party power struggles and conflicts between the central and local authorities also played an important role in the evolution of the cycle. Good harvests in 1958, 1964, and 1969 were associated not only with upswings in investment in general but also, more particularly, with the launching of new policies to promote small-scale industry at the local level. This occurred as Mao's faction, which advocated decentralized planning and self-reliance, gained the upper hand. Similarly, the low investment growth rates of the early 1960s corresponded not only to the emergence of famine conditions but also to the strengthening of Liu Shaoqi's faction, which favored a more centralized approach based on careful economic accounting.[44]

During the 1960s, national defense considerations also had important implications for the investment cycle. Increased US involvement in Vietnam following the 1964 Tonkin Gulf incident led to a massive effort to transfer defense-related production to relatively remote locations in the interior. These became known collectively as the "Third Front." Factories were moved inland from coastal cities, steel and weapons production facilities were built from scratch, and new railway lines were laid to provide transport links to the rest of the country. At the end of the decade, the

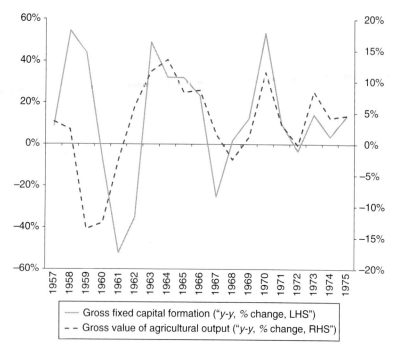

Figure 3.1   Cycles in agriculture and investment
Source: China Statistical Yearbook 1983.

possibility of a Soviet nuclear strike inspired a second Third Front–related boom, this time focusing on hydroelectric power, machine building, and additional rail lines.

From 1965 to 1971, such investment accounted for a significant share of nationwide fixed capital formation (FCF). Naughton has estimated that Third Front projects in Szechuan and Guizhou provinces alone accounted for some 15–20 percent of nationwide capital construction during the FCF peak years of 1965 and 1969.[45]

4.1. Small-Scale Industry and Decentralized Planning

The most extreme of the early investment booms was the 1958 Great Leap Forward, during which 240,000 backyard steel furnaces were set up throughout the country in a bizarre attempt to catch up with the UK in steel production. Nominal fixed capital investment growth reached 54 percent in that year but fell rapidly thereafter, finally bottoming at −52 percent in 1961.

The neglect of agriculture resulting from this industrialization drive, combined with various other policy mistakes and bad weather, led to one of the largest man-made famines on record. From 1958 to 1962, it is estimated that as many as 45 million people died of hunger and malnutrition.[46] Even the economic ups and downs of Keynes' day pale in comparison to this performance.

The Great Leap marked a dramatic turn from the Soviet-style central planning China had practiced in the early years of the People's Republic toward a more decentralized development strategy. This change may be dated from the beginning of 1958, when responsibility for a wide range of industrial sectors was transferred from central government ministries to provincial-level governments.[47] As a result, the share of locally con-trolled enterprises in total gross industrial output rose from 54 percent in 1957 to 74 percent in 1959.[48] This made it possible for local governments to respond to the central government's expansion drives by launching projects indiscriminately.

As the problems with the steel drive became obvious in February 1959, a *People's Daily* editorial titled "The Whole Country as a Chess Game" (*Quan Guo Yi Pan Qi*) called for a strengthening of central-ized leadership and unified planning and warned against "dispersionism" (*fensanzhuyi*) and "departmentalism" (*benweizhuyi*)—both terms refer-ring to the tendency of each unit to act on its own without regard for national priorities. Just as a chess game can only be won when the move-ments of each piece form part of a coherent overall strategy, so rapid growth could only be achieved when decision makers at every level prop-erly coordinated their development plans with those of the country as a whole.[49]

While this call for the restoration of economic discipline was clearly appropriate at the time, the chess game analogy suffers from the same difficulties as all other claims for the superiority of central planning. The economy is not like a chess board, where all of the relevant information is immediately visible to a single person. There are no economic laws analogous to the rules of a board game. Directing the activities of real people is nothing like moving pieces around on a chessboard. Chessmen move without either the promise of reward or the threat of punishment. Human beings do not act without incentives.

In any case, the failure of the Great Leap did not lead to the recen-tralization of decision making that the supporters of central planning among the leadership hoped to achieve. Mao mistrusted the kind of hierarchical organizations that would be needed to implement the chess-board strategy, regarding them as "a potential locus for the process of embourgeoisement."[50] At the same time, he believed that national priorities must originate from the masses. The role of the Party, as he saw it, was not to impose ideas on the people from above but rather to "take the ideas of the masses (scattered and unsystematic ideas) and concentrate them (through study turn them into concentrated and systematic ideas), then go to the masses and propagate and explain these ideas until the masses embrace them as their own."[51]

While Mao presented this "mass line" principle as his version of the Leninist doctrine of democratic centralism, it also has clear links to traditional Chinese political thought. Mencius held that "when a state is about to flourish, its ruler receives his lesson from the people."[52] Similarly, the idea of the masses embracing the Party's ideas as their own is echoed in Chapter 17 of the *Dao De Jing*, where the best form of government is described as one of whose accomplishments the people say "we did it ourselves."

Decentralized decision making also has a long history. During imperial times, while the emperor was honored as the "son of Heaven," in practice "the real rulers of China were the 'father and mother' officials; that is, the district magistrates who held both in theory and in fact a position as parents to the people."[53] Traditional Chinese hierarchies are "not command structures but rather prestige alignments" in which the "lower orders . . . pretend to comply but in practice . . . go on doing what they feel is in their best interests."[54]

During the 1960s and 1970s, responsibility for economic planning saw a significant devolution to lower levels of government, each responsible only for allocating resources among the political units immediately below it. The result has been described as "decentralized planning" or a "decentralized-command economy."[55]

In 1964, county governments were given the authority to create their own independent industrial sectors. After 1970, communes and brigades were encouraged to develop the so-called five small industries: iron and steel, cement, chemical fertilizer, energy, and machinery.[56] At the same time, the Cultural Revolution, which started in 1966, resulted in a major reduction in the size of the central government. Writing in 1972, Donnithorne found that two-thirds of the pre–Cultural Revolution ministries, commissions, and other offices under the State Council had "lost their separate identity," while the number of central government cadres had fallen from 60,000 to 10,000.[57] Decentralization even affected large-scale Third Front projects. Starting in 1969, many of these were transferred to lower administrative levels, resulting in severe management and coordination problems.[58]

Not surprisingly, the promotion of small-scale industry and indigenous techniques led to some highly inefficient outcomes. In the cement industry, for example, China came to rely increasingly on shaft kilns, a technology that had been obsolete since the early twentieth century. While in 1957 they accounted for less than 3 percent of total installed cement capacity, this share rose to 30 percent in 1960, 41 percent by 1970, and 68 percent by 1980.[59]

Similarly, by 1971 every province except Tibet had its own small- and medium-size iron mines and iron and steel plants. These produced one-fourth of China's iron ore and one-fifth of its pig iron.[60] The waste of resources implied by this state of affairs can easily be seen from the fact that modern smelters required only 70 percent as much coking coal per ton of iron as backward ones. Modern steel plants used only two-thirds the amount of iron per ton of steel.[61] And the output of these small-scale plants was not always even usable. Much of the steel produced in the Great Leap Forward backyard furnaces, for example, had to be resmelted in large "foreign" furnaces.[62]

4.2. SELF-SUFFICIENCY AS MERCANTILISM

In addition to the promotion of small-scale industry, which prevented the realization of economies of scale, the Cultural Revolution–era development model put considerable emphasis on self-reliance. This resulted in foregone gains from trade.

Here Mao's approach combined indigenous economic ideas and Marxist theory—both of which viewed commerce as unproductive—with national security considerations. In pre-modern China, the merchant class occupied the lowest rank in society, below gentry officials, peasants, and craftsman.[63] Similarly Marx, in *Das Kapital,* Volume I, Chapter V, wrote that "Circulation, or the exchange of commodities, begets no value."[64] Under full communism, trade was supposed to be a means of eliminating temporary supply shortfalls rather than a means of increasing economic efficiency through specialization.[65] Finally, the threat of nuclear attack from either the US or the Soviet Union meant that a dispersed industrial structure had obvious advantages. Decentralization helped to conceal production from foreign enemies, building factories in the hinterland shielded them from attack.[66] As an article in the October 1963 issue of the Party journal *Red Flag* put it, the goal was to have "many large and small industrial bases that can be relied upon," each a "war base indestructible."[67]

Small-scale industrial development does not necessarily imply regional autarky. An alternative would have been to encourage different areas to specialize in different products while promoting interregional trade. This was the approach taken in the development of the Third Front. New rail lines were built to connect a variety of manufacturing facilities in different locations—for example, to transport coal from western Guizhou province to the Panzhihua steel mill in southern Szechuan and to supply machine-building plants north of Chengdu, in central Szechuan, from Panzhihua.[68]

Counties and municipalities, however, strived for economic isolation, with enterprises using local raw materials to produce locally for local markets.[69] To take an extreme example, locally available iron ore and coal might be used to produce steel and generate electricity. These might then serve as inputs for the production of tools and spare parts at a repair station for agricultural equipment serving local farms producing for local consumers.

The emphasis on self sufficiency led inevitably to local protectionism. Local governments came to be evaluated on the extent to which they could independently produce various categories of products or even generate surpluses for "export" to other localities.[70] Protecting markets for local light industry was also desirable because high retail prices were often necessary in order to subsidize inefficient small-scale heavy industry.[71] Thus, in 1970 the Changchun Number One Department Store sourced all of its light industrial products from Jilin, its home province. Shanghai and Tianjin boasted of record shipments to the rest of China.[72] Hubei Province even had a program to grow all its own sugar.[73]

During the 1960s, China developed into what Donnithorne described as a "customs union but not a common market." It had, she wrote, "a common barrier against the outside world" but lacked "free trade within its national boundaries."[74] In the absence of either markets or effective central planning, the economy fragmented into multitude of autarkic localities while the ideology of self-sufficiency became an excuse for local-level mercantilism.

4.3. REESTABLISHING CENTRAL CONTROL

Under these circumstances, ending an investment boom required more than simply applying the brake by central control. Central control had first to be reestablished. The boom–bust cycle in investment was accompanied by expansions and contractions in the power of the central government. Unlike the countercyclical fiscal and monetary policy practiced elsewhere, this can hardly be called a system of economic management. The system itself was chaotic, lurching unpredictably from crisis to crisis without any of the stable institutional parameters normally imposed by private property rights and adherence to the rule of law.

Central planning became all but impossible during the Great Leap Forward and was only reestablished in 1962.[75] At that point much of the authority granted to localities to invest in small-scale projects was temporarily rescinded.[76] In December 1961, the Party halted all basic construction with the exception of specially authorized projects.[77] Most of the backyard furnaces, along with numerous small coal mines, fertilizer plants, power generating stations, and other "baby plants" ' were "axed out of existence," as one author aptly put it.[78] In some cases, then-president Liu Shaoqi is said to have personally intervened, in one county eliminating nearly 800 enterprises run by commune and production brigades.[79]

Unlike the process of creative destruction observed in a market economy, this kind of intervention was quite indiscriminate. Just as Hayek's man on the spot is the only person with the knowledge necessary for good investment decisions, he is also the only person really qualified to decide what projects should be halted. In Mao-era China, however, the man on the spot was a local official who could hardly be counted on to make such determinations objectively. The central government therefore often had no choice but to throw out the baby with the bathwater, issuing one-size-fits-all policies without regard for local circumstances.[80] In 1964 one visitor reported seeing construction equipment rusting on abandoned building sites throughout Beijing and other cities.[81]

Central planning was once again abandoned following the start of the Cultural Revolution in 1966. In 1968, it was noted that there had been no mention of the five-year plan in any of the official documents for the previous year.[82] A second investment boom ensued in 1969–1970, when small-scale local industries once again "sprang up like mushrooms"[83] and the stock of Third Front projects expanded to such an extent that they could not possibly all be completed.[84] It was hardly surprising that centralized economic management was reintroduced in 1972 and 1973. Then-premier Zhou Enlai launched a movement to combat "ultra-left thinking" (*jizuosichao*) and "anarchism." New measures were taken to prevent localities from launching projects indiscriminately. For example, the use of bank loans and enterprise working capital to finance basic construction was prohibited.[85]

5. SOCIALIST ANIMAL SPIRITS

Central planning never worked as advertised in any of the countries where it was tried. Even under ideal conditions it would never have been possible for central planners to identify optimal allocations of scarce resources.

It is unlikely that any such allocations could be realized in any case. With decision makers' incentives skewed by expansion drive and soft budget constraints, it is probably inevitable that socialist economic management was driven primarily by political considerations. Investment booms and busts have been the result.

In the Chinese case, these problems were compounded during the command economy era by attempts to limit the role of central planning itself. With self reliance as the watchword, lower-level authorities enjoyed a degree of autonomy that made it practically impossible for the central government to coordinate economic development. Even the Third Front, where many of the projects were national priorities, was not immune. The result was a pattern of decentralized boom followed by centrally imposed bust.

In an inversion of Keynes' assertion, the Chinese experience shows that the duty of ordering the current volume of investment cannot safely be left solely in public hands. Government entities are, if anything, even more at risk of possession by animal spirits than private sector companies. They almost invariably tend to prioritize ideological or political considerations over cost–benefit calculations.

What Keynes called the spontaneous optimism of the private sector quickly falters when people start to reevaluate expected returns. For investors not focused on profit maximization such a reevaluation is less likely and would make relatively little difference. For them, spontaneous pessimism sometimes sets in only when the food supply starts to give out and they find themselves, as Stalin put it in 1930 following an ill-fated collectivization drive, "dizzy with success."

In theory, socialism was supposed to eliminate anarchy in production. In China it had the opposite effect. Communist Party rule resulted in an investment cycle much like that described by the Austrian business-cycle theorists, with expansion drive on the part of local officials replacing bankers' expansion of the money supply as the driving force. In the Austrian model, below-equilibrium interest rates divert resources into investments with longer pay-off periods. Campaigns like the Great Leap Forward had the same effect, reducing the supply of goods available for current-period consumption in order to focus on investment in heavy industry. The resulting imbalances between the plans of consumers and producers eventually brought the expansions to an end, just as Mises and Hayek believed occurs under capitalism. In the absence of market prices, contractions were necessitated by shortages rather than inflation, but the underlying story is essentially the same.

Perhaps China's experience would not have surprised Bukharin and Preobrazhensky. They argued that "without a general plan, without a general directive system, and without careful calculation and book-keeping, there can be no organization."[86] Indeed, they might not have even recognized the Chinese system as communist. They might have instead seen it as a variety of what they termed "*lumpenproletarian socialism*" or "anarchism."

Their description of this type of economy actually fits pre-1978 China surprisingly well. "Anarchists," they wrote, "are far more concerned with dividing up than with the organization of production." As a consequence, "anarchism would not increase production, but would disintegrate it," by organizing the economy into a large number of small "self-governing communes" rather than as a "huge cooperative commonwealth."[87]

A HISTORY OF THE CYCLE

The past isn't dead. It isn't even past.

—Faulkner

CHINA'S TRANSITION TO TODAY'S "SOCIALIST MARKET" economy is generally considered to have started in 1978. In December of that year, the third plenum of the Chinese Communist Party's eleventh Central Committee declared economic development rather than class struggle to be the "basic line." This set in motion a new policy of "reform and opening."

During the next thirty years, the country would be transformed beyond recognition. Product markets replaced central planning. New forms of property ownership were introduced. The country opened its doors to international trade. Even Chairman Mao's most ambitious output targets were surpassed as China grew to become the world's second largest economy. By 2008, real GDP had risen to 16.5 times what it had been in 1978. For 1978–2008, the compound annual growth rate (CAGR) reached 9.8 percent, compared to a level of 6.4 percent for the 1952 to 1977 period.

Most analyses of this period tend to focus on the reasons for the acceleration in the average growth rate. This chapter looks instead at the volatility of growth, examining the history of the investment cycle from 1978 to 2009. The objective is not to account for the post-1978 changes but rather for continuities with the command economy era. As one might expect, these are attributable to the state's continued domination of the Chinese economic system.

The year 1978 does not mark any obvious change in the investment cycle, as Figure 4.1 shows. The figure tracks the growth in nominal fixed capital formation (FCF) from 1958 to 2010, along with estimated

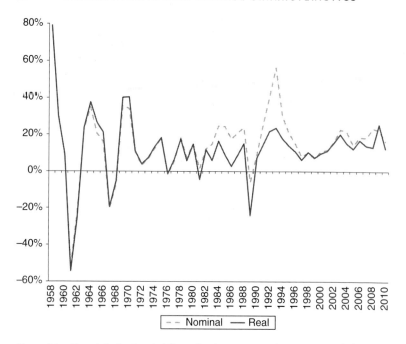

Figure 4.1   Growth in fixed capital formation (year-on-year changes in annual data)
Source: Bloomberg, author's calculations.

real (i.e., inflation-adjusted) growth. The latter is necessarily problematic because the official statistics do not include an FCF price index. The real growth series shown here is based on an index for ex-factory prices for manufactured goods prior to 1979,[1] a fixed asset investment (FAI) price index estimated by Jefferson, Rawski, and Zheng for 1979–1990,[2] and the FAI price index available in the *China Statistical Yearbook* that starts in 1991.

The use of these price indices to calculate real FCF growth presents several problems. First, FCF and FAI, while related, do not measure investment in the same way. FCF is a component of nominal GDP (as measured by the expenditure method) and therefore excludes expenditure on unproduced inputs such as land. FAI, on the other hand, includes these. The ex-factory price index is also based on an inappropriate basket of goods, though it is at least an improvement over the other indices available for the pre-1978 period, which track retail and agricultural procurement prices.[3]

The real FCF series is clearly preferable to the nominal one. Inflation was low or negative prior to 1978 but much higher subsequently. (See

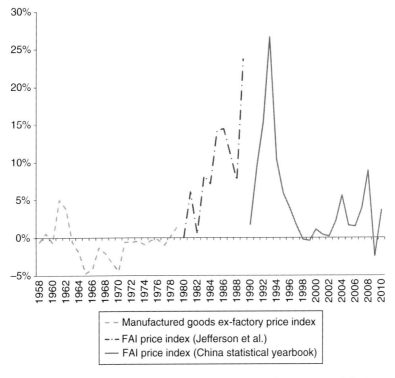

Figure 4.2   Measures of capital goods inflation (year-on-year changes in annual data)
Source: *Zhongguo Maoyi Wujia Tongji Ziliao 1952–1983*, Jefferson et al., China Statistical Yearbook 2011.

Figure 4.2.) A comparison of the pre- and post-reform periods that does not adjust for price changes would be like comparing "apples to oranges."

The real growth rate peaks also occur in the same years as the investment booms described in Chinese sources such as the *Zhongguo Jingji Nianjian* (Almanac of China's Economy). This suggests that using the ex-factory and FAI price indices as deflators does not lead to significant distortions in the chronology of the cycle.

While investment was less volatile after 1978, this shift in the pattern really occurred in the early 1970s. It predates the beginning of the reform period. The structural break corresponds not to the end of the command economy, but rather to the restoration of some semblance of central planning in the early 1970s. Our real FCF growth series reached its pre-1970 maximum of 79 percent in 1958 and a minimum of −54 percent in 1961. This compares to the post-1970 maximum of 23 percent that occurred in 1993 and the minimum of −24 percent in 1989.

The time between peaks in both series continued to be approximately five years until 1993, much as it had been ever since 1958. Again, there was no obvious change in 1978. The first and so far only significant change in the peak-to-peak period was the lengthening that occurred in the 1993–2003 cycle. As there was a subsequent peak six years later in 2009, it remains to be seen whether 1993 marked a real structural break or only a one-time aberration.

From 1978 to 2009, we can identify a number of swings in the investment cycle, with real FCF growth peaks in 1978, 1984, 1988, 1993, 2003, and 2009 and troughs in 1981, 1986, 1989, 1997, and 2005.

This chapter provides a brief history of these episodes, looking at the circumstances leading to the booms, the imbalances that subsequently emerged, and the policies the central government employed to address them.

In each case, the booms were driven primarily by local governments while the busts, as had generally been the case ever since 1949, were brought about by central government policy. At the same time, as product markets were introduced and the economy gradually became internationalized, inflation and trade deficits began to replace agricultural shortfalls as the primary constraints on investment. These problems became less severe as high rates of accumulation along with productivity growth resulting from the economic reforms led to excess capacity. This in turn generated both disinflation and a steady improvement in the balance of trade. One consequence was a second drop in FCF volatility starting around 1997.

The remainder of this chapter breaks up the post-1978 era into periods, each starting with an investment cycle peak and ending in the year immediately prior to the succeeding peak. There are four of these to consider: 1978–1983 (discussed in Section 1), 1984–1992 (Section 2, which treats the peaks in 1984 and 1988 as part of the same cycle), 1993–2002 (Section 3), and 2003–2008 (Section 4). Our story ends with the peak in 2009 (Section 5), while Section 6 concludes with a discussion of the impact of China's post-1978 transformation on the investment cycle.

1. LEAPING OUTWARD AND PULLING BACK (1978–1983)

In addition to marking the beginning of the reform and opening period, 1978 was the year of the "Great Leap Outward" (*Yang Mao Jin*), a Great Leap Forward-style attempt to catch up with and overtake the world's advanced economies. This time the focus was on the so-called Four Modernizations—of agriculture, industry, science, and defense. Specific objectives were established at the fifth National People's Congress in February 1978.

In his address to the Congress, Hua Guofeng, who became Party chairman after Mao's death in 1976, presented a ten-year plan covering the 1976–1985 time frame. In agriculture, the plan called for output to increase by 4–5 percent per year as a result of "mechanization, electrification, irrigation, and higher utilization of chemical fertilizers."[4] Planned industrial investment included 120 major projects requiring an amount comparable to the approximately 400 billion US dollar cumulative total for the preceding twenty-eight years.[5] Steel production was supposed to increase from 31.8 million tons in 1978 to 60 million tons by 1985, with a further increase to 180 million tons by 1999. By 1985 outputs of coal, crude oil, and cement were projected to rise by 46 percent, 381 percent, and 53 percent, respectively.[6]

Both the Great Leap Outward and the Great Leap Forward were crash programs designed to propel the Chinese economy to developed country status in as short a time as possible. However, the 1978 leap differed in two important respects from its 1958 predecessor.

First, leaping outward meant discarding Mao's principle of self-reliance. Rather than relying on "native methods" like the backyard steel furnace, advanced technology was to be imported from the very countries China was aiming to surpass. Vendors and banks from those countries were to provide the financing in many cases. Contracts were signed with foreign companies for capital goods including steel plants, textile machinery, oil rigs, and mining equipment.[7]

The second difference was that by the time of the Leap Outward, economic decision making had become considerably more centralized than it had been during the Leap Forward. And indeed it would have been practically impossible for local governments by themselves to carry out a program relying on high-tech imports. While any locality could arrange for the construction of a primitive steel smelter or cement plant using whatever materials happened to be available, only organs of the central government would have had access to the foreign exchange necessary to import equipment or been deemed good credit risks by foreign banks.

Despite the increased emphasis on planning, the resulting investment boom was once again due primarily to "investment enthusiasm" at the local level.[8] The system as it existed in the late 1970s encouraged not economic efficiency but rather attempts to "clamber into the plan" (as they used to say in Eastern Europe) by getting the project approvals needed to claim allocations of capital, raw materials, and equipment.[9] Projects tended to be submitted regardless of merit, and approvals often seemed to be based on the whim of the official in charge rather than on any economic calculation.[10]

As a result, investment goods allocations consistently exceeded what could actually be supplied. Supplies of steel, wood, and cement, for example, were subject to "three 80s": only 80 percent of demand would be allocated, only 80 percent of the amount allocated could actually be ordered, and only 80 percent of the amount ordered would actually be delivered. Similarly, orders for sets of mechanical and electrical equipment were often only partially filled. If key components were missing, even the items delivered might turn out to be unusable.[11]

Under these conditions, it was inevitable that the Leap Outward would lead to serious macroeconomic imbalances. Planned imports were far in excess of China's ability to generate the foreign exchange required to pay for them without a major increase in external debt.[12] Local resources were insufficient for the domestic investment necessary to bring all the new projects to completion. And the increased emphasis on heavy industry resulted in the neglect of the agricultural and consumer goods sectors.[13] The share of agriculture in the gross value of industrial and agricultural output (GVIAO) fell from 30.4 percent in 1976 to 27.8 percent in 1978, while that of light industry in the gross value of industrial output (GVIO) fell from 44.2 percent to 43.1 percent. Consequently light industrial products were in short supply and often of inferior quality.[14]

At the same time, household demand rose as a result of increased salaries and bonuses, forcing the government to increase state-set retail prices. With industrial raw materials in short supply, an increasing proportion of these began to be produced outside the plan and sold for higher off-plan prices. This resulted in upward pressure on producer prices as well. Year-on-year CPI inflation continued to rise until 1980, when it peaked out at 6 percent, the highest level since the early 1960s.[15]

Given the lack of a coordinated central plan and the poor incentives facing producers, it was also inevitable that the Leap Outward would result in considerable waste and inefficiency, just as earlier investment drives had done. "Newly built railways . . . failed to meet the needs of the shipment of commodities," materials such as steel products and electric motors were "seriously overstocked," and the drive to modernize agriculture led to "a tremendous waste of manpower, material and financial resources" as "many places engaged in farmland capital construction in a big way" producing "slipshod farm implements at high cost, of low efficiency."[16] In some cases expensive imported machinery was damaged simply because it wasn't properly stored after being delivered.[17]

When the third plenum convened, it had little choice but to call a halt to the Leap. A new policy of "readjustment, restructuring, consolidation and improvement" was announced, under which investment would be "commensurate with our capability."[18] In the heavy industry sector, 348 large-scale projects and 4,500 smaller ones were halted, in some cases leaving foreign investors with large losses.[19] Production targets were cut and the supply of available funds was curtailed through measures that included stronger management of bank credit, freezing enterprise deposits, and 4.8 billion yuan in government bond sales to enterprises.[20]

The Great Leap Outward was relatively constrained by the standards of the command economy era. Unlike the over 30 percent real FCF growth that had occurred in the peak years of 1958, 1964, and 1969, real FCF grew by only 18 percent in 1978 and decelerated rapidly thereafter. This reduction in volatility is perhaps unsurprising given that high-tech industrial imports had to be purchased from foreign companies and paid for in foreign currency. Unlike domestic enterprises, foreigners were not directly affected by the "investment enthusiasm" of China's central and local governments. And while the People's Bank of China (PBoC) could print any desired amount of yuan, the supply of US dollars could not exceed the sum of export receipts and external borrowing.

Leaping outward thus required the state to cede to overseas lenders and suppliers some of the economic power it normally enjoyed, with the (presumably unintended) result that some of the excesses of previous years were avoided.

During the period following the Leap, the emphasis shifted to improving incentives in the agricultural sector. The communes were broken up, with their assets reassigned to individual families under a "household responsibility system,"[21] which allowed farmers to keep any surpluses above a fixed quota.[22] This new system was introduced on a trial basis in 1978. By the end of 1984, essentially all of the communes' basic accounting units had adopted it.[23] At the same time, state-set agricultural procurement prices were increased and free markets for farm products were introduced.[24]

These developments led to dramatic increases in agricultural productivity. Average annualized growth in grain production increased from 2.1 percent for the 1957–1978 period to 4.9 percent from 1979 to 1984. Cotton production increased almost three times, from 2.16 to 6.25 million tons from 1980 to 1984. The output of oil-bearing crops more than doubled, from 5.21 to 11.91 million tons. China switched from being a net importer to a net exporter of grains, raw cotton, and soybeans, generating an agricultural trade surplus of 4 billion US dollars for the period from 1980 to 1984.[25]

The investment cycle during the period from 1978 to 1984 thus followed a pattern not unlike those described by Eckstein for the command economy period (see Chapter 3, Section 4). A boom in investment was followed by improved incentives in agriculture, which in turn created the necessary conditions for the next boom. But this time, the incentive changes were permanent—there was no subsequent return to the commune system or reversal of the policy on free markets. Instead of continuing to take "one step forward, two steps back," the policy makers had finally begun to move the economy steadily forward.

2. CLAMBERING OUT OF THE PLAN (1984–1992)

The success of the agricultural reforms encouraged the government to take on industrial liberalization. Following some early experiments in state-owned enterprise autonomy in the late seventies and early eighties, in 1984 the Party decided to begin phasing out central planning altogether.[26] This was not, as one might imagine, a matter of reducing the number of state-owned enterprises administered directly from Beijing. Even in 1978, there had been only 2,000 of these, accounting for just 2 percent of the total. Central government control was exercised primarily through control over investment funds and allocations of raw materials.[27] The key reforms were therefore (1) replacing investment financing from the state budget with bank lending and (2) allowing off-plan trading in raw materials at market prices. Both were gradually implemented throughout the 1980s and early 1990s.

Another important development in 1984 was the completion of a two-tier banking system. Under the command economy, the People's Bank of China (PBoC) had functioned not only as the country's central bank but also as a commercial bank. In addition to being responsible for managing the money supply, it also accepted deposits from individuals and state-owned enterprises and made working capital loans. This system began to change with the separation of the Bank of China and the Agricultural Bank of China from the PBoC in 1979.[28] On January 1, 1984, the PBoC finally became a true central bank, transferring its commercial banking businesses and much of its branch network and staff to the newly formed Industrial and Commercial Bank of China.[29]

Localities were also encouraged to develop collectively owned enterprises. Unlike state-owned enterprises, which are owned by the country as a whole even when they are administered at the local level, these entities are legally the collective property of their own workers. In practice, however, they were often little more than "mini-SOE's owned by local governments."[30] Their share in fixed asset investment rose from 5 percent in 1980 to 15 percent by 1988. It peaked at 18 percent in 1993.

The enterprise and banking reforms initiated in 1984 were at once an essential step toward building a market economy and a recapitulation of the command economy era mistake of devolving decision-making authority without hardening state sector budget constraints. The situation was exacerbated by an announcement in the last quarter of 1984 that the banks' lending quotas for the following year would be based on their 1984 levels. This resulted in a scramble by the newly independent commercial banks to expand their lending before the year end. As a result, year-on-year loan growth for 1984 reached 28.9 percent, with 48.8 percent of this increase occurring in the month of December alone.[31]

While the focus of the Leap Outward had been on heavy industry, in the mid-1980s most of the overinvestment occurred in the processing and building sectors. The combined share of power, transportation, and raw materials in total state sector basic construction fell from 53.7 percent in 1984 to a historic low of 48.8 percent in 1985.[32]

This change in emphasis reflected a fundamental change in the incentives faced by the local governments and the enterprises they controlled. In the late 1970s, the main objective had been to "clamber into" a central plan that included unrealistically high targets for products like steel and cement. Now that central planning was being eliminated, there was a shift into "prestige" projects like office buildings and exhibition halls, along with amenities, such as new employee housing, that decision makers could personally enjoy.[33] Production facilities that could take advantage of distortions in the price system were also popular. These used inputs available at low state-set prices to produce products such as home appliances[34] that could be sold at high market-set prices.[35]

Another contrast with the Leap Outward was the effect of consumption and investment growth on net exports of goods and services. In 1978, 1979, and 1980, deficits in this account of 1.1 billion, 2.0 billion, and 1.5 billion yuan had set records. In 1985, however, the deficit ballooned to 36.7 billion yuan from a surplus of 0.1 billion yuan in 1984. This was followed by a 25.5 billion yuan deficit in 1986, with a return to balanced trade only in 1987 when there was a 1.1 billion yuan surplus. The situation was exacerbated by a 1984 devaluation of the official exchange rate for the yuan from 1.99 to 2.80 yuan to the US dollar. This had the immediate effect of making imports 41 percent more expensive in yuan terms just as import demand was accelerating. The stimulative effect on exports from the cheaper currency would only be felt as more export-manufacturing capacity was brought online.

Over the course of 1985, the central government introduced a number of new policies to bring investment—particularly off-plan investment—under control. Banks were prohibited from lending to off-plan projects. Enterprises investing their own funds were required to deposit their entire project amounts with the Construction Bank and these deposits were frozen until the end of the year.[36] State-set interest rates were increased. For example the one-year deposit rate was raised from 5.76 percent to 6.84 percent on April 1 and to 7.2 percent on August 1. The required reserve rate saw its first use as a policy tool, being set initially at 10 percent.[37] Access to foreign exchange was also tightened in order to reduce imports of both factory equipment and consumer goods. And the authorities cracked down on illicit trading in quotas for foreign exchange and strengthened enforcement of limitations on foreign exchange retention by exporters.[38]

These measures were effective in the short term but did little to eliminate the new incentives to overinvest created by the market economy. And following a slowdown in real FCF growth from 1985 to 1987, policy was again relaxed starting at the beginning of 1988. Credit conditions eased dramatically—by mid-1988 bank lending was up 2.5 times year-on-year. A new round of economic liberalization got underway, providing a further stimulus. New profit-retention schemes for enterprises and preferential policies for investors in designated coastal cities were introduced.[39] Not surprisingly, real fixed capital formation rebounded sharply, rising by 15 percent for the full year. Net exports of goods and services swung back into the red as well, with 15.1 billion and 18.6 billion yuan deficits in 1988 and 1989, respectively, following the small surplus in 1987.

Inflation also became a serious problem, particularly following a decision in May 1988 to accelerate the transition to market pricing.[40] A price index including fifteen industrial raw materials rose by 18.5 percent from January to September, with coking coal up 15 percent; steel, 20.9 percent; lumber products, 26.5 percent; copper and aluminum, 40 percent; and caustic soda, 49.3 percent.[41] The Jefferson et al. (1996) FAI price index for 1988 was up only 7.6 percent but rose 23.6 percent in the following year. Full-year 1988 CPI inflation reached a record high of 18.7 percent as the share of retail prices set by the market rose to 49 percent from 38 percent the previous year.[42] Rapidly rising prices for everything from food to laundry detergent led to waves of panic buying in the big cities.[43]

In September new policies were announced to slow the economy and bring inflation under control. These were similar in many respects to the administrative measures employed following both the Leap Forward and the Leap Outward. Once again, the authorities relied primarily on the command economy method of simply stopping construction by fiat. Anything not part of the state budget was suspended. Banks were prohibited from lending for off-plan investment. Eighteen thousand existing projects were halted or postponed. Starts for new projects valued at more than 50,000 yuan fell to 41,000 in 1989—a 47 percent decrease from the previous year. Six million construction workers were wholly or partially left idle and debts to contractors totaling 10 billion yuan went unpaid.[44]

There were also increases in interest and required reserve rates. The one-year deposit rate was raised from 7.2 percent to 8.6 percent in September 1988 and to an all-time high of 11.3 percent in February 1989. The required reserve rate, which had already been increased to 12 percent in 1987, was raised to 13 percent, also in September 1988. The People's Bank of China ceased using this rate as a monetary policy tool for the following ten years, keeping it unchanged at 13 percent until 1998.

Investment growth remained relatively subdued during the two years following the June 4, 1989, suppression of the Tiananmen Square student movement. As had been the case following the two Great Leaps, more conservative forces within the Party took control of economic policy. The replacement of Zhao Ziyang by Jiang Zemin as Party secretary signaled the beginning of a period of relatively strict central government control over investment, not unlike the periods following Mao's retreat from the Great Leap policy at the 1959 Lushan Conference or Hua Guofeng's replacement by Deng Xiaoping at the end of 1978.

The post-Tiananmen period also saw a dramatic falloff in consumer demand, which meant that expansion of production lines for items such as home appliances dropped sharply. After growing rapidly in the years after 1985, these markets were basically saturated. Falling inflation also meant that consumers were no longer buying products such as refrigerators and washing machines as a hedge against rising prices. While refrigerator capacity had increased by 1.1 million sets in 1988, it rose by only 0.5 million sets in 1989.[45] Production fell from 7.6 million to 6.7 million sets[46] as "mountains of refrigerators choked warehouses all over China."[47]

Declining demand for both consumption and investment goods, combined with a recentralization of control over imports, also resulted in a turnaround in net exports of goods and services. Following an 18.6 million yuan deficit in 1989, there were surpluses of 51.0 billion and 61.8 billion yuan in 1990 and 1991, respectively. The official yuan rate, which had remained fixed at 3.73 to the US dollar from 1986 to 1988, was raised to 4.73 by the end of 1989 and to 5.23 the following year. This move partially reduced the gap with the market rate, which had already reached 5.5–5.8 by November 1990.[48]

3. FROM SOUTHERN TOUR TO LONG LANDING (1993–2002)

Local-level "investment enthusiasm" reemerged with a vengeance after Deng Xiaoping's January 1992 "Tour of the South." The Tour, which included visits to the Shenzhen Stock Exchange and a variety of high-tech factories, signaled support for continued "reform and opening" and marked the start of a new phase of economic reform.

As markets for most products had been liberalized during the 1980s, the next step was to allow trading in real estate and financial assets. An unprecedented incentive for property investment was created. Local governments and enterprises were given the opportunity to convert their land holdings into marketable projects. While previous construction booms had been limited to buildings for the investor's own use and prestige projects, the focus now turned to condominiums, luxury "villas," and leasable office towers. In 1992 investment in property development rose by 117 percent year-on-year. The floor area of commercial buildings completed increased by 58 percent, developer's operating revenues by 87 percent.[49]

A craze for "development zones," inspired by Deng's endorsement of the Shenzhen Special Economic Zone (across the border from Hong Kong), quickly got underway as well. Localities around the country designated areas within which investors enjoyed tax breaks and other incentives. By March 1993, when the central government finally began to crack down on the practice, governments at the county level or higher had set up some 6,000 such zones covering a total area of 15,000 square kilometers—enough to cover almost half of Taiwan. Many existed in name only as they lacked sufficient funds for site development.[50]

Although the ostensible purpose of these zones was to draw foreign capital into the manufacturing sector, in practice they catered primarily to local and off-shore real estate speculators. From 1991 to 1993 real estate accounted for 90 percent of foreign investment inflows.[51] In many cases promoters' claims about attracting overseas money had more to do with getting approvals for incentive schemes than with any real marketing plans. Much of the office and high-end residential space constructed, particularly in subprime areas, was purchased by locals betting that some "greater fool"—possibly but not necessarily foreign—would eventually take it off their hands at a higher price.

The year 1992 also saw the beginning of an important new phase in enterprise reform—the conversion of state- and collectively owned enterprises into joint stock corporations. This process continued throughout the decade and eventually led to the listing of many of China's largest state-owned enterprises on local and foreign stock exchanges. The result has fallen far short of genuine privatization, however. Either the central or local governments continue to hold controlling stakes in almost all of the companies.

Financial sector supervision following the Southern Tour became exceptionally lax. By some estimates, as much as 30 percent of the financial system was unofficial and unregulated. Each state bank had a number of nonbank financial institutions (NBFIs) as wholly owned subsidiaries.[52]

These had ready access to funds through the market for interbank lending. Loans that would normally be made to help maintain banks' reserve levels on a short-term basis (e.g., overnight) were available for periods of anywhere from three months to three years.[53] Lending at 20–30 percent, some two to three times the official loan rate, NBFIs became a major source of financing for property investment and other speculative projects in coastal cities. This happened even while credit was so tight in the interior provinces that some state grain-trading companies had to pay farmers with IOUs.[54]

Year-on-year real FCF growth rose to 22 percent in 1992 and peaked out at 23 percent in 1993. While foreign direct investment played a more important role than it had in previous booms, the Southern Tour craze was primarily a local phenomenon. It was driven less by FDI than by out-of-control lending at the state sector banks. M2 growth rose from a low of 20.0 percent in 1989 to a high of 33.3 percent in 1992, pushing CPI inflation from a low of only 3.1 percent in 1990 to a post-1949 record high of 24.1 percent in 1994. (M2 is a measure of the money supply that includes currency in circulation, demand deposits, and savings deposits.)

By mid-1993 it was again time to "apply the brakes by central control." In addition to shutting down development zones and delaying new project starts,[55] cutting off financing for investment projects proved to be particularly effective. Lending quotas for financial institutions were strictly enforced. An abrupt switch to a stricter prudential supervision regime resulted in a massive credit crunch as loans that had been improperly used to finance investment were abruptly recalled. Property projects throughout the country ground to a halt as developers ran out of working capital and speculators lost access to credit.[56] Interest rates, which the People's Bank of China had been cutting since 1990, were increased dramatically as well. The one-year deposit rate, which had been reduced to 7.6 percent by 1991, was raised to 11.0 percent by July 1993.

The Southern Tour property craze relied more on illicit financial flows than had been the case with previous booms. These flows served as a major source of funds both for the activities of developers and for their customers' pre-purchases. The subsequent policy tightening thus made more use of measures that affected the supply of credit. But it would be a mistake to characterize these measures as market based or to confuse the 1993 strengthening of prudential supervision with conventional monetary policy. The essential feature of market-based monetary policy is that creditors make their own decisions about which projects to fund. In contrast, credit controls imposed by the central government are better described as a new application of command economy-style macro-management techniques.

The tightening policy remained in place through 1996, when full-year CPI inflation finally fell back below 10 percent. With Chinese exports threatened by the 1997 Asian financial crisis, the policy priority began to shift toward "continued rapid and healthy development."[57] In mid-1998 an aggressive series of fiscal stimuli were announced including state investment in highways, hydropower, granaries, and irrigation. Meanwhile the People's Bank of China continued with a series of interest rate cuts it had started in 1996, bringing the one-year deposit rate from 11.0 percent at the beginning of 1996 to 3.8 percent by the end of 1998. It cut the required reserve rate for the first time in a decade in April of that year, from 13 percent to 8 percent. It was cut again, to 6 percent, in 1999.

Unlike in 1992, however, prudential supervision of the financial system continued to be relatively strong. The central government was simultaneously carrying out plans to clean up the banks and close loss-making state-owned enterprises. Measures were taken to mitigate credit risk, for example, by moving loan-approval authority to higher levels within the banks' bureaucracies. This limited the ability of localities to get financing, cutting off most projects lacking central government sponsorship.[58]

Conditions in the late 1990s were not particularly favorable for investment in any event as excess capacity had emerged in a variety of industries by mid-1997. In the first half of that year excess supply was reported for only 5.5 percent of 613 product categories. However, by the second half this share had risen to 31.8 percent. Similarly, statistics for 900 product categories revealed that more than half had capacity utilization rates for 1997 of 60 percent or less. An analysis of 140 basic industrial commodities found that inventories had increased for 109.[59]

The emergence of excess supply marked a major turning point for the Chinese economy with important implications for the investment cycle. By the late 1990s, China had not only become self-sufficient in a wide variety of products but had also considerably expanded its export markets. The share of finished manufactured goods as a proportion of total exports rose from 74 percent in 1990 to 87 percent in 1997.[60]

Chronic shortages and trade deficits were a thing of the past. Following a record 68 billion yuan deficit in 1993, net exports of goods and services were consistently in the black, reaching a record 355 billion yuan in 1997 and remaining in a range of 200 to 400 billion yuan until 2003. The yuan peaked at 8.45 to the US dollar in 1994, following a devaluation that unified official and market rates. After several small revaluations it remained pegged at approximately 8.28 from 1997 until 2005.

The period from 1997 to 2002 marked a notable departure from the pattern of booms and busts up to that time. Since 1978, peaks in investment growth accompanied by trade deficits, rising inflation, and shortages of power and industrial raw materials had occurred about every five years. Six years after the Southern Tour craze, however, the overheating previously observed at this point in the cycle did not recur. Instead, the "soft landing" on which government officials were congratulating themselves in 1996 was prolonged by an unprecedented period of deflation, excess supply, and trade surpluses lasting another six years.

4. Overheating and Magic Weapons (2003–2008)

Investment growth finally took off again in 2003. Real FCF growth reached 20 percent for the full year. Nominal FAI growth peaked at 43 percent in the first quarter of 2004.[61] In addition to the usual overheating in the property sector, overinvestment was most severe in heavy industry. Statistics for projects valued at 5 million yuan or higher showed increases in full-year 2003 investment of 96.6 percent for steel, 92.9 percent for aluminum, 121.9 percent for cement, 87.2 percent for autos, 80.4 percent for textiles, and 52.3 percent for coal.[62]

An important catalyst for the 2003 boom appears to have been a change in local-level personnel. From late 2002 to early 2003, there were leadership changes in the majority of localities. The new leaders, expecting to be judged primarily on economic growth within their jurisdictions, immediately launched new projects. During the height of the boom, in the first quarter of 2004, FAI by the central government rose by just 4.8 percent, but investment in local government-sponsored projects was up 60.2 percent.[63]

The local leaders' investment enthusiasm was matched by a newfound eagerness to lend on the part of the state-owned banks. By this time they had transferred large portions of their nonperforming loans to state-owned asset management companies as part of their preparation for listings on the Shanghai and Hong Kong stock exchanges. Lending to local projects helped to generate the high loan-growth numbers they would need to attract investors for their initial public offerings. It also lowered the banks' nonperforming loan ratios by increasing the denominator of the bad loans/total loans fraction.[64] Local government-backed projects were also considered to be relatively safe, as they were perceived to enjoy an implicit central government guarantee. Thus the supply of loans increased to meet the demand. Quarterly loan growth remained at 20 percent or higher from the first quarter of 2003 to the first quarter of 2004.

The jump in investment was accompanied by serious shortages of coal, electricity, and fuel. By the beginning of 2004, twenty-four of China's thirty-one provinces and provincial-level municipalities were suffering from frequent power outages. By the summer it was estimated that the shortfall had reached a historic high of 30–35 gigawatts nationwide, more than the 22.5 GW installed capacity of the entire Three Gorges Dam project.

Rapid growth in demand for coal in the first half of 2004 also put a severe strain on the rail system, with many trunk lines operating at 100 percent capacity. In July some power plants reported coal inventories sufficient for only three days. The so-called electricity drought (*dianhuang*) also led to tight conditions in the markets for refined oil products as enterprises in a number of places turned to small diesel-powered generators for extra power.[65]

By mid-2003, policy makers were already warning about overheating in various sectors. The economy was beginning to run up against obvious resource constraints. And the banking system was at risk because of the use of bank loans to finance potentially unprofitable investment. The central government's response was initially limited by concerns about possible economic effects of the SARS epidemic, however, and no really effective measures were taken until 2004.[66]

At the beginning of that year, the People's Bank of China instructed the commercial banks to limit lending to steel, aluminum, and cement projects. Then, following the first quarter's 43 percent FAI growth, additional policies were rolled out. The National Development and Reform Commission (NDRC) began requiring promoters to reduce the share of bank loans in the financing of investment in overheated sectors. The State Council announced a half-year freeze on the conversion of agricultural land to industrial use along with a nationwide "cleanup" of projects in a variety of sectors. These included not only iron and steel, aluminum, and cement plants but also Party and government offices and training centers, high-speed rail schemes, golf courses, convention centers, logistics hubs, and large-scale shopping centers.[67]

The PBoC, which had already raised the required reserve rate from 6 percent to 7 percent in 1999, increased this rate to 7.5 percent in 2003 and to 8 percent in 2004. Interest rates were also increased, though only slightly. The one-year deposit rate, which had been cut to a low of 2.0 percent in 2002, was hiked to 2.3 percent in October 2004. It remained at this level until 2006.

All these measures—particularly the so-called magic weapons (*fabao*) of restrictions on land and credit and ad hoc official interventions—brought FAI growth down to 28.6 percent in the second quarter of 2004. It remained below 30 percent until the second quarter of 2009.

Investment continued to outpace GDP growth, however, with the result that the share of FCF in GDP continued to set records.

At the same time excess capacity persisted in many sectors. Despite the 2004 project cleanups, in September 2009 the NDRC was still expressing concern about overinvestment in steel, cement, and aluminum. In 2008 these industries had capacity utilization rates of only 76 percent, 75 percent, and 73 percent. New overheated sectors had emerged as well. 2008 capacity utilization was 88 percent for flat glass, 40 percent for methanol, and just 20 percent for poly-crystalline silicon (a key raw material for solar cells).[68]

Excess investment in property also became particularly apparent in the years leading up to the global financial crisis. By the end of 2008, JPMorgan Chase estimated nationwide inventories of residential property at twenty-four months sales. A report by the property consultancy firm King and Wood found that Beijing alone had 100 million square feet of vacant office space, an amount that would take fourteen years to absorb even at the peak pre-crisis take-up rates.

The period from 2004 to 2008 also saw an unprecedented expansion in the trade surplus. (See Figure 4.3.) Net exports of goods and services

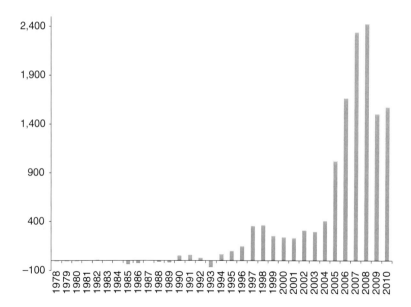

Figure 4.3   Net exports of goods and services (billion yuan)
Source: Bloomberg.

went up almost six times from 408 billion yuan in 2004 to 2.4 trillion
yuan in 2008. While the exchange rate was allowed to appreciate from
8.27 to the US dollar at the end of 2004 to 6.83 at the end of 2008,
the PBoC had to intervene continuously to keep the currency from rising even faster. It bought massive amounts of foreign currency (mainly
US dollars) from the commercial banks and then sterilized the resulting
money supply increase, primarily through reserve rate increases and sales
of central bank paper. (See Chapter 7 for a detailed discussion.)

5. GROWTH AT ANY COST (2009)

In the wake of the global financial crisis, China faced a potentially
disastrous economic situation. From June 2008 to February 2009,
year-on-year export growth plummeted from 19.2 percent to negative
25.7 percent. Growth in real estate investment, which by that point
accounted for about a third of total FAI, fell from 30.1 percent to 4.9
percent. As many as 40 million migrants were reported to have lost jobs
in manufacturing and construction, often with their wages still unpaid, as
business owners disappeared with whatever cash their companies had left.

In the absence of any effective bankruptcy procedure, banks, suppliers,
and employees were sometimes left with no alternative but to loot abandoned factories. In some cases they even dismantled and removed parts
of whole buildings. In Dongguan, an electronics manufacturing center in
the Pearl River Delta famous as the world's largest manufacturer of computer mice, some creditors were even reported to have recruited members
of the People's Armed Police to remove assets at gunpoint.[69]

The central government's response included many of the same measures that had been adopted following the 1997 Asian financial crisis.
As had been the case then, the goal was to keep real GDP growing at
8 percent. This was the rate the policy makers believed was necessary to
prevent widespread unemployment and social unrest.

In the last quarter of 2008, the central government announced a four
trillion yuan spending package. Thirty-eight percent of this amount was
allocated for transportation, 25 percent for earthquake reconstruction,
10 percent for housing, 9 percent for rural infrastructure, 9 percent for
technical innovation, 5 percent for energy/environment, and 4 percent
for health and education.[70] Monetary policy was loosened as well. The
required reserve rate was lowered from 17.5 percent in June 2008 to
14.5 percent by December; the one-year deposit rate from 4.14 percent in
September 2008 to 2.25 percent in December. As was the case after 1997,
the exchange rate was kept constant, in effect suspending the gradual
appreciation the People's Bank of China had allowed starting in 2005.

Central government spending alone was only expected to contribute two percentage points to GDP growth.[71] This was hardly enough to meet the 8 percent target if the collapse in exports and property investment that began at the end of 2008 were to continue throughout the whole of 2009. To give an added jolt to the economy, the authorities resorted to a tactic that they had been unable to try in 1998—relaxing financial sector prudential supervision. With the big state-owned banks recapitalized following their listings on the securities exchanges in 2005 and 2006, it was now possible to take the risk that unrestrained loan growth would result in large increases in nonperforming loans.

Encouraging lending had an immediate and unmistakable effect, with monthly year-on-year loan growth rising above 25 percent early in 2009 and remaining above 30 percent for much of the year. New yuan loans for the full year came to 9.6 trillion yuan, or 29 percent of GDP, dwarfing the 4 trillion yuan stimulus and the official fiscal deficit of only 2 percent of GDP.

It was clearly this dramatic expansion of the banks' loan books, rather than central government spending, that made it possible for year-on-year quarterly FAI growth to rise above 30 percent in the second quarter of 2009 for the first time since 2004 and to remain above that level until the end of the year, ensuring that the 8 percent growth target would be met.

As was the case during earlier credit booms, much of the new money made its way into risky investment projects. By some estimates, a quarter of the total went into the property market. As much as 40 percent may have been loaned to local governments through vehicles known as local government investment platforms (LGIPs).[72]

LGIPs were backed primarily by the localities' expected revenues from future land sales rather than by cashflow from their investments. Many of those investments reportedly consisted of redundant infrastructure projects or were in sectors with excess capacity. By the end of 2009, some 8,221 LGIPs were reported to have borrowed the equivalent of 240 percent of total nationwide local government annual revenue. Seventy percent of the investments were said to be unprofitable.[73]

6. INVESTMENT AS AN ENGINE OF GROWTH

Despite the dramatic changes that have occurred in China since 1978, the investment cycle for the last thirty years has displayed a remarkable degree of continuity with the pre-reform era. All six of the cycle peaks that followed the introduction of the reform and opening policy were the product of local-level "enthusiasm." All five of the slowdowns were primarily the result of administrative measures imposed by Beijing.

As the country moved into the twenty-first century, it seemed almost as though the clock had been turned back to 1958. Despite all the reforms that had taken place, in 2003 the localities engaged in yet another steel drive. And in 2009 the policy makers even required local governments and state-owned enterprises and banks to contribute to the fulfillment of growth targets. Both of these strategies were strangely reminiscent of Mao-era moves.

At the same time, it is evident that the cycle has been transformed by the introduction of markets, by new forms of ownership, and by China's entry into the global economy.

Markets and new forms of ownership led to dramatic improvements in incentives. These developments eventually made it possible for China to transition from chronic excess demand for producer and consumer goods to the unprecedented levels of excess supply observed in many sectors by the late 1990s. Market pricing also meant that rising inflation became a prominent feature of all the post-1978 booms and created opportunities for profitable arbitrage between prices for state-controlled inputs and finished products. The profit motive became a key determinant of the character of investment overheating, giving rise to excess capacity in sectors as diverse as home appliances in the 1980s and high-end real estate today.

Internationalization has allowed China to transcend the limits of its indigenous resources. This development, together with the emergence of excess industrial capacity, has meant that high rates of investment growth have become less inflationary. In 2003, for example, real FCF grew at 20 percent year-on-year, but CPI inflation peaked at only 4 percent in the following year. Compare this to the situation in 1993 when the 23 percent real FCF growth resulting from the Southern Tour craze was followed by 24 percent inflation in 1994. The shift from excess demand to excess supply that made this change possible can easily be seen from the net export statistics. While the Southern Tour led to a 68 billion yuan trade deficit, ten years later the balance of trade had swung to a 299 billion yuan surplus.

With excess supply and high trade surpluses, it has become much easier for the central government to carry out countercyclical policy. During the 1980s and early 1990s, measures to slow investment growth had to be sufficiently draconian not only to eliminate ill-conceived projects but also to bring down excessive trade deficits and high inflation. Today the authorities are much better able to adhere to their oft-repeated policy desideratum of "preserving while suppressing" (*you bao you ya*)—cracking down on particular sectors while continuing to support others. As a result, post-boom declines became noticeably less pronounced starting in the late 1990s and the FCF series became less volatile.

It should be noted, however, that as Chinese demand has begun to push up world commodity prices these have increasingly begun to play the constraining role on investment formerly played by rises in the domestic price level. As China's share in the global economy has continued to rise, its excess-demand era investment/inflation cycle has begun to reemerge, this time on a worldwide scale.

An important though often overlooked consequence of the reform and opening strategy has been to increase the scope for expansion drive, one of the main drivers of the socialist booms and busts described in Chapter 3. While the post-1978 economic policies tend to be presented as a complete break with what came before, it would be more accurate to characterize them as simply a more successful method of "building socialism with Chinese characteristics." Ironically, now that excess supply has replaced excess demand the old dreams of the command economy, for example, being number one in steel production, are finally coming true. Yet the very efficiency gains that made it possible for Chinese industry to expand successfully have at the same time given the old boom–bust cycle a new lease on life.

Further evidence for this view of the reform and opening approach comes from the relative ineffectiveness of conventional monetary and fiscal policy measures in the Chinese context. While these invariably accompany the central government's efforts to smooth the cycle, it has never been possible for them to take the place of command economy-style administrative interventions.

While interest and/or reserve rate increases have been implemented during every episode of overheating since the mid-1980s, lending quotas and tightened prudential supervision continue to be the monetary authorities' primary policy tools. Similarly, in the late 1990s attempts to stimulate investment with fiscal policy were unsuccessful in the absence of a relaxation in the prudential supervision regime. The 2009 investment rebound clearly had more to do with out-of-control bank lending than with Beijing's much ballyhooed stimulus package. The ineffectiveness of conventional monetary and fiscal policy is arguably the clearest indication that even after thirty years of reform and opening there has yet to be a truly fundamental transformation in the nature of China's economic system.

It is often said that exports and investment are the "twin engines" of Chinese economic growth. The analysis presented here implies that the real engine of growth is investment, just as it was under the command economy. The primary function of the export sector is to generate the foreign exchange necessary to import goods that would otherwise be in shortage during a boom—not only the capital goods and raw materials used directly in investment projects but also agricultural products that would be undersupplied when farmers took jobs on building sites or when their land was expropriated by property developers. To extend the metaphor, exports might be better thought of as a lubricant or a coolant than as a separate propulsion mechanism.

In this regard China is perhaps not that different from Korea and Taiwan during their "take-offs" in the 1960s and 1970s. In those cases, Rodrik has argued that export growth was primarily a response to increased import demand resulting from investment booms. While one might imagine that investment grew as a result of factory construction by exporters, Rodrik finds that the causality went the other way. "Export orientation," he notes, "enables growth (by allowing imports [e.g., of capital goods] to increase), but is not its ultimate determinant. Ultimately, the reasons for growth must be traced back to why it became profitable to invest."[74]

In the Korean and Taiwanese cases, these reasons included government interventions that increased the return on private capital. In the Chinese case, the role of the state is even more direct. With the majority of the investing being done by either wholly or partially state-owned locally controlled entities, stimulating investment does not even necessarily require an increase in its profitability. The issue becomes not why it became profitable to invest but simply what motivated the local governments to do so. We take up this question in the next chapter.

CHAPTER 5

WARPED INCENTIVES AND "SECOND-BEST" EFFICIENCY

Shang you zhengce, xia you duice.

[Above there are policies, below there are counterpolicies.]

—Chinese saying

CHINESE INVESTMENT BOOMS SINCE 1978 have invariably been led by local governments—governments at the provincial, municipality, county, township, and village levels—rather than by the central government. They may invest either directly, for example, in public works or through the enterprises they control. They may also act indirectly—by offering incentives to enterprises outside their jurisdictions or to the private sector.

To understand the Chinese investment cycle we must first understand what motivates local government investment policy. As institutions, local governments benefit from investment because they can claim a portion of the return it generates, either as profits from their own enterprises or as taxes. But the distorted incentives facing local-level officials as individuals are even more important than those they face in their official capacities.

Chapter I, Article 3, of the Chinese Communist Party constitution requires Party members to "adhere to the principle that the interests of the Party and the people stand above everything else" and "subordinate their personal interests" to them. In practice personal interests are nearly always paramount, as career advancement and financial gain take precedence over "serving the people." This makes the stimulus for investment in today's China largely a product of prospects for promotion within the government/Party hierarchy along with opportunities to amass wealth through corruption.

This chapter examines the incentives motivating local officials and shows why these result in investment booms whenever they are not checked by Beijing. The basic problem is that the system incentivizes maximizing local GDP and fiscal revenue at the expense of economic rationality. The emphasis is "on quantifiable results, rather than process."[1] Officials rise through the system on the basis of statistical indicators that may convey little information about whether resources are being used efficiently. Fiscal revenue maximization results in a race to the bottom among localities. Corruption only makes things worse, replacing benefit to society with kickbacks and bribes as the criteria for deciding which projects get done and which don't.

The relative importance of local GDP, fiscal revenue, and corruption as motivators naturally varies from case to case. These factors may be mutually reinforcing, for example, when projects simultaneously deliver both kickbacks and GDP growth. They may also lead to contradictions. GDP maximization will not necessarily be revenue maximizing if it has to be incentivized by tax breaks. Similarly, revenue will not be maximized when investors pay bribes. Generally they will enjoy some corresponding reduction in their obligations to the government.

Such contradictions may in some cases ameliorate economic distortions. Even the most dishonest officials will not be in a position to give away state land to developers in exchange for a bribe when their locality is relying on land sales to cover expenses. Constraints like this are insufficient to correct the problems with the incentive structure, however. They force officials to prioritize among suboptimal strategies rather than to adopt optimal ones.

The existence of perverse incentives does not imply that all investment is irrational. Indeed if investment generally served no real purpose, China's post-1978 economic transformation would not have been possible. Perverse incentives do, however, help to explain the extraordinarily irrational character of Chinese booms and the extreme levels of excess capacity that typically result. They explain vacant apartments, idle or inefficient industrial plants, and empty airports, not the entire capital stock. But it is these failures, rather than the obvious success stories, for which a theory of the boom–bust cycle must account.

In recent years, the central government has repeatedly emphasized the importance of "scientific development" and "putting people first" in its attempt to make Chinese investment less wasteful. (See Chapter 9 for a detailed discussion of the scientific development concept.) Unfortunately, under the current system these slogans are little more than empty words.

As Hayek argued, economic rationality cannot be imposed from above. Putting people first is an illusory goal if they are not allowed to participate in decision making.

Under the current system there is no way to maximize social welfare because individuals are unable to express their preferences. Inevitably, the public's priorities are subordinated to those of the Party, while the priorities of the Party as an institution are subordinated to those of its members. Thus the system generates suboptimal results from the point of view of social welfare while producing optimal outcomes for the politically powerful. Irrationality at the macroeconomic level goes hand in hand with rationality on the part of individual decision makers.

The effective control of local government/Party officials over most investment decisions trump any theoretical advantage Beijing's technocrats might otherwise have. While their interventions can be efficiency improving, this is only relative to the grossly inefficient outcomes that would result from leaving lower-level officials to their own devices.

The remainder of this chapter looks at these forces in detail. Section 1 shows how fiscal considerations and the promotion process shape the incentives facing local officials. Section 2 describes some examples of the resulting excess investment. These include inefficient small-scale plants, facilities that exceed the optimal scale, and even projects that appear to serve no purpose at all. Section 3 explores another consequence of the system—intense competition among jurisdictions for investment from private sector and outside investors. Section 4 examines the role of corruption in investment decision making, looking at cases involving roads, railways, and public buildings. Finally, Section 5 presents a "second-best" efficiency argument in favor of central government intervention.

1. TAX-REVENUE MAXIMIZATION AND "TRACK-RECORD" BUILDING

The Chinese literature on local government expansionism tends to focus on the fiscal situation of the localities and the promotion process for officials. Both are undoubtedly important, and they generally create complementary incentives. Career prospects are better for those who can achieve larger budget surpluses. Fiscal revenue maximization alone, however, cannot explain the low level of economic cooperation observed among local governments. Competition for promotion appears to be the more fundamental of the two explanations.

The fiscal case for investment is easy to state: when a new business locates in a community it increases local government revenue. The new revenue may consist either of profits, when the investor is one of the local government's own enterprises, or of taxes. The latter became increasingly important after 1994, when the central government's share in tax revenues was increased without a corresponding decrease in the local governments' obligations.

This policy change had the unintended consequence of exacerbating local protectionism and redundant investment as localities stepped up efforts to defend their fiscal turf. Consider the value-added tax, for example. Since this is collected from the factory where a product is made, rather than at the point of sale, jurisdictions where production takes place capture income from those where the output is sold. Defending the tax base therefore requires producing as much as possible locally, even at the cost of building plants that are too small to realize economies of scale.[2]

The tax-revenue maximization theory is consistent with much of the anecdotal evidence. However, this explanation is not completely satisfactory because it implicitly assumes that localities cannot cooperate. Instead of replicating each other's inefficiently small plants, couldn't neighboring governments build a variety of different large-scale plants and take advantage of gains from trade and specialization? The Chinese economist Zhou Li'an has solved this puzzle by showing how competition for promotions makes officials unwilling to work together even when doing so might produce win-win outcomes for their local economies.[3,4]

The promotion process is a solution to the "hidden action" problem faced by the leadership in overseeing China's vast government/Party hierarchy. While outcomes at lower levels such as grain production or GDP growth can easily be observed, it is generally not so easy to account for them. A high growth number, for example, might be attributable to effective economic management but might also be due mainly to other factors. Incentivizing officials requires a system of rewards and punishments that motivates them to take desired actions even when these cannot be directly monitored.

One straightforward way to solve this problem is simply to reward good outcomes, much as a salesperson who had a good year might be rewarded with a bonus. But when many people are involved, a cheaper solution is to set up a tournament that rewards the person who achieves the highest ranking relative to his peers. This creates incentives by forcing the participants to compete against each other. While each of them might prefer to take actions that are suboptimal from the point of view of his superiors, anyone who did so would only lose out to his rivals. The situation is analogous to the "prisoner's dilemma," where two accomplices in a crime are made to confess in separate interrogations because neither can trust the other not to do so.

Zhou's account of investment promotion begins with the observation that Chinese officials compete in tournaments where the rankings are based mainly on indicators of economic growth, principally GDP, and the reward is promotion. The system is not unlike that used during the Great Leap Forward, when grain deliveries were the measure of success, or those employed in the Soviet Union and Eastern Europe to stimulate the fulfillment of production targets for various products. It shares an obvious weakness with those earlier socialist incentive schemes—the emphasis is on quantity rather than quality. Cooperation is discouraged.

Measures such as GDP or the production of particular commodities are unsatisfactory proxies for economic performance and become even less reliable when used to rate the effectiveness of individual officials. An ideal tournament-scoring method would instead make use of Hayek's "knowledge of the particular circumstances of time and place." But this is ruled out because, as Hayek argued, it is not generally possible to convey such information to any central authority in statistical form. (See Chapter 3, Section 2.)

In addition, indicators used as a basis for promotion become unreliable because people invariably discover ways to game the system. In the Soviet Union, for example, steel manufactures found that the easiest way to meet their targets for a certain volume in tons was to produce thicker sheets. Similarly, trucks made unnecessary trips to help fulfill quotas measured in ton-kilometers. Furniture makers built oversized sofas to meet quotas in rubles.[5] And when "numbers produce officials and officials produce numbers," as the Chinese say, outright fraud will be an issue as well.

The problems with the tournament system are further exacerbated when officials using tournaments to motivate their subordinates are themselves involved in similar competitions for promotion. For example, a county-level Party secretary who is going to be ranked on the basis of his county's GDP growth will naturally choose to rank the heads of the townships in his jurisdiction in the same way. Even if he could use more rational criteria for assessing their performance, he would find it counterproductive to do so. If they don't maximize GDP, neither will he.

One result is that targets set by provincial-level governments routinely exceed Beijing's nationwide targets. Zhou gives as an example the Eleventh Five-Year Plan, which targeted real GDP growth of 7.5 percent per annum. All of China's thirty-one provinces and provincial-level cities set targets higher than this. The average provincial target was 10.1 percent; the highest was 13.0 percent, the lowest, 8.5 percent.[6]

In addition to maximizing economic growth, officials may also be expected to meet other more specific objectives handed down by their superiors. For example, villages may be required to build new schools or police substations that meet precise specifications or to surface all highways with pitch and bitumen.[7] Typically these requirements are uniformly imposed regardless of need, the ability of the village governments to pay for them, or the possibility that there might be more pressing local priorities.

Targets like these are necessary because Hayekian decentralized knowledge is inaccessible. Numbers replace need as the basis for decision making regardless of their practical relevance. The goal of improving the local school system is considered to be met if every school has "six coats of paint, brick walls, an iron gate, and a garden environment."[8] Public safety is enhanced if each police substation has five rooms.[9] Under such a system, efficient resource allocation is a practical impossibility.

At the national level, policy on renewable energy is similarly misguided. This involves not only local governments but also managers at central government-controlled enterprises, who compete in tournaments similar to those for local-level officials.

In 2006 it was decided that non-hydroelectric alternative energy sources must account for 3 percent of total installed capacity at the large state-owned power producers by 2010, reaching 8 percent by 2020. The power companies generally chose to build wind farms, as these are more economical than solar or biomass facilities. As the targets are for capacity rather than annual production, an incentive was created to build in the windiest locations regardless of their proximity to the existing transmission network or the economic feasibility of installing new power lines.[10] As a result, 26 percent of China's wind-power capacity was not connected to the grid at the end of 2010.[11]

At the same time, local governments around the country have gotten into the wind-turbine-manufacturing business, thanks in large part to a central government subsidy to support local production. In 2010, China had more than a hundred turbine manufacturers. Most of these are quite small, with the top thirteen accounting for 98 percent of supply. 2010 excess capacity in this sector is believed to have been as high as 50 percent.[12]

Local governments are also eager to promote wind-farm investment within their jurisdictions, making land available almost free of charge for this purpose. Whether or not there is a connection to the grid makes no more difference to the officials than it does to the power company managers. The fact that much of the offline capacity is susceptible to damage from windblown sand also does not matter.

Even a Ministry of Industry and Information Technology vice-minister has admitted that one of China's largest wind farms, a 10 GW project in

Gansu Province dubbed the "Three Gorges of the Land," is "a typical image project" (i.e., a project done primarily for the purpose of making officials look good).[13] It could take years for all of this capacity, which is scheduled to be completed by 2015, to be brought online. Meanwhile the project's idle turbines are being continuously blasted by sand from the Gobi desert.

China has become the world's leading wind-power investor, a fact which many foreign commentators have cited as an example of the efficiency of its authoritarian government. Other countries, we are sometimes told, should study and learn from this program to develop alternative energy sources. But those making such claims are mistaking the power companies' rush to meet state-set targets for the development of an effective alternative to fossil fuels. While China's massive investment in wind power seems at first glance to be part of the solution to the problem of global climate change, on closer inspection much of it turns out to be little more than Potemkin environmentalism.

2. REDUNDANT CAPACITY AND INEFFICIENT INVESTMENT

Zhou finds that using tournaments to rank officials has two important consequences for investment:[14]

(1) Cooperation among localities occurs only when it does not affect the relative rankings of the officials involved.

(2) Local government entry into any particular sector will continue as long as it benefits someone's relative ranking, regardless of whether or not new entrants are likely to be profitable. This implies that unprofitable new entries may even occur solely for the purpose of reducing the profitability of existing players.

These two laws of Chinese economic life create distortions not unlike those resulting from Chairman Mao's principle of self-reliance. The situation is surprisingly similar to the "customs union without a common market" that Donnithorne described in 1972. (See Chapter 3, Section 4.2.) More than thirty years later, Zhou still finds that localities are less able to cooperate than the many independent countries that have entered into bilateral and multilateral trade agreements.[15]

One important implication of Zhou's analysis is that the more similar two areas are, the more difficult it will be for them to cooperate. Localities within the Pearl and Yangtze River Deltas, the Beijing/Tianjin/Hebei area, and the Northeast all have a tendency to invest in the same industries and to engage separately in every category of investment designated by the central government as a national priority. Zhou cites as an example the three northeastern provinces of Liaoning, Jilin, and Heilongjiang, each of which has designated a similar set of "pillar industries" in the petrochemical sector.[16]

Such redundant capacity is typical of other heavy-industry sectors as well and often includes plants that are too small to realize economies of scale. The steel boom in 2003, for example, included investment in numerous small smelters, many built by private companies with local government incentives. By 2004, China had a total of 280 steel enterprises, of which 200 had an annual capacity of less than 100,000 tons.[17] This compares to capacity of about 3 million tons at even the smallest international producers.

Small-scale cement plants have also continued to be popular with local governments, much as was the case during the command economy period. While cement companies in other countries typically produce millions of tons a year, in China most cement is still made in plants with capacities of only 50,000–200,000 tons a year. The majority of these are owned by local government-controlled entities, which in many cases are still installing shaft kilns not unlike those used in the 1960s. (See Chapter 3, Section 4.1.) The product is of poor and uneven quality and generally used only within the locality where it is produced.[18]

Local governments are also responsible for small and inefficient capacity in a variety of other industrial sectors, including oil refining, auto manufacturing, and aluminum and zinc smelting, to mention just a few examples. Occasionally there may be some justification for these investments. For example, cement is uneconomical to transport over long distances because its value per unit volume is low. Thus in remote areas not easily accessible by road, a small-scale kiln might make economic sense. But in most cases, a more efficient industrial structure could be achieved with large modern plants supplying multiple localities. Such plants would also emit much less pollution per unit of output, thereby helping to bring down the considerable health costs associated with Chinese industry.

Investment manias generally involve, almost by definition, the emergence of excess capacity in particular sectors. However, this does not typically include plants that are too small to achieve economies of scale. Booms in market economies, even where the investors might be accused of "irrational exuberance," do not tend to result in overinvestment in small-scale facilities producing inferior products using out-of-date technology. In the absence of the distorted incentives facing China's local officials, it seems unlikely that such overinvestment would be a feature of Chinese booms either.

Localities may also strive to be in the leading position in as many sectors as possible. This can easily lead to investment in facilities that far exceed the optimal scale. For example, during the opening years of the twenty-first century many municipalities in the Yangtze and Pearl River Deltas built what were supposed to be "first-tier" airports, even in cases where it should have been clear at the outset that they would be underutilized and lose money. As one indicator of the extent of the overbuilding, Zhou cites a calculation of the airport density in the Yangtze Delta, which found 0.8 airports per 10,000 square kilometers. This compared with 0.6 for the United States, despite its much less dense and more affluent population.[19]

It might be imagined that most Chinese airports would be profitable given the rapid growth in air travel since 2004. This is not the case, however. In 2010, 130 out of China's 175 airports, or 74 percent, were losing money. Their combined losses for the year came to 1.68 billion yuan. Most of them were in second-tier cities; many have only a few flights a week.[20]

Consider the city of Fuyang in Northeastern Anhui Province, for example. Located in a relatively remote location in one of China's poorer interior provinces, the city originally had only a small landing field for flights to Hefei, the provincial capital. In the 1990s, the local government decided to "raise the city's profile" by building an international airport. The original airport's 400-meter runway was expanded to 2,400 meters (long enough for commercial flights to most Asian destinations) and a 7,200-square-meter terminal and other amenities were built at a total cost of 320 million yuan.[21]

In 2004, after being open only a year, the new facility had to be closed because there was not enough traffic to keep it operating. While it was finally reopened in 2008, as of 2011 its website showed only three flights a day.

Local governments appear to have remained surprisingly optimistic about the prospects for airport projects. Despite China's recent development of a new high-speed rail network, which presumably will reduce growth in air travel, the Twelfth Five-Year Plan includes forty-five new airports.[22] One of these will be built in Jiaxiang, Zhejiang Province—just an hour's drive from two airports in Shanghai and another in Hangzhou, cities to which Jiaxiang has also recently been connected by high-speed rail. Total investment in this project comes to 300 million yuan.[23]

Such optimism seems hard to explain in terms of conventional economic rationality. Perhaps it is simply the result of a blind faith in the idea that "if you build it they will come." However, from the point of view of officials competing for promotions it may in fact be quite reasonable.

If each official's main objective is simply to outrank his peers during his tenure in office, what counts is the short-term boost to GDP growth that can be realized during the construction phase, rather than long-term profitability. After all, if the officials are successful in the short term, in the long term they will have moved on to other postings. Furthermore, if a municipality doesn't have an airport but its neighbor does, it may not want to take the risk that the neighbor will be able to use its transportation advantage to outcompete it in attracting outside investment.

A similar "build-it-and-they-will-come" spirit seems to have motivated a craze for theme park investment that began in the mid-1990s. Here again, the number of badly conceived, poorly sited projects is hard to understand if their main purpose is to increase local government revenues.

In 2009, it was reported that only 25 percent of China's 1,000 theme parks were profitable. Of the remaining 75 percent, 60 percent just broke even, while the remainder generated losses. Up until 2006, most were built by local governments. Since then, real estate developers, generally more interested in obtaining local government land cheaply than in making money from park attractions, have become the main investors.[24] Like the airports, the profitable parks tend to be in major metropolitan areas; the failures in second- and third-tier cities.

In addition to poor location, the losses in the sector are also attributable to lack of innovation. This can easily be seen from the tendency of new parks to imitate existing ones. Following the success of Shenzhen's "Windows on the World," which features miniature replicas of famous sites from various countries, a series of copycats were built throughout China. Neighboring Guangzhou has a (now bankrupt) "View of the World" (*Shijie Daguan*); Changsha, its own "Windows on the World"; Chengdu, a "World Paradise" (*Shijie Leyuan*); Beijing, a "World Park"; Tianjin, a "Miniworld Amusement Park"; and Wuxi, "Wonders of the World."

Parks generally do well at first but have trouble keeping the public's interest once their initial novelty has worn off. Again, lack of innovation is the problem—generally they fail to introduce new attractions or even to maintain the existing ones properly.[25]

From an ordinary business point of view it is hard to see why Chinese theme parks should be so poorly conceived and managed. But as political "track-record" projects they make perfect sense. In the short term, like the airports, they contribute to GDP growth during the construction phase. They also typically generate revenue and stimulate local tourism when they are first opened. Their poor long-term prospects are perhaps not really relevant as long as the promotion opportunities of the officials involved are not affected. Their successors in office are likely to be more interested in promoting similar projects with big short-term payoffs, possibly even building new theme parks, than in improving the return on their predecessors' investments.

Even when theme parks are built by property developers, the situation may be much the same. In the city of Baoji, for example, a Beijing developer reportedly invested 200 million yuan in a theme park in exchange for the right to develop retail space in the surrounding area, which it subsequently sold for 800 million yuan. The project was little more than an excuse for officials to trade land-use rights for a short-term economic stimulus. Neither they nor the developer had much incentive to worry about whether or not the idea made any economic sense.[26]

Some "image projects" have no discernable rationale at all aside from creating the impression that officials are getting things done. These contribute to GDP growth while they are being built, but subsequently have little prospect of contributing anything either to GDP or to fiscal revenues. The most that could be said in their favor is that they might help to create an environment conducive to economic development. Many seem to be built for the ostensible purpose of promoting the tourism and entertainment sectors.

In Funing County, Jiangsu Province, for example, the local government spent 3.5 million yuan on a 23-meter-tall replica of the China Pavilion at the Shanghai 2010 Expo. The replica, which is one-third the size of the original, sits in the middle of an 8,000-square-meter paved square along a roadside in the middle of an impoverished farming community.[27]

Similarly, in 2011 it was reported that Beijing's Grand National Theater, a landmark built for the 2008 Olympics, has inspired numerous imitators. Some thirty cities have invested a total of around 10 billion yuan in their own grandiose theater projects, though few have any need for them. Many are in relatively inaccessible development zones, making them even less likely to attract visitors. Needless to say, such venues host few events and generally do not earn sufficient revenue to cover their costs.[28]

One of the strangest examples of an image project is the 10,000-meter "green corridor" built in Huagou Township, Anhui Province, in 1998. This consisted of two rows of cement posts—one on each side of a main road—that were supposed to serve as supports for grape vines: Seventy-eight families were displaced and their homes demolished. Some ended up living under a bridge or in makeshift shelters. Two years later, reporters from China Central Television found no evidence of any viticulture—just a road lined with thousands of cement posts.[29]

These are not isolated incidents. Unnecessary landmarks, public squares, office buildings, sports complexes, cultural centers, road improvements, and even libraries can be found throughout the country. In 2010, a vice-minister for housing and rural development estimated that a fifth of China's cities and towns had such projects.[30]

D. COMPETING FOR INVESTMENT

In addition to investing directly, local governments also compete with each other to attract outside and private sector investors. In doing so, they can provide a much stronger stimulus to investment than can typically be achieved in a private enterprise economy through monetary or fiscal policy. Promoted projects, which may be undertaken by state or collectively owned enterprises from elsewhere or by privately owned entities, may be offered incentives such as tax breaks, cheap or free land, and low-cost credit. They are also often allowed to violate labor and environmental regulations.

As one official put it, "every area acts as though it were a separate country." Attracting investment from neighboring cities tends to be seen as a zero-sum game, where the score is simply the total investment value of new projects. In the Yangtze River Delta, local governments have even been known to send undercover development zone "touts" (*huangniu*) to hotels and restaurants frequented by businesspeople. Their mission is to find out what deals have been reached with rival districts and offer the investors even better terms.[31]

Officials who are successful in bringing in investors may be rewarded with bonuses, those that don't get punished with demotions. A study of "Benghai" County in Anhui Province revealed that "every county agency and every township government" had "quotas for the amount of investment they should attract each year."[32] (Note that "Benghai" is a pseudonym used to protect the author's sources.) Officials could earn commissions set at 0.5 percent of the investment in each project they successfully attracted.[33]

While there are strong incentives to maximize the quantity of investment, incentives to maximize its quality are lacking. Benghai officials, for example, made a deal with a "Taiwanese" individual to build a five-star hotel, despite the low likelihood of its attracting any visitors. 13.3 hectares of agricultural land were cleared and the farmers evicted before it was discovered that the investor was a fraud. He had no money to invest and came not from Taiwan but from Fuyang (home of the airport described in the last section). He had apparently conceived the whole idea simply as a way of enjoying the local nightlife at the county's expense.

Nothing daunted, the government simply renamed the area an "Eco-Industrial Park." This provided a new use for the land, which could no longer be farmed. At the same time, the officials presumably were able to get points for promoting environmentally friendly development. The park was subsequently expanded and is now a 15-square-kilometer provincial-level development zone.[34]

Competition for tax revenues seems an inadequate explanation for local government investment decisions in cases like this. If fiscal considerations were the Benghai officials' primary motivation, why would they have started such a project without making more of an effort to determine whether it was likely to generate any taxable earnings?

The tax-revenue explanation is also inconsistent with the common practice of granting investors multiyear tax-free periods. By the time these have expired, factory equipment is sometimes already obsolete. Investors may even insist on having expired tax-free periods extended, threatening that they will otherwise move to another locality.

Tax breaks can easily end up worsening local finances because the taxes that investments are supposed to generate may be necessary to cover the localities' investment-related expenses. This is often true, for example, of compensation owed to families that have to be relocated, which may be spread out over as many as fifteen years to match expected tax-revenue streams.[35]

In the short term, providing investors with discounted or free land is practically guaranteed to create net losses for local governments because land is not generally free. In Zhejiang province, for example, compensation for farmers and site preparation together are reported to have come to as much as 100,000 yuan/*mu* in the late 1990s while the average sale price was only 86,000 yuan/*mu*. (A *mu* is about one-fifteenth of a hectare.) The situation was even more extreme in the province's development zones, one-quarter of which did not recover even half of their costs from land sales.[36]

One of the best-documented examples of local government project promotion was that of the Tieben Steel Mill in Changzhou, a city on the Yangtze River in Jiangsu Province. In the early 2000s, Changzhou was urgently in need of large-scale investment. Its GDP growth had failed to keep up with its larger rivals Suzhou and Wuxi. In terms of economic size, it was even in danger of falling behind Nantong and Xuzhou, which had formerly been counted among the province's second-tier cities.[37] Not only was the city losing out to its neighbors in the competition for tax revenue, but its officials were losing the race for GDP.

To remedy the problem, the Changzhou government's 2003 work report called for the approval of 100 new projects of 10 million US dollars or more, of which three to five were to require 100 million US dollars or more. One of the projects selected to help meet this quota was a new steel plant, to be built by Tieben Steel, a privately owned company that already had a small existing factory in the city. The major shareholder was eager to expand, as the steel market was booming, and in 2002 had already proposed building a blast furnace with capacity of 2 million tons per year. With the encouragement of the local officials, this was eventually expanded to 8.4 million tons per year. Farmers were evicted from a site along the river and construction began in June 2003.

Work was halted in April 2004 in the midst of that year's crackdown on investment overheating. A team including representatives of nine different central government ministries and committees found that local officials had allowed the project to go ahead without required approvals from the State Council (for appropriating agricultural land) or the State Environmental Protection Administration. The local government also provided land at below-market prices—contrary to regulations requiring an open tender—and looked the other way as Tieben delayed compensation for 1,400 households (about 4,000 people) who had been forced off their farms along with payments owed to several thousand construction workers and various raw materials suppliers.[38]

The displaced farmers were left without any way to earn a living or any place to live. While the government offered to sell them discounted apartments, few had the cash to pay for them. Some moved in with relatives; others were less fortunate. Reporters from the New China News Agency visited an elderly couple who had been living for eight months with a few pigs in a shelter made out of an old boat, some bricks, and scrap lumber. They also visited four or five families who were living under a bridge and a 90-year-old woman who had taken refuge in an abandoned classroom. When her son complained to the township he was simply told, "Don't make trouble for us, the project must go ahead."[39]

An article by Jin Sanlin in the June 2004 issue of *China Investment* (a publication of the National Development and Reform Commission, China's top economic planning body) gives a detailed breakdown of the savings Tieben realized as a result of the local government's failure to enforce central government rules and regulations. His analysis is useful not only because of the significance of the Tieben case but also because it helps to quantify the magnitude of the stimulus to investment that local governments can provide.

The most important item in Jin's calculation was land acquisition. While the average price for land in Changzhou at that time was 400,000 yuan per *mu,* the project's location within a development zone meant the company would have acquired the site for no more than the zone's posted price of a 100,000 yuan per *mu.* For Tieben's 6,000-*mu* site, this savings of 300,000 yuan per *mu* translates into a total savings of 1.8 billion yuan (about 225 million US dollars at the then-prevailing exchange rate). The actual savings may have been even greater. If the land was offered at the 10–50 percent discount commonly given to large projects, the true figure could have been as much as 2.1 billion yuan. Savings on land acquisition thus were likely to have been in the range of 17.3–20.2 percent of Tieben's total 10.4-billion-yuan investment.

Proceeding without the necessary environmental-protection approvals was the second biggest source of savings. Here Jin bases his calculation on the experience of Beijing-based Capital Steel, which produced 8 million tons of steel in 1994—an amount close to Tieben's total installed capacity. Capital Steel spent 1.6 billion yuan from 1995 to 2002 on pollution abatement in preparation for the Beijing Olympics. Assuming (perhaps somewhat charitably) that Tieben's pollution-abatement systems were similar to what Capital Steel initially had in place, Jin believes that bringing it into full compliance with the regulations would also have cost at least this same 1.6 billion yuan amount and probably more, as sites along the Yangtze are subject to more stringent regulations. Thus savings on pollution abatement would have come to at least 14.9 percent of the total project value.

Finally, Jin considers the cost of capital. Assuming that the investors put up 40 percent of the financing, the project would have been capitalized at 4.1 billion yuan. With total investment of 10.4 billion yuan but only 3.4 billion yuan in bank loans, he believes that payables of one sort or another must have accounted for $10.4 - 4.1 - 3.4 = 2.9$ billion yuan. In other words, by delaying payments to workers and suppliers, the company enjoyed the equivalent of an interest-free loan equal to 28 percent of its total assets. Assuming an interest rate of 5 percent over the three-year construction period, Jin estimates a total savings in interest expense of 450 million yuan, or 4.3 percent of the project value. Adding in savings from delayed compensation to the displaced farmers, he finds that the total interest expense saved must have been at least 5 percent of the total.

This account of the cost of capital is not entirely satisfactory. Most companies have some payables on their balance sheets. It would make more sense to compute the savings based on the amount by which Tieben's payables can be considered to have exceeded some normal level. At the same time, however, Jin also doesn't consider the potentially much greater cost-of-capital savings resulting from the reduced expenditures on land and pollution abatement. If Tieben had paid the full cost Jin estimates for these two items, it would have needed an additional $1.8 + 1.6 = 3.4$ billion yuan.

Assume for the sake of argument that the company would have financed this amount with a five-year loan at an annual interest rate of 5 percent. The net present value of the resulting interest payments (also using 5 percent for the discount rate) would have come to 736 million yuan, or 7.1 percent of the project value. Jin's 5 percent figure is, if anything, on the low side.

Without the savings he has identified, Jin finds that the total cost would have been at least $17.3 + 14.9 + 5.0 = 37.2$ percent higher. This is an extraordinary figure but apparently not atypical. Jin believes that such cases are quite common, not only in the steel sector but also in the cement and aluminum industries, with many projects enjoying cost savings in the 20–40 percent range.

The majority of such projects go ahead. Tieben's shareholders were just unlucky. Had there not been a campaign to control excess capacity in the steel sector just as construction was getting underway, had the project size been smaller, and had the displaced families been more fairly treated, the plant would most likely have been completed and gone into operation.

Chinese economists generally refer to incentives such as those enjoyed by the Tieben project as "soft budget constraints." This is clearly not consistent with what Kornai meant by the term. According to Kornai's definition, a budget constraint is soft when "the strict relationship between expenditure and earnings has been relaxed, because excess expenditure over earnings will be paid by some other institution, typically by the State." The more likely the decision maker expects this external assistance to be available, the softer the budget constraint.[40]

Local government investment incentives generally do not provide this kind of support. They are a subsidy, not a soft budget constraint. Discounted land and waivers of regulations are offered ex ante, not as ex post assistance to keep a company from going bankrupt. Ad hoc extensions of tax-free periods do not really count as soft taxation either. These typically have more to do with opportunistic behavior on the part of investors than with the avoidance of bankruptcy. The alternative to ex post assistance in these cases is not that companies will have to close but rather that they will move somewhere else.

It is easy to understand why investment incentives might be confused with soft budget constraints, however, as they have similar consequences. Under a soft budget constraint, the investor has two probabilities to consider: (1) the probability that revenues will not cover expenses and (2) the probability that there will be external assistance if this happens. We can think of the decision to invest as being based on the product of these two probabilities. With a subsidy such as discounted land, only probability (1) may be relevant. If the cost reduction reduces this to the same level as the product of (1) and (2) in the soft-budget-constraint scenario, however, the investor's calculation of a project's expected value, and his choice of what action to take, will be the same.

Alternatively, while soft budget constraints raise the probability that the firm will be rescued if it gets into trouble, investment incentives lower the probability that the firm will get into trouble in the first place. From the investor's point of view, these are equivalent.

An important implication of Jin's analysis of the Tiehen project is that local government investment incentives can significantly reduce the need for financial leverage. Consider, for example, the impact of a 30 percent increase in costs on a project that had originally been relying on bank loans for 30 percent of its financing. If additional funds were borrowed to cover the entire amount of the cost overrun, debt and interest expense would both double.

As a result, even private investors with relatively hard budget constraints can take greater risks than would otherwise be the case. They can operate at a smaller percentage of capacity without making losses and can survive bigger downturns without defaulting on loans and other obligations. They thus have strong incentives to overinvest, making them willing participants in the economically irrational drive for new investment of their local government hosts.

Naturally, Chinese private investors will not put money into projects that have no chance of succeeding. Like investors anywhere, however, they do not have perfect foresight. Investment decision making is a matter of calculating odds, not certainties. The problem with promotional incentives is not so much that they subsidize obviously hopeless causes as that they encourage betting on long shots.

4. INVESTMENT AS A VEHICLE FOR CORRUPTION

Worldwide, Transparency International has reported that corruption is typically a bigger problem in construction than in any other sector. This is due to the technological and organizational complexity of most large projects, which makes it relatively easy to conceal illicit payments. The problem is worse when "there are insufficient controls on how officials behave." Overbuilding then becomes unavoidable, with many projects "conceived solely as vehicles for corruption."[41]

China is no exception. Controls on official behavior are generally inadequate and the country's rapidly growing economy has made rent seeking a highly profitable activity. The problem is exacerbated by the murky ownership status of most of China's firms, financial institutions, land, and natural resources (see Chapter 2). In the absence of individual owners, there is often no one with a strong incentive to monitor publicly owned assets. Chinese officials are not any more "ethically challenged" than their counterparts in other countries. They are just in a much better position to enrich themselves at their country's expense.

While there have been numerous well-publicized corruption cases, most of the time officials find that they can "wet their beaks" with impunity. As one official explained, "If someone gets caught, they've either been isolated in a factional struggle or got too greedy and kept too much for themselves."[42] Under these circumstances, bribes and kickbacks inevitably reinforce the stimulus to investment provided by officials' attempts to maximize tax revenues and build their track records.

This has clearly been the case at the provincial-level transportation departments. Since 1996, department heads at about half of the provinces have faced corruption charges. In an address to the fifth plenum of the Central Commission for Discipline Inspection in 2003, General Secretary Hu Jintao put the blame on "loopholes" in the investment and finance, project tendering and approval, and personnel systems. Of these, the tendering process has been particularly prone to abuse.

Bid rigging is exceptionally easy to get away with because the same officials are often in charge both of inviting bids, in their capacity as transportation department employees, and submitting bids, in their capacity as managers of department-owned construction companies. It is straightforward for them to award contracts to companies they control and then arrange payments to themselves either from these entities or from subcontractors. Alternatively, they may award contracts to outside companies in exchange for kickbacks or extract revenue from particular subcontractors or suppliers after making it mandatory for bid winners to purchase their products and services.

Henan Province has one of the worst records. Since 1997, four successive Henan transportation department heads have been sacked for economic crimes. These primarily involved bribes and kickbacks connected with project tendering.

A case from Zhengzhou, the provincial capital, provides a revealing glimpse into abuses in road building. In 2002, seven companies won contracts for the southwest section of a Zhengzhou ring road project. After being selected, they were told that they had to share the work with two other contractors. One of these had submitted a losing bid; the other, an agency under the provincial transportation department, had not even participated in the bidding. The seven winners were also required to purchase steel products through a middleman that charged them 17–24 percent markups over prevailing market prices.[43]

While the province has reformed the bidding process in various ways over the years, problems persist, with collusion among officials and bidders still commonplace. Draconian punishments also do not seem to have been much of a deterrent. The first of the four department heads got a fifteen-year sentence. The next two got life imprisonment. Apparently, ex post penalties are no substitute for effective ex ante internal controls.

There is no way to know how much of Henan's over 5,000-kilometer expressway network falls into Transparency International's category of "projects conceived solely as vehicles for corruption." But perhaps it is no coincidence that, in addition to holding the record for consecutive dismissals of corrupt transportation department heads, Henan also led the nation in expressway mileage from 2006 to 2010 despite being only seventeenth among the Chinese provinces in land area.

Even China's much vaunted high-speed rail network may, at least in part, fall into the "vehicle-for-corruption" category. Total investment in this project, which was launched as part of the central government's stimulus package in late 2008, was set at 300 billion US dollars. The original plan called for 16,000 kilometers of track by 2015.

Whether or not high-speed rail makes economic sense for China is open to question. Ticket prices are far in excess of what China's 200 million migrant workers, the country's largest group of train travelers, can afford. Not surprisingly, the five lines opened in 2011 had many empty seats. There seems to be little doubt that the system is operating deep in the red.

These problems are not unprecedented. While the entire investment in Japan's famous Tokyo–Osaka Shinkansen (sometimes called the "bullet train") was recovered just four years after it opened in 1964, five subsequent Shinkansen lines all lost money.[44] Covering the cost of high-speed rail requires a combination of affluence and population density that can be found in relatively few places. China does not seem to be one of them.

Perhaps, as the *Economist* suggested, "Chinese Communist Party leaders' economic priorities are defined by a different kind of cost-benefit analysis than that familiar to politicians in capitalist democracies." In the short term, the project might be worth doing for the sake of the jobs created. In the long term, ridership should gradually increase with rising incomes. And think of the boost to national prestige.[45]

Indeed Party leaders' economic priorities are different—but not always in the way that the *Economist's* commentator had in mind. In February 2011, both the railway minister, Liu Zhijin, and his deputy general engineer, Zhang Shuguang, were removed from their posts in a corruption scandal involving high-speed rail construction. Liu was reportedly charged with taking bribes totaling 2.1 billion yuan. Zhang, known as the "father of Chinese high-speed rail," was said to have had the equivalent of 2.8 billion US dollars in US and Swiss bank accounts.

We may never know why these two officials originally promoted this project. Since the costs to society may well exceed the benefits, it seems likely that opportunities to benefit personally may have played a role in their decision making. In the absence of such opportunities, it is possible that high-speed rail might never have been proposed in the first place or have been conceived on a much smaller scale. It is also possible that many of the safety issues that have subsequently come to light, including the signaling problem that led to the fatal Wenzhou collision of July 24, 2011, might have been avoided.

In many cases, both corruption and track-record building may influence investment decision making. Many projects can potentially play a dual role, allowing officials to improve their chances for promotion while at the same time feathering their own nests.

Consider, for example, the bizarre case of the "Loudi White House," a domed, six-story municipal government headquarters completed at a cost of 500 million yuan in 2006 in the small, relatively poor city of Loudi in Hunan province. (If anything, it actually looks more like the US Capitol than the White House.) This building, which included sufficient space for thirty agencies, with 50 square meters per employee, was phase one of a planned redevelopment covering 5.5 square kilometers, 2 square kilometers of which were taken from local farmers. Total investment was eventually expected to reach 1.5 billion yuan. In addition to the White House, the plans called for new roads, public buildings, and even a fire station.

This scheme had all the characteristics of a typical image project. In 2007, it also became the focus of a corruption probe. Eighteen cases were brought against twenty-six people involving illicit payments totaling 20 million yuan. Local Party secretary Shen Qinghua alone was alleged to have received bribes exceeding 1 million yuan, including 344,000 yuan in exchange for construction contracts for the building itself and 548,000 yuan for a 13-million-yuan contract to build a 40,000-square-meter wall. Construction and landscaping companies were also said to have paid over a 100 million yuan in bribes to Shen and Xie Wensheng, a local Party standing-committee member.[46]

Interestingly, these officials' successors have shown no less appetite for image projects. In July 2011, Bloomberg News reported that the city was building "a 30,000-seat stadium, bulb-shaped gymnasium and swimming complex" at a total cost of 1.2 billion yuan. The justification: Loudi will be a stop on the Shanghai–Kunming high-speed rail line. This out-of-the-way town, Bloomberg's reporter was told, is now an "emerging city."[47]

The relationship between corruption and promotion as motivating factors is, in the final analysis, not a straightforward one. Corruption may, for example, undermine the incentives provided by the promotion system if officials have opportunities to collect bribes and kickbacks in their current positions or can move up by bribing their superiors. Moreover, the sale of public office is not uncommon. In "Benghai County" some 80 percent of department heads were believed to have paid for their positions. In another county, in Henan Province, prices ranged from 60,000 yuan for township Party secretaries to 400,000 yuan for Finance Bureau heads.[48]

At the same time, however, corruption may also be an important incentive for individuals to seek promotion in the first place. Otherwise, why would positions with official salaries of only a few thousand yuan per month be for sale?

5. A "SECOND-BEST" CASE FOR INTERVENTION

It might be argued that most of China's excess investment is ultimately motivated by the opportunities it provides officials for personal financial gain. They may benefit either immediately, by taking bribes or using increased tax revenues to benefit themselves, or at a later date, if their track records have helped them to move to a more powerful position. They may also benefit in both the short and the long term. Alternatively, they may simply be responding to pressure from superiors who will be the real beneficiaries.

In any event, such investment hardly promotes economic efficiency. Unlike the activities of private entrepreneurs in a market economy, there is no presumption that the machinations of local officials stimulated by dreams of personal gain will create value.

In fact, investment in today's China is prone to inefficiency for two reasons. First, the soft budget constraints enjoyed by the governments themselves and the enterprises they control naturally result in overbuilding, as was the case under the planned economy. Second, investment-promotion incentives lead investors to take on risk that would otherwise be unacceptable. These incentives limit the downside by reducing financial leverage.

In both cases, inaccurate or deliberately distorted predictions of future demand result in excess capacity, just as would be the case in a market economy. But the magnitude of the problem is greater because investors are in a position to take on riskier projects.

There will also be inefficiency, even in a world of perfect certainty, simply because resources are not allocated optimally. Distortions in the land market are a case in point. Generally, localities provide industrial land at a discount while at the same time restricting the supply of commercial and residential land in order to maximize revenue from the sale of land-use rights to developers. The result can only be too many factories relative to the number of apartments.

This outcome will fail to maximize social welfare regardless of whether or not the factories are running at full capacity. Were all land to be sold at market prices, the increase in the supply of housing would more than make up for the loss to consumers from the reduction in the supply of manufactured goods. (This loss might result either from consuming fewer locally produced goods or from reduced export revenues.) In the language of welfare economics, society would move to a higher social-indifference curve at which the marginal rate of substitution in consumption became equal to the marginal rate of transformation in production.

A similar argument could be made about the conversion of agricultural land to industrial land, which has resulted in the displacement of 2–3 million farmers a year since the turn of the twenty-first century.[49] Here, in addition to the losses to the displaced people themselves, there is also less agricultural production than would be optimal.

When investment promotion allows manufacturers to pollute indiscriminately, the inefficiency is even more obvious. Clearly the optimal trade-off between environmental amenities and manufactured goods will not be achieved in the absence of any effective pollution-abatement incentives.

Periodic intervention by the central government to slow investment growth is generally seen as necessary in order to achieve goals such as lowering inflation, alleviating power and transportation sector bottlenecks, and preventing the build-up of nonperforming loans at the banks. When the incentives facing local officials make it impossible to reach an optimal outcome, there is also an efficiency argument for intervention. By reducing the allocation of resources such as land and clean air and water to investment, central government-led busts partially correct for local government-sponsored inefficiencies.

Naturally, such interventions would be inefficient in a world without perverse incentives—the so-called first-best world of the economics textbook. But this is not necessarily the case in a world where such distortions must be taken as a given. There the "theory of the second best" tells us that one form of inefficiency may offset another, thereby making it possible for a constrained optimum to be achieved. If it were possible to correct local government incentives and thereby eliminate the drive for expansion not justified by market forces, central government action might not be desirable. But given China's political and economic realities, applying the brakes "by central control" is clearly optimal from a "second-best" point of view.

CHAPTER 6

BANKING AND FINANCE RUN AMOK

> Money is a creature of the state.
>
> —Abba Lerner

THE CHINESE BANKS HAVE ALWAYS BEEN ENTHUSIASTIC participants in investment booms. They are the most important source of external financing for the construction of infrastructure, industrial capacity expansion, and speculation in real estate and financial assets. Without their active involvement China's boom–bust cycle would be considerably less extreme.

The close proximity of fixed capital formation and credit growth peaks shown in Figure 6.1 has persisted despite three decades of legal and regulatory reform as well as the introduction of "state of the art" risk management systems. This chapter describes these changes and shows why they have failed to stem the flow of bank funds into excess investment.

The banks participate in investment booms in various ways. They not only lend directly to speculative projects but also support them through loans for other purposes, loans their clients use to play the asset markets. In both cases, the banks' risk management failures are primarily due to political interference and soft budget constraints. With state-owned entities holding the controlling stake in practically every bank and all top-level personnel decisions made by the Communist Party, the bankers are not in a position to act independently. At the same time, they can always count on being bailed out when things go wrong.

The potential for their clients to be bailed out also warps lending decisions. Cash-flow considerations are relatively unimportant when the borrower is perceived to have at least an implicit government guarantee.

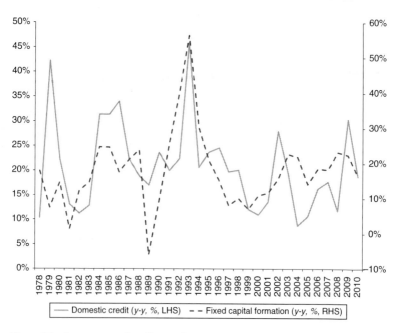

Figure 6.1   Investment and credit growth
Source: Bloomberg.

Small- and medium-sized private firms are thus at a severe disadvantage in applying for loans. Underground high-interest lenders are often their only option, regardless of the merits of their business plans.

Attempts to reduce the banking system's exposure to the investment cycle through technical fixes have been unsuccessful. When political considerations at the central government level call for an expansion in lending, laws and regulations, the interests of minority shareholders, and the banks' own internal control procedures make little difference. Even calls for restraint from the People's Bank of China (PBoC, China's central bank) and the China Bank Regulatory Commission (CBRC, the central government's top bank regulator) go unheeded.

In any case it would be difficult for external regulation and internal controls to work properly. Many loans are misclassified due to borrowers' misrepresentations and insufficient due diligence or deliberate misreporting by bank staff. Working capital financing may be used for fixed capital investment. The identity and principal business activities of the borrower may be disguised. Collateral may be overvalued or even nonexistent. Nonperforming loans may be refinanced so that they appear to be performing. While the CBRC and the banks' head offices now have world-class IT systems, there is still considerable uncertainty regarding the nature and extent of the risks to which the banks are exposed.

The Chinese banks and their regulators face a very different set of problems from their foreign counterparts. In China, bank staff cannot be isolated from political considerations and consequently have less incentive to take risk management seriously. For the large internationally active banks, unreliable employees are a relatively minor concern, despite the large losses that occasionally result from the activities of "rogue traders." As the 2008 financial crisis made clear, credit, liquidity, and market risk are their Achilles' heel.

In the first half of the 2000s, foreign financial institutions took equity stakes in a number of Chinese banks. They were not allowed to acquire controlling shares, but it was hoped that they could help to improve the banks' performance by introducing "international best practices." Indeed such an improvement would certainly have been possible under political and economic conditions similar to those for which these best practices were designed. They would normally be sufficient for the "plain vanilla" lending that accounts for most of China's banking business, even if they have not protected financial institutions elsewhere from the hazards of trading in complex derivatives products.

In practice, however, the adoption of international best practices has not raised the quality of the Chinese banks' operational risk management to the level of their international peers. The problem is not that the new systems are inadequate. It is rather that managing risk is not always a priority for the people implementing them.

Similarly, while China's regulatory institutions are not unlike those in other countries, they lack the political power to function effectively. The economic rationale for Western-style bank supervision is also less clear in the Chinese context. When banks are privately owned and their management is relatively independent of political pressures, regulators can credibly threaten to wind up insolvent institutions. The managers of such banks can keep this from happening by acting prudently. In China, insolvent institutions will simply be recapitalized. And poor lending decisions may be due as much to politics as to moral hazard.

With Chinese investment booms driven primarily by the state, it is inevitable that the banks, as state-controlled entities, help to finance them. The remainder of this chapter looks at the influence of politics on bank lending (Section 1), then turns to the failure of governance reform (Section 2), internal controls (Section 3), and external supervision (Section 4) to reduce the banks' exposure to overinvestment. Section 5 concludes with a discussion of the implications for money and credit of continued state and Party control of the banking sector.

I. POLICY-DRIVEN LENDING

Since the founding of the People's Republic in 1949, China's banking sector has been an integral part of the state. During the command economy period, the banks had no independent decision-making powers. Subsequently, they were transformed into separate entities responsible for their own profits and losses but also subject to direct interference by both the central and local governments. In 1998 the system was centralized in order to reduce local government influence, but the central government's commitment to prudential supervision proved to be inconsistent. Lending and the money supply have continued to accommodate investment booms much as they always did.

Before 1978, China had a "mono-bank" system similar to those in the Soviet Union and other socialist countries. The term "mono-bank" does not mean that there was literally only one bank, but rather that there was no distinction between the normally distinct functions of central and commercial banking. The People's Bank of China issued currency, and, at the same time, accepted deposits from households and enterprises and made short-term working capital loans. Bank of China, which specialized in foreign exchange transactions, and Agricultural Bank of China were both divisions of the PBoC. Investment financing took the form of budgetary appropriations, which were disbursed by the People's Construction Bank of China, a division of the Capital Construction Finance Department of the Ministry of Finance.[1]

There was no independent role for either the PBoC or the specialist banks. The mono-bank system was simply part of the bureaucracy. It facilitated the flow of funds among administrative units and state-owned enterprises, and provided currency to and accepted deposits from households. With government officials in charge of allocating funds, the money supply invariably accommodated the state's economic policy. During the Great Leap Forward, for example, the banks provided all the money required for commercial departments to buy "anything on offer regardless of quality."[2] Booms and busts were a political, not a monetary, phenomenon.

The Chinese economy was to a large extent unmonetized, particularly in the countryside. The Maoist emphasis on self-sufficiency meant there was relatively little need for money to finance domestic trade. Rural households also did not need much cash. They received a significant part of their income in the form of free goods and services[3] and could in any case find only a limited selection of items for sale. The underdeveloped condition of the retail sector is evident from the number of shops. By 1978 this had fallen to only 54 percent of the total for 1957.[4]

Another important feature of the mono-bank system was that funds deposited with banks were, in theory at least, not fungible among different accounts belonging to the same entity. Money designated for paying salaries or purchasing raw materials, for example, was supposed to be segregated from money for fixed asset investment. Even if an enterprise had a surplus in one account, it could not use it for any other purpose. Thus, as Kornai tells us, money was not a "universal means of exchange . . . even within the state-owned sector."[5] A parallel situation existed for households, which had to present ration tickets when purchasing many basic staples.[6] Neither firms nor individuals could freely convert their cash holdings into goods.

Mono-bank money was an extreme example of what the monetary theorist G. F. Knapp termed a "chartal" means of payment—one that is accepted by the public primarily because it can be used to discharge obligations to the state.[7] In the countries Knapp considered, such obligations mainly took the form of taxes. In traditional socialist economies, however, practically all obligations among firms and from households to firms were obligations to the state. In the absence of private businesses, households were bound to accept the state's preferred means of payment. Anything else would be worthless simply because there would be nowhere to spend it.

In China, chartal money was not always limited to the official currency issued by the central bank. In the latter half of the 1950s, many agricultural cooperatives issued "vegetable tickets," "cash circulation notes," and "co-operative currency." These were widely accepted as cash substitutes within their home areas. Later, during the Great Leap Forward, many communes issued their own notes as well.[8] Naturally the government had not declared any of this paper to be "legal tender for all debts public and private." Quite the opposite. As the minister of finance wrote in a 1959 article, "the issue of any disguised forms of money" was "absolutely prohibited." The emergence of such alternative media of exchange was due entirely to the willingness of local governments to accept such media as payment.

After 1978, loans began to replace budgetary appropriations as a source of funds for investment.[9] This change was a logical consequence of economic liberalization. Enterprises began to retain more of their profits and households to make money in the market economy. At the same time, localities and enterprises gained more autonomy in investment decision making. It was natural for the banks to intermediate between these emerging sources and uses of credit.

The mono-bank system was formally replaced by a "two-tier" system in 1984. The People's Bank of China became a true central bank (the first "tier"), responsible only for managing the money supply and supervising the commercial banks (the second "tier"). Its commercial banking operations were separated into a new entity, Industrial and Commercial Bank of China, which took over most of the PBoC branches and their staff.[10] In addition to ICBC, the second tier now included Agricultural Bank of China and Bank of China, which became independent entities in 1979, and the People's Construction Bank of China (now known as China Construction Bank), following its 1984 separation from the Ministry of Finance.[11]

Reform of the banks did not keep pace with the reform of the economy as a whole, however. The banks continued to be responsible for supporting both national and local government economic development priorities. Nor were they free to make their own lending decisions. Starting in the 1980s, they were subject to an annual credit plan that not only set total lending levels in each province but also specified the percentages to be allocated to fixed asset investment and to working capital loans.[12]

This system worked poorly because local governments could generally provide political cover for bankers to exceed their quotas. When this happened, the PBoC would simply have to provide additional funds.[13] Formerly the PBoC had funded enterprises and government units directly. Now they borrowed from the commercial banks, which then turned to the central bank for funding. From the point of view of monetary policy, this was a distinction without a difference. As one contemporary commentator observed, the new arrangement had simply made the credit plan "even more arbitrary" (*suiyixing geng da*).[14]

At the same time, the bankers were happy to expand deposits and lending in any way they could. Without hard budget constraints, they focused on capturing business from their competitors rather than on maximizing profits. Loans were given out regardless of credit risk, while depositors were rewarded with payments of various kinds that increased effective returns above the officially set interest rates.[15] While financial liberalization should in theory have promoted economic efficiency, political pressure and the absence of bankruptcy risk resulted in the banks becoming the main source of financing for speculative investment and failing state-owned enterprises.

A second round of bank sector reform began in 1998 when the credit plan was abolished and local governments ceased to participate directly in the lending decisions of bank branches in their jurisdictions.[16] Decision making was centralized within banks while supervision was concentrated at higher levels of government.

At the same time, steps were taken to recapitalize the banks and address their nonperforming loan (NPL) problems. In 1998, the Ministry of Finance injected 270 billion yuan in equity into Agricultural Bank of China (ABC), Bank of China (BoC), Industrial and Commercial Bank of China (ICBC), and China Construction Bank (CCB)—the so-called Big Four. In the following year, the Ministry initiated a plan to transfer state-owned bank NPLs to newly established asset management companies. By 2005, these AMCs had removed a total of 3.2 trillion yuan in NPLs from the banks' balance sheets. Finally, in 2003–2004, Central Huijin Investment, at that time an arm of the State Administration for Foreign Exchange, drew on China's foreign exchange reserves to inject a total of 60 billion US dollars into BoC, CCB, and ICBC.[17]

Importantly, however, the Party remained in control of selecting bank personnel. Party approval is required for the appointment of top officials at all the banks, even the privately owned Minsheng Bank.[18] The Party can also transfer or fire bank executives at will. If they are suspected of corruption, they, like other Party members, face the wrath of the Party's Central Commission for Discipline Inspection, which can hold them for months in secret extra-legal administrative detention (*shuanggui*).

The state also continued to be the controlling shareholder in practically all of the banks (see Chapter 2, Section 3). Even though most now have stock exchange listings, it is not possible for outside investors to act as a force for change. The disciplining effects of a market for corporate control are entirely absent.

Centralizing banking administration and supervision freed the banks from formal local government control. Nevertheless, they have continued to finance local government-led investment booms.

There are two main reasons for this. First, centralization is only a restraining force when the central government desires restraint. When faster economic growth is the central government's main priority, the bankers, whose primary allegiance is to the Party rather than to their institutions, still have little choice but to support local government projects. Second, the banks consider projects promoted by local governments to be relatively safe. Local governments not only have land and other assets to offer as collateral but also can usually count on a bailout from Beijing if they get into trouble.

The post-1998 centralized control mechanisms failed to reduce the banks' exposure to the investment cycle because they are not applied consistently. When the economy begins to overheat, they strengthen the central government's ability to put on the brakes. But when the central government wants to "step on the gas," it is willing to sacrifice control for the sake of faster growth. Then the banks are allowed to set aside prudential considerations and lend aggressively for whatever investments the local governments decide to promote.

At the Sixteenth Party Congress in November 2002, for example, local governments were given the green light for a new investment drive in the name of building a "well off society" (*xiaokang shehui*). The bankers and their regulators fell into line immediately as the Central Finance Work Commission, at that time the Party's top organ for financial regulation, called upon the banks to "guarantee" the accomplishment of this goal.[19] Similarly, following the 2008 global financial crisis, the banks responded to Beijing's call to maintain 8 percent growth with an orgy of new lending to local government investment platforms. Many of these will not generate sufficient cashflow to repay their loans, which, in many cases, were backed by local government loan guarantees of questionable legality. (See Chapter 4, Section 5.)

The banks have undoubtedly become considerably more independent than they were under the old mono-bank system. Ironically, however, this newfound independence has only changed them from passive to active participants in investment booms. Formerly local governments played a direct role in lending decisions. Today the banks compete actively for local government business. The ill-fated Tieben Steel mill, for example, received loans from three of the Big Four—BoC, CCB, and ABC—along with two of the larger second-tier banks—Guangdong Development Bank and Pudong Development Bank. (See Chapter 5, Section 3, for more on the Tieben case.) These institutions needed no prompting to participate and apparently put little effort into assessing credit risk or verifying that the project had the necessary central government approvals. They were also unconcerned when loans ostensibly for working capital were used for fixed asset investment. The local government's support was all that mattered.[20]

2. THE FAILURE OF GOVERNANCE REFORM

The banks' 2009 lending boom followed the partial privatization of the sector, which began in 2005 with China Construction Bank's initial public offerings (IPOs) in Shanghai and Hong Kong. By 2009, Bank of China, Industrial and Commercial Bank of China, and a number of their smaller competitors had gone public as well. (Agricultural Bank of China, by all accounts the worst managed of the Big Four, did not come to market until 2010.) According to their listing documents, these lenders had all completed major corporate governance reforms as part of their IPO preparation. They also had new responsibilities to minority shareholders, which now included global heavyweights such as Bank of America, HSBC, Royal Bank of Scotland, Goldman Sachs, Allianz, and American Express. Continuing to play their traditional role as local government piggy banks should not have been an option.

New corporate governance guidelines were promulgated by the PBoC in 2002 and the CBRC in 2005. These required the banks to appoint independent directors and set up audit, risk management, and related party transaction control committees.[21] In 2002, the PBoC also introduced new internal control requirements, which included establishing audit and risk management departments.[22] These were followed, in 2005, by additional internal control measures from the CBRC covering everything from compulsory vacations for branch officers to "segregating persons in charge of account-keeping and persons in charge of account reconciliation."[23] (Compulsory vacations create opportunities to uncover fraud while the employee in question is away.)

BoC's IPO prospectus gives a detailed account of the kinds of organizational changes that the banks carried out prior to listing. In 2004, BoC restricted loan-approval authority to its head office and tier-one branches.[24] Newly established risk management departments took over due diligence work from loan origination teams. Credit review committees at the head office and tier-one branches began reviewing credit applications for compliance with "relevant laws, rules, and regulations."[25] All corporate credit applications now had to be approved by "authorized credit application approvers" with the exception of "loans sufficiently secured by PRC [People's Republic of China] treasury bonds, bills, or pledged funds as collateral or loans supported by the credit of financial institutions...within pre-approved credit limits."[26] Following branch approval, a specialized team at the head office risk management department was put in charge of monitoring for "discrepancies or noncompliance with the required procedures or credit policies."[27]

ICBC, BoC, CCB, and Bank of Communications (BOCOM) were among the banks that had help implementing their new systems from foreign strategic shareholders. Goldman Sachs, which had a 5.75 percent stake in ICBC, provided "appropriate risk management tools and models" and assisted in developing "risk management systems and analytical models in order to provide...tools to develop a rigorous risk management infrastructure."[28] Royal Bank of Scotland, which took 9.609 percent of BoC, "seconded professionals" to take "advisory roles" in BoC's "operational risk and credit risk operations."[29] Bank of America, which bought 8.739 percent of CCB, helped develop a "comprehensive risk management framework" as part of an effort to "adopt international best practices."[30] As part of HSBC's deal to purchase 19.9 percent of BOCOM, the British lender agreed to provide "advice and guidance in relation to international practices" in areas including risk management, corporate governance, and internal audit and control.[31]

Under the new regime, analysis of credit risk was supposed to be carried out in an objective and standardized manner. BoC's IPO prospectus gives a detailed list of the relevant factors. They include expected cashflow, repayment ability, the purpose of the loan, and the quality of the borrower's guarantor and collateral.[32]

None of these seem to have been particularly important when the banks began lending to local governments in the wake of the global financial crisis. At that point, the criterion for lending seems to have changed from making a profit to keeping China's GDP growth above 8 percent. Strong cashflow and repayment potential cannot have been prerequisites for local platform loans. The majority of local platforms were not expected to generate enough operating cashflow to satisfy their obligations. They were to rely instead on revenue from local government land sales.

In many cases, the purpose of the loans does not seem to have mattered either. Many were for projects with long payback periods that subsequently had to borrow more money to make principal and interest payments. In an audit of local government debt released in June 2011, the National Audit Office found that this problem was particularly severe in the areas of road and hospital construction. Nationwide, 55 percent of the 2010 debt servicing for highway construction loans guaranteed by local governments and "other related loans" had to be covered by new borrowing. A third of the hospitals with such financing were "evergreening" over half of their debt.[33]

The case of Yunnan Highway Development Investment Ltd., a local financing platform of the Yunnan provincial government, is apparently not unusual. This company was formed in 2006 to carry out the expansion of Yunnan's provincial highway network. By 2010, the size of the network had doubled, making Yunnan third among Chinese provinces in terms of total mileage even as it remains one of the country's poorest and least densely populated areas. Many of Yunnan Highway's projects were little more than "roads to nowhere," linking the isolated hamlets of the Yunnan-Guizhou Plateau with China's Vietnamese and Burmese borderlands.

Not surprisingly, toll revenue could not cover debt servicing costs. In April 2011 Yunnan Highway notified its banks that it would be "repaying interest but not principal." By that point, it had 90 billion yuan in bank loans, compared to just 5 billion in capital. The company's bankers—China Development Bank, a centrally controlled policy bank, China Construction Bank, and Industrial and Commercial Bank of China—had kept the money flowing long after the company had violated central government regulations on highway financing. These mandate a debt to equity ratio of no more than three.[34]

Lenders to the 185 local platforms set up by the government of Liaoning Province had a similar experience. Eighty-five percent of these financing vehicles missed payments in 2010. 120 of the 185 were loss making. The provincial auditor also found evidence of fraud. 17.6 billion yuan of these platforms' bank loans had been "misappropriated."[35]

The local platforms' lack of creditworthiness was not the only problem the banks seem to have overlooked. The quality of the guarantors was frequently unsatisfactory as well. These were generally the local governments themselves despite the fact that they were prohibited by law from guaranteeing loans. In many cases, they circumvented this prohibition by offering the banks "promissory letters" or "letters of comfort," in which they pledged to prioritize the repayment of platform loans in allocating future revenue, particularly land sales proceeds. It was far from clear, however, that these letters did not constitute guarantees for legal purposes. Some also used fiscal revenues or state-owned assets belonging to their own administrative units to back local platform loan guarantees. All of these practices were explicitly prohibited in a State Council notification dated June 13, 2010. By the end of that year, however, the National Audit Office found that seven provinces, forty cities, and 107 counties were continuing to use such financing strategies.

There were also problems with land posted as collateral. In some cases the same plot was pledged for multiple loans. In others, incorrect valuation was an issue. One locality was reported to have taken out a 10-million yuan loan using land with a market value of only 3 million yuan. As Chinese banks generally only lend 60–80 percent of the value of collateral, this particular site must have been overvalued by at least 300 percent. Sometimes the registration status of the land was also in doubt. Some local government entities pledged city parks, land under administrative offices and stadiums, farmland illegally converted to other uses, or sites to which they did not even own the land-use rights.[36]

Out of a total of 6,576 local platforms, 1,033 were not properly capitalized. These included cases in which the capital had not actually been contributed, was illegally contributed by local governments or entities they controlled, or was subsequently withdrawn.[37]

The banks' credit review committees can hardly have failed to notice such obvious failures to comply with the "relevant laws, rules, and regulations." Yet of the 10.7 trillion yuan in financing covered by the National Audit Office report, bank loans accounted for 79 percent.

A look at China's regulations on related party transactions makes it easy to see what went wrong. According to the CBRC's May 2004 *Administrative Measures on Related Party Transactions Between Commercial Banks and Insiders or Shareholders,* related parties include "legal persons or other organizations under direct or indirect common control with the bank."[38] Naturally lending to such parties creates the risk that the entity controlling both the lender and the borrower will interfere in the lending decision.

The *Measures on Related Party Transactions* specify that total related party credit may not exceed 50 percent of a bank's net capital.[39] In most countries, this would be considered an unacceptably high limit. But the CBRC could not possibly have set a lower one. In the case of the Big Four, all of the central government-controlled state-owned enterprises meet the definition of "related party" because all have the central government as a controlling shareholder. More prudent regulation would deprive China's biggest banks of some of their most important customers.

In fact, while this was clearly not the CBRC's intention, its definition of related party really includes local governments and local government-controlled enterprises as well. All of these are controlled by the Party. They therefore should logically be considered as being under "common control" with the banks. If the *Measures on Related Party Transactions* were interpreted in this way, most of the banks' existing loans would have to be recalled.

Effective control of related party transactions would require either genuine privatization of the banks or the privatization of their customers. Absent either of these alternatives, most of the Chinese banks' business will inevitably be done with related parties. And the Party, rather than the "authorized credit approvers," will have the final say on what loans get made.

Governance reform never really had a chance to succeed because the political prerequisites for it were lacking. Administrative tinkering could not have effected fundamental changes without any corresponding limitations to the Party's economic power. The banks' failure to control lending to local government platforms strongly suggests that their new committees, departments, and regulations were more effective as talking points for marketing IPOs than as a line of defense against NPLs. While the risk management systems introduced by foreign strategic investors allowed the banks to write about "international best practices" in their offering documents, these practices evidently do not work as well in China as in those investors' home countries.

3. LAX DUE DILIGENCE AND SPECULATIVE INVESTMENT

The local platform lending boom was not the first evidence that the banks' new risk management systems were not working as advertised. In the years leading up to the global financial crisis, the banks were a major source of funds for real estate and stock market speculation. Both were important contributors to fixed asset investment. In the mid-2000s, property development accounted for as much as a third of FAI. Bank funds diverted into the stock market contributed indirectly by making it easy for listed companies to raise capital.

Commercial bills provided one of the most popular means of accessing credit for speculative purposes. These are essentially corporate IOUs, documents in which one Party (the drawee) undertakes to pay another (the drawer) a specified sum on a particular date. Chinese law requires that commercial bills must be backed by genuine commercial contracts. The drawee is generally supposed to be a buyer, the drawer, a vendor.

The drawee can turn a bill into a readily negotiable instrument by arranging to have it "accepted" by a bank. The accepting bank agrees to make the payment on the drawee's behalf. The drawee agrees to pay back the bank, pays a fee, and deposits a percentage of the bill amount as margin. With a 100 percent margin, acceptance serves solely to guarantee payment. Smaller margin percentages also make it possible for the drawee to purchase more than it would immediately have the cash to cover.

Acceptance makes it easier for the drawer to finance its operations because the bill becomes the bank's obligation rather than the drawee's. The drawer can easily have an accepted bill discounted, selling it to a financial institution for less than the full amount prior to the due date. The discounting bank can also easily rediscount the bill, selling it to an investor (in China this will typically be another bank), again at a discount to face value. (Naturally the rediscount rate will have to be lower than the discount rate for this to be profitable.) Ownership is transferred by endorsement. The accepting bank's obligation will be to whoever is holding the bill on the due date, the so-called "holder in due course."

Proper due diligence for acceptance, discounting, and rediscounting is relatively straightforward. In addition to verifying the corporate identity and creditworthiness of the drawee, the accepting bank must ascertain that the underlying contract is genuine. Discounting and rediscounting require checking that accepted bills are genuine. Such precautions ensure that bills financing is backed by real commercial activity. Acceptance is connected with the drawee's operating business via the underlying contract between the drawee and the drawer. Discounting and rediscounting

ANIMAL SPIRITS WITH CHINESE CHARACTERISTICS

are linked, via the accepting bank's contract with the drawee, to payments
for goods and services.

In China, lax due diligence has made bills financing a convenient
method for defrauding the banks. The problem is particularly severe at
the acceptance stage. Relatively simple frauds involve forging or alter-
ing contracts or value-added tax receipts or presenting multiple copies
of the same documents to different lenders. (VAT receipts are commonly
accepted as evidence that a contract is genuine.) Alternatively, corporate
officials may sell their firms' contract documents to outsiders. Sometimes
two firms collude, entering into phony contracts in order to get a bill
accepted.[40]

The bills financing share of total lending rose from just 2 percent
in January 2002 to a peak of 9 percent in April 2006. By that point,
the market was clearly out of control, with year-on-year growth topping
50 percent. New bills financed in the first quarter of 2006 alone reached
three quarters of the total for all of 2005. On April 18, the CBRC called
a halt, issuing an "urgent notification" that called the banks to task for
"blindly" developing the sector without proper regard for risk management. It also made public eleven cases of illegal bills financing at Bank
of China, Agricultural Bank of China, and China Construction Bank
involving a total of 750 million yuan. These cases had occurred during
the period from July 2005 to March 2006, just as BoC and CCB IPO
subscribers were reading about the new risk management systems that
should have prevented such lapses from occurring.

Most were surprisingly simple frauds that even elementary due diligence should have detected. Many of the bills were found to have improb-
able chains of endorsements, indicating that they had changed hands with
extraordinary frequency, sometimes between endorsers and endorsees in
widely separated parts of the country. At some banks, bills were discounted before being accepted. The funds received were then posted as
margin at the accepting bank, after which the completed acceptance documents were forwarded to the discounter. At others, staff used official
seals and forms to forge accepted bills or receipts for margin deposits.

Poorly implemented internal controls were a common problem. Bank
staff discounted bills without seeing them, relying only on faxes or
telephone calls for authentication. They also neglected basic audit and
accounting procedures that would normally alert staff members to incon-
sistencies in each other's work. Sometimes such mutual supervision was
even left to employees with personal relationships, for example, husbands
and wives. In one case, at a Bank of China branch in Shuangyashan,
Heilongjiang Province, the branch manager, assistant branch manager,
and three other management-level staff members were all involved in

a cover up. Together, the five had control of all aspects of the branch's bills business. It was a foregone conclusion that no "red flags" would be raised.[41]

One of the largest cases to be made public came to light almost immediately following the CBRC's urgent notification. The Huanghe Road branch of the China Construction Bank in Luohe, Henan Province, was found to have accepted 319 million yuan worth of bills without authorization. As a "second tier" branch, it was only authorized to accept bills with 100 percent margin deposits. To get around this requirement, the management simply began to do an off balance sheet business, accepting bills with less than 100 percent margin and not reporting them to the head office.[42]

The People's Bank of China called for stronger risk management in the bills market at its "window guidance" conferences on April 27 and June 13, 2006, and also began sending out teams of inspectors to look into the problem at the local level. Growth in bills financing and its share in total lending then declined rapidly. Some bank branches even temporarily suspended this business entirely.

One effect of the crackdown was that stock market speculators using discounted bills to finance trades were suddenly forced to liquidate their positions. This appears to have been one of the main reasons for the 9 percent decline in the Shanghai Stock Exchange index from July 3 to July 31, 2006.

The bills market remained relatively subdued until the global financial crisis. Then, starting in October 2008, the central government ordered the banks to increase lending even though their customers initially had relatively little demand for new loans. To raise their loan-growth numbers, the bankers began to discount bills so aggressively that discount rates fell below the comparable deposit rates. By the end of the year, three-month deposits were paying 1.98 percent while the bills rate was only 1.5 percent to 1.6 percent. Enterprises holding bills they would not normally have chosen to discount now found it advantageous to do so. They could borrow at a low rate by discounting, then put the cash they received on deposit at a higher rate. In a bizarre inversion of normal banking practice, lenders were effectively paying interest to borrowers.[43]

It is unclear exactly what happened to the flood of new cash released by this remarkable development. Much of it appears to have been used to buy shares, thereby helping to fuel the 34 percent jump in the Shanghai Stock Exchange index from October 11, 2008, to February 11, 2009. The Hong Kong paper *Apple Daily* (*PingguoRibao*) reported that some of this money may also have gone into year-end government and state-owned enterprise employee bonuses.[44]

The use of bank credit for stock speculation has been a problem ever since the mainland stock market reopened in the early 1990s. At the end of 2006, the CBRC drew attention to the problem in a circular on "Risks Relating to the Interaction of Bank Sector Financial Institutions and Securities Companies." This called for an end to the "misappropriation" of bank credit "either directly or indirectly" for stock trades and ordered the banks to recall any such loans.

In addition to bills financing, personal consumption loans were also popular with share punters. For the powerful and well connected, such financing could be surprisingly easy to get. In January 2007 the *21st Century Business Herald* described one bank branch where credit limits for government officials were typically based simply on rank—800,000 yuan for officials at the prefecture level, 400,000 for those at the county level, and 200,000–300,000 for those at lower levels. The branch's employees also had little trouble taking out consumption loans for themselves. While new hires might require some collateral, those who had been at the bank for several years could easily borrow "hundreds of thousands" of yuan with few conditions for just about any purpose they cared to put down on the application form.

In early 2007, the CBRC was also warning about the use of fraudulent mortgages to finance property development projects. In one version of this scam, developers sold units to their own investors or entities they controlled (in effect to themselves), with the "buyers" using mortgage loans to pay the "sellers." The resulting sales, often done at above market prices, made it appear that projects were selling well. The banks would only be repaid if real sales could subsequently be made, however. In other cases, multiple mortgages were taken out on the same property or on property that did not even exist at all.

The CBRC revealed that an investigation in the second half of 2006 had found fraudulent mortgages totaling "billions" of yuan. At one state-owned bank (presumably the worst offender), 1.309 billion yuan in such loans were discovered; a further 734 million yuan turned up at another. These amounts were 6.05 percent and 3.23 percent, respectively, of the personal housing credit examined at each lender. The regulator blamed the problem on "perfunctory due diligence investigations," in which bank staff merely "went through the motions" of examining loan applications without doing enough to detect irregularities.

When bank funds are used to buy property or shares in the secondary market (i.e., from investors rather than from the developer or the issuer), it is sometimes imagined that there is no effect on the "real economy." The money, it seems, is simply "sloshing" back and forth between bank accounts as investments change hands. This analysis is faulty, however, because it implicitly assumes that the supply of assets is fixed.

Suppose, for example, there is an increase in bank credit that can be used to purchase condominiums. Initially, this will push up prices. In the slightly longer run, however, developers will start building additional units. Then the new money will start being used to take up developers' pre-sales, thereby funding an increase in fixed asset investment. Similarly, a bull market in stocks opens a "window" for companies to increase capital to finance expansion projects. Again, the new money will not stay "bottled up" in the secondary market for long.

We might think of a secondary asset market as a line of traders continuously exchanging suitcases full of cash for others containing share certificates or title deeds. As long as no seller ever takes out her cash and spends it, the money is "stuck" in the suitcases. Sooner or later, however, a company will send someone to join the line of speculators with a suitcase full of newly issued shares or titles. Once this has been exchanged for one of the cash suitcases, he will return to his employer. The employer will open the suitcase, take out the money, and invest it in a real asset, possibly even levering up the initial amount with a bank loan.

The banks' risk management failures thus have important implications for investment even when they result in lending for real estate and stock punting. While those borrowing under false pretenses to finance speculation may not be putting up high rises or factories themselves, their money soon makes its way to people who are.

4. Collusion, Risk Management, and Prudential Supervision

It is often claimed that the Chinese banks passed the test of the 2008 "financial tsunami" with flying colors. This is only half true. Thanks to China's closed capital account they were relatively unaffected by events such as the Lehman Brothers bankruptcy. They were instead, however, made responsible for helping local governments to keep GDP growth from falling below 8 percent. Ironically, the leadership responded to a crisis brought on by reckless lending overseas by forcing its own institutions to lend recklessly. The response to the bursting of a credit bubble in the United States was to release a deluge of liquidity at home through local government financing platforms and the commercial bills market. The banks' "international best practices" were swept aside by the flood.

Risk management systems can only be effective when those in control of the banks want them to work. This is generally the case at the internationally active institutions, where political interference and operational risk management failures are relatively infrequent. There, the main problem is not that systems will be undermined but rather that they will not work properly. For example, the "toxic assets" on the US banks' balance sheets at the end of 2008 were the result of flawed assumptions built into derivatives valuation models rather than employee fraud or government meddling.

For the Chinese banks, such "model risk" is relatively unimportant because they have little exposure to derivatives. Large deposit bases and strong government support also make liquidity crises of the type that brought down Lehman Brothers unlikely. Spectacular collapses were unheard of even at the end of the 1990s when the ratio of NPLs to total lending at the Big Four was estimated to be as high as 50 percent.

In China, credit and operational risk are the most serious issues. The former, as the evidence on local government platform loans makes clear, is not only a matter of lax due diligence. It is primarily the result of state-directed lending, which renders due diligence procedures irrelevant. Similarly, operational risk is difficult to control because employees are able to collude with each other and with outsiders to cover up irregularities. In this case, too, due diligence procedures are irrelevant. Reporting protocols and IT systems serve no purpose if the people responsible for acting on the data they generate are themselves "on the take."

A study published in the July 2005 edition of the Chinese journal *International Finance Research* found that frauds perpetrated by employees are considerably more common at Chinese banks than at their internationally active counterparts. In China, fraud accounted for 99 percent of losses due to operational risk management failures, compared with only 23 percent internationally. Only one-third of the fraud losses at foreign banks involved insiders, compared with two-thirds in China. And while the insiders at foreign banks typically consist of a small number of relatively low-ranking individuals acting in secret, in China much of the staff, including higher-level managers, is often implicated.[45]

Poor operational risk management at the state-owned banks tends to be the result of widespread collusion among employees at all levels, as occurred at the Bank of China branch in Shuangyashan mentioned in the last section. The problem is therefore considerably more difficult to solve than it is at foreign banks. The adoption of new internal control policies by the head office or the regulator is unlikely to make much difference if there is organized resistance to carrying them out at the branch level.

Widespread fraud perpetrated by colluding employees also weakens credit, liquidity, and market risk management because it hinders an accurate analysis of the risks to which banks are exposed. A bank accepting bills used to finance stock trades rather than commercial transactions, for example, will underestimate the extent of its stock market exposure. It also will not hold appropriate collateral. The amount in its margin accounts for the bills will not fluctuate with the market valuation of the borrower's share portfolio.

Prudential supervision will be undermined in the same way. Consider the CBRC's "Project 1104," for example. (The name comes from the date on which the program was inaugurated, November 4, 2003.) This is an off-site inspection program that gathers information from supervised institutions on their financial health, risk exposure, and capital adequacy. In a presentation in June 2006, when the system first began to "go live," CBRC Statistics Department Director Liu Chengxiang explained that the institutions were providing the basic data in a series of twenty-four standard forms and twenty-five special forms customized for particular situations, which the CBRC then subjected to further analysis, including the compilation of twenty-three "core indicators." These, he claimed, made it possible to see the main risks facing the banking system "at a glance."[46]

Liu described Project 1104 as a "revolutionary reform" in bank supervision, with the potential to mitigate threats to the financial system before they materialized. The output of any such undertaking, however, can only be as good as the inputs. With the banks recording the land under local governments' administrative offices as collateral, evergreening platform loans, and accepting and discounting fraudulent commercial bills, many of the most significant risks they face will be left unreported.

In any case, the bankers do not seem to have been particularly cooperative. In the CBRC's April 2011 "Notification on Correctly Performing the Work of 'Supervisory Data Quality Control,'" the regulator noted that, due to the lack of a "standardized data quality control process," the banks frequently submit inaccurate and incomplete reports. Six years into the program, it was necessary for the CBRC to designate 2011 as the "Year of Data Quality." Improving data quality, however, will require more than better adherence to the Project 1104 reporting requirements. It will require an improvement in the banks' own internal controls. This will be impossible as long as bankers, local governments, and the Communist Party itself have other conflicting priorities.

5. Money as a Creature of the State

Over twenty-five years since the end of the mono-bank system, the commercial banks have yet to become truly independent. The state is still their controlling shareholder. The Party still has the final say in top-level personnel decisions. Political considerations still take priority over sound lending practices. When macroeconomic policy is expansionary, prudential supervision is loose. Bank credit then increases at the behest of officials and their cronies, financing booms in local government investment, property development, and the stock market.

The economist Abba Lerner once famously characterized money as a "creature of the state." It is issued by the state and circulates because the state accepts it as payment. This is particularly true in China. While the state is no longer the sole source of the goods and services on which money may be spent, it is still the primary provider and recipient of credit and the main holder of assets that can be used as collateral. To a much greater extent than is the case in the developed economies, monetary flows within the banking sector take the form of payments to and from state-owned entities.

Under the mono-bank system, these flows were supposed to be confined within officially designated channels through the segregation of enterprise funds into special purpose deposit accounts. Even before 1978, the boundaries between such accounts—particularly between working capital and fixed asset investment accounts—were often porous. Today, as a result of poor operational risk management at the banks, the diversion of financing into unauthorized uses has become commonplace. While the creature of the state has not slipped the leash entirely, it has become much more difficult to control.

Chinese economists tend to imagine that the problems with the banks can be fixed by making them more like their Western counterparts. A 2006 article in the journal *Nankai Economic Studies,* for example, proposed a variety of reforms such as strengthening the powers of boards of directors; breaking up the Big Four into smaller, separately listed, companies; and introducing employee stock option plans. Such measures, it was felt, could be part of an effective strategy to improve the banks' performance. More powerful boards could discipline managers more effectively. Corporate reorganization would break up networks of corrupt employees. Employee stock options would incentivize management to maximize profits.[47]

Such reforms, however, would not weaken the Party's ability to override internal controls whenever it believes economic policy goals should take precedence over bank sector asset quality. This makes it impossible to make lending decisions conform to a standardized set of norms. Instead, the banks' risk management culture is corrupted by ad hoc interventions by the politically powerful, whose power to act in an official capacity is easily abused for the sake of personal gain. Under these circumstances, corruption on the part of bank managers is hardly surprising.

Improving risk management would inevitably weaken Party control. It is therefore easy to understand why the economists' recommendations were not taken up. They were, in any case, based on a mischaracterization of the problem. Like the "international best practices" adopted ahead of the banks' IPOs, these policy proposals were predicated on the idea that the Party would willingly relinquish power to an independent bureaucracy of boards of directors and risk management committees.

In fact, however, the leadership continues to view prudential supervision of the banking sector primarily as a tool of countercyclical macroeconomic policy. Internal controls may be strengthened as a temporary measure when the economy is overheating. They are, however, just as likely to be relaxed when stimulus is called for. As long as this is the case, bank credit will continue to be readily available to finance investment booms, both through official and unofficial channels.

CHAPTER 7

TAKING AWAY THE LADLE

> The job of a good central banker is to take away the punch bowl just as the party gets going.
> —Attributed to former Federal Reserve chairman
> William McChesney Martin

SMOOTHING INVESTMENT FLUCTUATIONS IS A PRIORITY for central banks around the world. The People's Bank of China (PBoC) is no exception. Its approach to macro-management is fundamentally different from that of its Western counterparts, however. The state's dominant role in investment decision making and China's inflexible foreign exchange rate regime make it difficult for the PBoC to use interest rate policy effectively. It must instead rely on more unconventional strategies to mitigate booms and busts.

The PBoC's policy tools include open market operations (OMOs) and a variety of administrative measures. The former affect investment through changes to the base money supply—currency in circulation or in bank vaults and reserves held by commercial banks at the central bank. The latter leave base money unchanged but make it more difficult for investors to access credit. This chapter describes these options and analyzes their effectiveness as instruments of countercyclical monetary policy.

Open market operations are transactions between the central bank and commercial banks. They consist of sales or purchases of assets, typically government debt or central bank paper (CBP). OMOs change the monetary base by changing the amounts held in the banks' reserve accounts. In the case of a sale of government debt, for example, there will be a decrease in commercial bank reserves matched by a corresponding decrease in the central bank's assets. (The central bank no longer holds the debt; the commercial banks no longer hold the reserves they used to pay for it.) A CBP sale has the same effect on reserves but replaces one type of central bank liability (commercial bank reserves) with another (CBP).

Monetary policy is carried out almost entirely through open market operations in countries with well-developed financial markets. There, OMOs work through their effect on interest rates. Slower investment growth can be achieved by reducing commercial bank reserves. This pushes interest rates up, thereby increasing investors' funding costs and reducing the net present values of their projects.

For the PBoC, however, interest rates are of only secondary importance. Their effectiveness is blunted both by the insensitivity of state-subsidized investors to the cost of capital and by "hot money" inflows. The latter occur when Chinese rates rise relative to foreign rates, creating an incentive for individuals and firms to convert foreign exchange to yuan. Such conversions add to the local money supply, quickly undoing the central bank's attempts at tightening.

The PBoC's main administrative policy options include changes to the commercial banks' benchmark deposit and lending rates, adjustments to the required reserve rate (the percentage of deposits banks are required to hold as central bank reserves), and a variety of ad hoc credit-control policies.

Increases in the required reserve rate (RRR) have become particularly common in recent years. These were relatively unimportant until the take-off in China's trade surplus in 2004. Since then, the PBoC has routinely purchased foreign currency from the commercial banks to defend its exchange rate targets. Such purchases increase the money supply because the central bank pays for them by crediting the commercial banks' reserve accounts. RRR increases "sterilize" this new money by preventing the banks from withdrawing it.

In a market economy, monetary policy can be based primarily on money supply changes. During slumps, central banks create new money to stimulate economic activity. In boom times they endeavor to limit economic excesses by taking away the liquidity punch bowl "just as the party gets going."

The PBoC relies instead on administrative interventions. These leave the money supply unchanged but impose or remove artificial restrictions on borrowers and lenders. When investment is growing too fast, to extend Martin's metaphor, the PBoC leaves the punch on the table but takes away the ladle. This approach is undesirable because it does not allow market forces to operate. It is, however, the most effective option for an economy that is not primarily based on private enterprise.

The remainder of this chapter considers the PBoC's efforts to slow investment booms with "Chinese characteristics." Sections 1–4 cover the use of interest rates, required reserve rates, open market operations, and credit controls. Section 5 concludes with a look at the future of Chinese monetary policy.

1. INTEREST RATE DILEMMAS

The PBoC dictates commercial bank rates directly, setting ceilings on deposit rates and floors under lending rates. In the process, it also sets a minimum level for the banks' loan-deposit spreads (the difference between comparable deposit and lending rates), thereby mandating a key determinant of bank sector profitability. However, administrative rate setting is not a powerful tool for macroeconomic management. Rate hikes alone are never enough to bring Chinese investment booms to an end.

In China, the local government-controlled or promoted entities that do most of the investing are relatively immune to higher rates. Consider the effect of the two 27 basis point increases in the one-year loan rate that occurred during 2006, for example. (A basis point is 0.01 percentage points.) For anyone starting a project enjoying promotional incentives similar to those the local authorities gave to the Tieben steel mill, these moves would have had a negligible impact. They were, after all, two orders of magnitude smaller than the 20–40 percent cost savings that investors would typically have been able to realize through discounts on state-owned land and other inputs. The central bank's attempts to tighten using interest rate policy could easily have been reversed through a marginal amount of additional local government stimulus. (The Tieben case is described in Chapter 5, Section 3.)

Local government financing platforms would have been similarly unaffected by the twenty-five basis point one-year loan rate increase that occurred in the first half of 2011. For them, higher interest payments could, in a worst case scenario, simply have been covered through additional borrowing. (See Chapter 6, Section 2, for more on local platforms.)

The existence of a large amount of local platform debt is a significant constraint on the PBoC's ability to raise interest rates. If the local platforms get into trouble, they will have to be bailed out by the banks. The banks also cannot be allowed to fail. If higher loan rates exacerbate the local platforms' financial problems—through increasing interest expenses or pushing down demand for the land they will have to sell to service their debt—their lenders will also have to be bailed out.

Such bailouts would require, among other things, a cut in deposit rates relative to lending rates. By making the banks' performing loans more profitable, the resulting higher lending spreads would help to cover nonperforming loan losses. At the same time, however, the higher spreads would also give the banks an additional incentive to lend. Whatever tightening the PBoC might originally have intended to achieve would be at least partially neutralized.

The existence of soft budget constraints for both the banks and many of their customers creates an obvious conflict between the PBoC's macroeconomic objectives and its responsibility for subsidizing the state sector. The kind of aggressive tightening that would be required for the "creative destruction" of inefficient capacity is not really an option when the central bank is also responsible for keeping lenders and borrowers afloat.

For the PBoC to use its interest rate tools effectively, it would have to enjoy the same degree of independence that characterizes Western central banks. Such independence is ruled out by the "Law of the People's Republic of China on the People's Bank of China." This tasks the central bank with "formulating and implementing monetary policies" but only "under the leadership of the State Council" (Article 2).

The PBoC's Monetary Policy Committee thus bears only a superficial resemblance to bodies like the Federal Reserve's Federal Open Market Committee or the European Central Bank's Governing Council. While the latter are relatively independent of national governments, the role of the former is limited to "consultation and discussion."[1] In China, the State Council, rather than the central bank, sets the overall direction of monetary policy and has the final say on interest and exchange rate changes.

The PBoC's attempts to slow investment with higher interest rates are also incompatible with China's foreign exchange rate regime. The yuan exchange rate is set by the PBoC rather than the market. If the commercial banks find themselves with an excess supply of foreign currency, the central bank must increase the supply of yuan to keep its value from rising.

Interest rate increases have the counterproductive effect of encouraging the conversion of foreign currency to local currency, both by onshore holders of foreign exchange and offshore holders with the option to transfer funds onshore. Following a rate hike both will be able to get a higher return on their deposits by exchanging some of their forex holdings for yuan with the commercial banks. The banks will then become net sellers of foreign currency to the PBoC, which will have to create new local currency in order to satisfy the demand for yuan at its existing exchange rate target. As the central bank buys up the excess foreign exchange, the increase in its foreign exchange reserves on the asset side of its balance sheet will be matched by an increase in commercial bank reserves on the liabilities side. It will have to increase the money supply even as it is trying to tighten.

This problem is an example of the general rule that countries with open capital accounts cannot target both the money supply and the exchange rate at the same time. If they target the money supply, they will lose control of the exchange rate. When there is an excess supply of foreign currency, the local currency will have to appreciate to restore equilibrium. Countries that target the exchange rate lose control of the money supply. Exchange rate targeting requires the central bank to purchase foreign currency surpluses. It will unavoidably create new money in the process. Similarly when there are deficits, the central bank will have to defend the exchange rate by selling foreign currency. This will reduce the money supply.

This rule does not strictly apply to China because it has a closed capital account. The scenario in which the central bank loses control of the money supply assumes that foreign exchange can freely be brought onshore. In theory, China's foreign exchange controls should limit such non-trade-related inflows.

In practice there are many ways to evade these controls. One of the most common is by using phony export invoices. These can be presented to a bank to justify the conversion of the invoiced forex amount into yuan. Similarly, inward transfers ostensibly for foreign direct investment are often converted into local currency to finance stock and property market speculation.

A popular way to estimate the size of such hot money inflows is to identify increases in the US dollar value of the PBoC's forex reserves that cannot be explained by (1) net exports, (2) foreign direct investment, and (3) US dollar-denominated gains on the PBoC's non-US dollar reserves. This method is easy to use because (1) and (2) are available on a monthly basis while (3) can be estimated from data on US dollar exchange rate movements.

Unfortunately defining hot money as the difference between forex reserve changes and the sum of (1), (2), and (3) is not entirely satisfactory. Net exports of services are left out as the relevant data are only available semiannually. There may also be timing differences between the movement of money between offshore and onshore accounts and its conversion into or out of yuan. These omissions mean that the estimate may be quite misleading in particular months although it should be a reasonably reliable indicator of the magnitude and direction of movements in hot money over longer periods.

US dollar-denominated gains and losses on non-US dollar reserves cannot be known with certainty because the currency composition of

China's forex reserves is a state secret. The easiest way to estimate this item is to make two simplifying assumptions. First, following Roubini Global Economics,[2] assume that 64 percent of the reserves is denominated in US dollars, 30 percent in euros, and 3 percent each in Japanese yen and British pounds. These shares are likely to have changed over time as the PBoC has looked for ways to move out of the dollar. Nonetheless, such changes have probably not been large enough to affect general conclusions about relatively recent hot money trends. Second, assume that at the end of each month the central bank revalues its non-US dollar reserves and then immediately returns the ratio of dollars, euros, yen, and pounds to 64:30:3:3 by buying and selling the necessary amounts of the four currencies.

Calculations based on these assumptions suggest that the magnitude of China's hot money inflows has been significant. (See Figure 7.1.) The quarterly average for the period from the first quarter of 2004 to the third quarter of 2011 was 25 billion US dollars, or 28 percent of the 90 billion

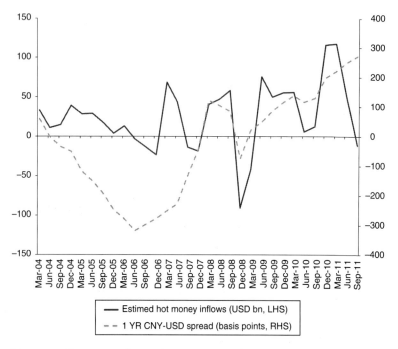

Figure 7.1   Hot money inflows and interest rate spreads

Source: Bloomberg, author's calculations.

US dollar average quarterly increase in China's foreign exchange reserves during that period.

Figure 7.1 also shows the difference between yuan and US dollar one-year deposit rates. In the years prior to the financial crisis, the yuan deposit rate was consistently below the dollar rate (in other words, the spread was negative). Starting in 2008, however, the dollar rate began to fall dramatically as the Federal Reserve began cutting rates while the yuan rate remained high as the PBoC continued to worry about inflation. The spread moved into positive territory at the end of 2007 and remained there until the fourth quarter of 2008. At that point, dramatic cuts to the yuan rate briefly brought it to a level slightly below the dollar rate. Subsequently, while the yuan rate was kept constant throughout 2009 and 2010, the dollar rate continued to decline, pushing the spread back to pre-crisis levels. It moved even higher in 2011 as the PBoC once again began raising deposit rates.

Naturally interest rates are not the only factor influencing hot money inflows. Expected returns in the asset markets and expected exchange rate appreciation also play a role. The lack of significant outflows despite the negative spread prior to 2008 is likely due to the bullish outlook for the yuan during that period along with the high returns that could be earned by holding stocks and property. The problem facing the PBoC is easy to see starting in 2008, however, when widening positive spreads coincide with progressively higher peaks in hot money.

Hot money inflows can lead to investment bubbles regardless of the reasons for which the inflows initially take place. Money brought onshore by property speculators has a direct effect on fixed asset investment. Money moved into higher-yielding deposit accounts contributes to asset bubbles indirectly by increasing the banks' supply of loanable funds.

It would thus be very difficult for the PBoC to smooth the investment cycle simply by administratively setting deposit and lending rates. Rate hikes have a weak effect on investment because of soft budget constraints, while their effect on hot money inflows is likely to be much more powerful. At the same time, rate cuts are unlikely to lead to outflows as long as the yuan is expected to appreciate.

2. STERILIZING HOT MONEY

Required reserve rate increases and money supply reducing open market operations are often described as activist policies with which the PBoC can carry out macroeconomic adjustments. In reality these tools are used almost exclusively to sterilize the new money created by the

PBoC's interventions in the foreign exchange market. In raising reserve rates or selling central bank paper, the central bank is generally responding passively to hot money inflows rather than actively "fine tuning" the economy.

Regulators require banks to hold a certain percentage of deposits as reserves in order to ensure that they will have enough cash to meet depositors' demands for withdrawals. The required reserve rate is thus part of the prudential supervision regime. But in China, as in many other developing countries, the RRR has instead become a tool for liquidity management.

A 100 yuan increase in the commercial banks' reserves at the PBoC will generally increase the system-wide deposit base by considerably more than 100 yuan because the new money can be loaned out multiple times. If every borrower deposits the entire amount of his loan in a bank account, total deposits will go up by the amount of every new loan that is made. The same will be true if borrowers use the new money to make purchases and remit their payments to their vendors' bank accounts. After deducting the reserve amount required for the new deposits, the banks can lend them out again, further increasing deposits and making possible yet another round of new lending.

This process can continue until the entire 100 yuan initial increase in the monetary base has been added to the banks' required reserves. The final amount of new deposits will be 1/RRR times 100. (The factor 1/RRR is known as the "money multiplier." Note that this gives the maximum amount by which deposits can increase, not an amount by which they are necessarily likely to increase in practice.)

As an example of how the PBoC uses the RRR, suppose that the central bank purchases 1 billion US dollars from the commercial banks as part of an intervention to keep the exchange rate at 7.00 yuan to the US dollar. The monetary base would initially rise by 7 billion yuan. If the RRR were 10 percent, the money multiplier would be $1/0.10 = 10$, and the potential increase in deposits would be 70 billion yuan.

Sterilizing this 7 billion yuan monetary base increase with an RRR hike would require that, at the new rate, 7 billion yuan would have to be added to the amount of reserves required for the banks' original deposit base. Then no additional deposits could be created. Starting with deposits of 10 trillion yuan and 1 trillion yuan in reserves, for example, the RRR would have to be increased to 10.07 percent. This would increase required reserves to 1.007 trillion yuan, with the increase in the reserve requirement exactly matching the size of the PBoC's 7 billion yuan forex intervention.

Alternatively, the PBoC may remove the new money using open market operations. In that case, it would sell 7 billion yuan in securities to the commercial banks, reducing their reserves and the monetary base by this amount rather than increasing required reserves.

The PBoC carries out open market operations at regular auctions, which generally occur on Tuesdays and Thursdays. These primarily involve sales of three-month, one-year, and occasionally three-year central bank paper. Like the developed country central banks, the PBoC also buys and sells government debt under repurchase agreements. These transactions, usually referred to simply as "repos," are effectively loans from the purchaser to the buyer, with the interest rate being the difference between the sale price and the higher repurchase price.

PBoC repos are for durations of one, two, three, or four weeks or three months, with the latter being the most common. Usually the PBoC is selling but it occasionally also does "reverse repos," buying securities in order to increase the money supply for short periods—for example, just prior to the Chinese New Year holiday. (Note that the US Federal Reserve describes repo transactions from the commercial banks' point of view, while the PBoC describes them from that of the central bank. What the PBoC calls "repos" (*zheng huigou*), the Fed calls "reverse repos"; the PBoC's "reverse repos" (*ni huigou*) are the Fed's "repos.")

As a means of sterilizing money creation following foreign exchange market interventions, an RRR hike that increases required reserves by a given amount is a more powerful move than an open market operation involving the same amount of CBP or repo sales. While both have the same initial effect on loanable reserves, the former also reduces the money multiplier on any increase in the monetary base that is left unsterilized.

Open market operations, however, allow the central bank to take a more nuanced approach to liquidity management by varying the durations of its CBP and repo obligations. During periods when the PBoC was concerned about excess investment, it has increased issuance of longer-dated CBP in (largely unsuccessful) attempts to reduce the availability of long-term financing. The issuance of three-year CBP was resumed in January 2007 following a one-and-a-half year hiatus, discontinued in June of 2008 as the global financial crisis began to intensify, and resumed once more in April 2010. From December 2008 to July 2009, even one-year CBP issuance was halted.

While it is unclear how effective such tactics can be, the time to maturity of the central bank's outstanding CBP and repo obligations is nevertheless a useful indicator of the PBoC's policy bias. This statistic rose from around 200 days at the beginning of 2006 to over 500 days in mid-2008, fell back below 200 days in early 2010 and had again risen above 400 days by the end of 2011. (See Figure 7.2.)

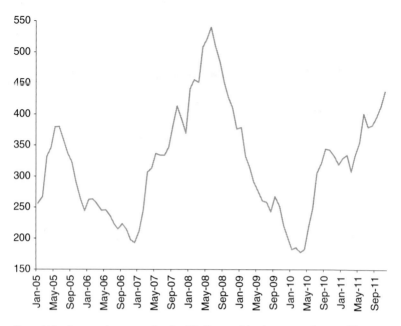

Figure 7.2   Average time to expiry for PBoC central bank paper and repo obligations (days)

Source: People's Bank of China, author's calculations.

Required reserve rate increases, central bank paper sales, and repos all create expenses for the central bank because it must compensate the commercial banks for the use of their deposits. Otherwise, monetary tightening would have significant adverse effects on the banks' profitability. As of the end of 2010, the PBoC was paying interest on required reserves at an annual rate of 1.62 percent. The weighted average annual rate on its outstanding repos and CBP was 1.23 percent.

At these rates, the approximately 12 trillion yuan in required reserves and about 4 trillion in CBP and repos on the PBoC's balance sheet as of year-end 2010 implied interest expenses for the central bank of 200 billion and 49 billion yuan, respectively, on an annualized basis. At the same time, the PBoC would also have been earning interest on a corresponding 16 trillion yuan amount of foreign exchange assets. Whether or not its interventions were profitable depends on what returns were available offshore and on how its forex reserves were invested.

Changes in the PBoC's balance sheet reveal that commercial bank reserve increases, CBP sales, and repos financed most of the 18-trillion-yuan build-up in China's foreign exchange reserves during the seven years from year-end 2003 to year-end 2010. During that period, the central bank's reserve deposits liability rose from 2.2 to 13.6 trillion yuan. This 11.4-trillion-yuan increase accounted for 64 percent of the forex reserve change. A 3.7-trillion-yuan increase in CBP and repos outstanding, from about 600 billion to 4.3 trillion yuan, accounted for a further 21 percent.

None of this intervention can be characterized as fine-tuning. It was rather an effort to maintain the status quo in the face of an explosion in forex inflows resulting from an undervalued currency. In the looking glass world of Chinese monetary policy it takes, as the Red Queen told Alice, "all the running you can do to keep in the same place."

3. DIFFERENTIAL LIQUIDITY MANAGEMENT

As long as the PBoC is targeting the exchange rate, it has little choice regarding the magnitude of its sterilization program. It can, however, sterilize more money at some institutions than at others. For example, it can force particular banks to purchase large amounts of CBP or raise their required reserve rates above the benchmark level. Such tactics give the central bank a "stick" with which to penalize those that lend "too much" or to the "wrong" sectors.

The PBoC periodically sold "targeted" CBP from May 2006 until September 2007, requiring banks to purchase special CBP issues and hold them to maturity. In 2006, there were four such sales, all of one-year paper, totaling 370 billion yuan, with an average discount to the comparable market yield of twenty-seven basis points. There were five sales in 2007, all of three-year paper. These totaled 555 billion yuan. The average discount was five basis points.

The institutions involved were not officially identified. The relevant PBoC announcements invariably reported that the sales were made to "certain open market primary dealers," however, which implies that only the largest institutions could have been affected. Newspaper reports claimed that the targets included the Big Four and some of the larger second-tier banks such as the Bank of Communications and China Merchants' Bank.

The amounts involved would have been significant for any of these institutions. Three hundred and seventy billion yuan was 12 percent of total CBP and repos outstanding at the end of 2006 and 37 percent of the increase in financial institutions' PBoC reserves for that year. Similarly, 555 billion yuan represented 14 percent of year-end 2007 CBP and repos outstanding and 28 percent of that year's reserves increase.

Following the 2008 financial crisis, targeted bill sales were replaced with a "differential reserve rate" policy (*chabie cunkuan zhunbeijin lu*), under which required reserve rates can be raised or lowered on a case-by-case basis.[3] This policy was originally introduced in April 2004 and is reportedly unique to China. A combination of monetary policy with prudential supervision, it is particularly appropriate when excess money supply growth is driven by lax lending standards. Assigning the highest RRR to the banks with the lowest standards should increase the effectiveness of any given aggregate increase in required reserves and make the central bank's interventions more efficient.

Until early 2011, the policy was implemented sporadically and applied only to the larger banks. In February 2011, a central bank spokesperson revealed that the system was being extended to smaller banks and would henceforth be based on a consistent formula. Forty banks with low capital adequacy rates and excessively high loan growth were reported to have been "differentialed" (*bei chabie le,* as the Chinese newspapers put it). The penalties ranged from 50 to 300 basis point increases to the RRR benchmark. The central bank was also said to be considering paying interest at reduced rates or, in extreme cases, even not at all, on the additional reserves.[4]

In an article in the March 1, 2011, edition of the PBoC publication *China Finance,*[5] the new formula for determining a bank's RRR differential (R) was given as:

$$R = a(C^* - C)$$

Here a is a bank-specific "stability adjustment parameter" that takes into account factors such as the bank's "liquidity situation, leverage, provisioning, financial reports, credit rating, internal controls, history of payments and settlements problems, credit policy, and operational situation."

C^* is the standard minimum capital adequacy ratio of 8 percent plus an additional percentage based on the systemic importance of the bank plus a "countercyclical buffer" (presumably a percentage that may be either positive or negative). C is the bank's actual capital adequacy ratio. (A bank's a capital adequacy ratio is the ratio of its capital to a risk-weighted sum of its assets. In China, examples of risk weightings include 100 percent for ordinary loans, 50 percent for residential mortgages, 20 percent for loans to local banks for periods of four months or more, and 0 percent for government bonds and PBoC reserves.[6])

The logic of this approach is straightforward for cases where C^* is greater than C. Poorly run banks will be assigned a high value of a and their RRR differentials will go up to the extent that they are poorly capitalized. It is also conceivable, however, that $(C^* - C)$ might be less than zero. For example, for banks with no systemic importance during a period when the countercyclical buffer was negative, C^* might be less than 8 percent while C (at least on paper) might be 8 percent or higher. In that case, the more poorly run banks (those with the highest values of a) would get the biggest reductions in their required reserve rates!

This formula is supposed to provide a "predictable, fair, and transparent" standard for the application of the new policy. The method for calculating the stability adjustment parameter (a) seems far from transparent, however. It is unclear how numerical values are assigned to the various factors on which it is based or how these values are to be aggregated into a single number.

From the point of view of conventional prudential supervision, it does not really make sense to base a bank's RRR on its capital adequacy ratio. Reserves are an asset with which a bank can fund withdrawals. This is money that has not been lent out. Capital, on the other hand, is used to finance lending and other banking operations. It is an equity item with which a bank can cover losses, for example, losses on bad loans. It is not a fund from which deposits can be withdrawn.

In fact, the PBoC is using its RRR tool for an entirely different task from that for which it was originally designed. RRR differentials have become a blunt instrument for disciplining small- and medium-sized banks. Since the 2008 financial crisis these lenders have become, as the authors of the *China Finance* article put it, the "main striking force" behind credit expansion, because of their "intimate connections with local governments." The new regime, it is hoped, will help to rein in loan growth by targeting them directly. As they are among the most poorly capitalized and badly managed of China's financial institutions, the $a(C^* - C)$ formula would assign them the highest required reserve rates.

The PBoC drew attention to problems with capital adequacy in a special section of its "China Monetary Policy Report" for the second quarter of 2010. Following the international financial crisis, it said, "relatively loose monetary policy enabled rapid growth in bank credit." Many banks "expanded their assets" to the point at which they had "diluted and undermined capital adequacy," secure in the knowledge that they could rely on "state-owned shareholders and the government" to top up their capital. While capital adequacy considerations ordinarily serve to limit lending, in this case "the capital discipline mechanism was not put into full play."[7]

The declines in the banks' capital adequacy ratios probably did not even fully reflect the magnitude of the problem, because the banks have found ways to report higher ratios than their real circumstances warrant. One of the most straightforward methods is to under provision for nonperforming loans. A proper accounting for local platform lending, for example, would reduce the banks' capital by requiring them to recognize additional losses in cases where platforms lack sufficient cashflow to service their debt.

Lenders have also been able to decrease the denominators of their capital adequacy ratios using "wealth-management products." These have become popular with both banks and their wealthy clients alike because they provide a way to bypass the PBoC's administratively set lending and deposit rates. Available products range from fixed-income guaranteed principal offerings to high risk/high reward investments. Typically the banks invest wealth management funds in a "capital pool," which may invest in anything from real estate to highway construction. These pools will typically be financed by a wide variety of products, with money from new products continuously being added as old products fall due.[8] By the end of 2011, Fitch Ratings put total outstanding risk management product issuance at almost 10 percent of system-wide deposits.

Until mid-2011, the banks could reduce their risk assets by including capital pool contributions in "other assets." These had a risk weighting of zero because they normally include nonrisky items such as fixed assets (e.g., bank buildings) and amortizable income. As a result, even principal-guaranteed products were being treated as though they posed no threat to bank capital in the event that their underlying investments made losses. In August 2011, it was reported that the China Bank Regulatory Commission would finally be closing this loophole by raising the "other assets" weighting to 100 percent.[9]

When customers shift deposits into wealth management products, the banks also benefit because the funds in question disappear from the denominator of the RRR, reducing required reserves. At the same time, however, with fewer deposits loan-deposit ratios rise, creating the risk that this metric may exceed the 75 percent limit specified in Article 39 (2) of China's Commercial Bank Law. To get around this difficulty, some institutions have issued products with maturities of a month or less, timing their maturity dates to fall after the RRR reporting date and before the loan-deposit ratio reporting date.[10]

In practice, an official at the PBoC's Taiyuan branch told the *21st Century Economic Herald* in February 2011 that the RRR differential was based on monthly loan growth rather than capital adequacy. Loan growth, he said, had been the main criterion for selecting the forty banks penalized that month by the PBoC. His account was confirmed by a source at a financial institution in Hunan Province, who described the new policy as little more than a de facto quota. New lending for a given month, he said, could "only be less and not more" than that for the same month in the previous year. Thus, as lending in January 2011 had slowed at the large centrally controlled banks but was still strong at the smaller regional lenders, the former reportedly escaped punishment.[11]

4. CONTROLLING CREDIT BY FIAT

When interest rate hikes, open market operations, and required reserve rate adjustments fail to slow investment, the PBoC has one final card to play. It can simply order the banks to limit their overall lending and/or loans to particular sectors. Such command economy style measures are undesirable from the point of view of economic efficiency and bank sector profitability and cannot be continued indefinitely. They nevertheless continue to be the central bank's most effective tool. Indeed, all three of the major tightenings that the PBoC has undertaken in the past ten years—in 2004, early 2008, and 2011—owed their success to credit controls.

The PBoC typically undertakes sectoral lending controls together with other central government organs as part of an overall policy to limit excess capacity. In 2004, for example, the central bank, the National Development and Reform Commission, and the China Bank Regulatory Commission jointly issued a notification on "Strengthening the Coordination of Industrial and Credit Policy." This targeted overinvestment in the steel, nonferrous metals (e.g., aluminum), machinery, building materials, petrochemical, light industry, textile, pharmaceutical, and printing sectors.

The notification was accompanied by an index categorizing various project types as either "prohibited" or "restricted." Projects included in the former category had serious occupational safety or environmental protection issues, required excessive amounts of energy and raw materials, or would produce substandard output. The latter category included projects that would exacerbate excess capacity problems, use backward technology, fail to conserve resources, or were considered to be environmentally unfriendly.

The banks were instructed to terminate all new lending to prohibited projects. They were also to "take appropriate measures" to recall any such loans that had already been made. Restricted projects were to undergo a "cleanup" period during which their compliance with the relevant rules and regulations would be reassessed. Financial institutions were to cease "all forms of credit support" until this reassessment was completed.[12]

Similarly, the PBoC's June 2003 notification on "Strengthening the Management of Real Estate Credit" formed part of a series of central government measures designed to rein in excess investment in property development. In this case, the goal was to crack down on speculation without impeding the genuine end user's access to mortgage loans. Banks were prohibited from extending loans to developers for land acquisition while loans to home buyers were limited to buildings where "the roof had already been put on the principal structure."[13]

Controls on aggregate credit formed a key part of the PBoC's anti-inflation strategy in the first half of 2008. Following the failure of a series of tightening measures to reverse an upward trend in CPI inflation, which had risen from 1.5 percent in 2006 to 4.8 percent in 2007, the central bank required the commercial banks to limit full-year new lending to 2007 levels. This implied that 2008 loan growth should not exceed 13.9 percent. This target was to be monitored on a quarterly basis. Offenders, it was rumored, would be punished with targeted CBP sales.

Administrative tightening can be quite disruptive. At the end of 2007, it was reported that some banks, in anticipation of the new policy, had ordered their provincial-level branches to stop making new loans altogether. Normally these branches would be free to lend provided that they remained within specified limits for total lending and loan-deposit ratios. Now they were only allowed to accept principal and interest payments on existing loans. The funds received could not be lent out again.[14]

This year-end lending halt is a good example of Smith's observation that the Chinese system emphasizes "quantifiable results, rather than process". (See the introduction to Chapter 5.) The primary motivation could only have been to impress the regulators by lowering December 2007 year-on-year loan growth. Such a policy would have had too many adverse side-effects to be continued beyond the few weeks necessary for the bankers to "make their numbers."

Refusing to make new loans makes no sense as "process" because a bank's corporate clients do not generally take out loans on a one-off basis. Their relationship with the bank is ongoing. Working capital loans, for example, are an integral part of many firms' cash-flow cycles. Similarly, investment plans may be predicated on the expectation that new credit will become available as each phase of a project is completed and a new one begins. In China, this is particularly true in the many cases where short-term borrowing is used to finance long-term investments. A ban on new lending upsets business arrangements throughout the entire economy, halting ordinary operating businesses and speculative ventures alike. Chains of bad debts may also be created as customers find themselves unable to pay their suppliers, who in turn become unable to repay their own creditors.

Strict enforcement of quarterly lending targets was discontinued in the second half of 2008 when the PBoC began easing monetary policy in response to the global financial crisis. Subsequently, the effects of the earlier credit rationing were quickly undone. The bankers' priority now shifted to producing high loan-growth numbers in order to demonstrate support for the central government's 8 percent GDP growth target. At the same time, their clients had significant pent-up demand for loans. They were eager to borrow once the banks were again able to lend freely.

The runaway money supply and loan growth of 2009 was thus yet another example of the power of credit controls. In this case, the PBoC stimulated investment by removing them.

PBoC tightening in 2011 relied heavily on loan quotas and also involved credit controls targeting speculative property projects. The use of the former was surprising because the central bank was initially reported to be moving away from its traditional emphasis on lending targets. By the second half of the year, however, many banks were reported to be restricting lending because they were approaching their annual limits.[15]

Banks subject to yearly quotas will seek to use them up as early in the year as possible. All other things being equal, the sooner the new loans are made the greater the full-year interest income they will generate. In many cases, the banks may also expect the regulators to let them go over quota once their original amount is used up. For these reasons, Chinese bank lending typically exhibits a pronounced seasonal pattern, with the strongest loan growth in the first quarter.

2011 was no exception. Relatively high loan growth at the start of the year was followed by extraordinarily tight conditions in the second half as the PBoC stuck to its full-year goal of 7.5 trillion yuan in new loans. Despite the PBoC's repeated calls for the banks to support small- and medium-sized enterprises (SMEs), these were the hardest hit. Large numbers of SME bankruptcies were reported in some areas, notably in the city of Wenzhou, a leading producer of items such as cigarette lighters, footwear, and felt-tip pens. There, tight monetary conditions led to a crisis in the informal financial sector upon which many of the city's manufacturers depended for funding.

The impact on the property sector was also particularly severe. In this case, the central bank largely followed the lead of the State Council, which began a major campaign to bring down housing prices in April 2010 by setting the minimum down payment on purchases of second homes at 50 percent. In September, the PBoC banned lending for third-home purchases and limited mortgage borrowing to individuals buying homes in cities where they had lived for at least a year. Banks were also ordered to stop lending to developers holding sites on which they were not actively building. This measure was designed to crack down on land speculation.

By the end of 2011, even ordinary home buyers were having difficulty getting mortgages as the banks began to slow their mortgage-lending businesses. In some cases, loan approvals were reportedly taking as long as three months. Some branches had even stopped mortgage lending altogether. Ironically, the same policies that were beginning to make housing more affordable were at the same time making it harder for households to get financing.

5. THE FUTURE OF CHINESE MONETARY POLICY

The PBoC has many of the same tools as the developed country central banks but it uses them differently and they generally are less effective as instruments of countercyclical policy. Like an old mallet that can get the job done when all else fails—though not without some collateral damage—credit controls invariably become the tool of choice when attempts at fine-tuning with more market-oriented policies prove unsuccessful.

It might be imagined that the Chinese way of doing things, while unsuitable for developed countries, is the right way for China. PBoC officials and Chinese academics typically do not take this view, however. For years they have reiterated that monetary policy should make more use of interest rates and rely less on command economy methods. The latter tends to be thought of as a "solution when there is no solution" (*meiyou banfa de banfa*).[16]

Unfortunately, the PBoC does not really have the option of replacing its toolbox. As long as the investment cycle is driven by the state sector and the central bank is targeting the exchange rate, interest rate changes are not going to be the right tools for the task of moderating China's booms and busts.

Chinese monetary policy continues to evolve, but it is moving toward new forms of administrative intervention rather than increased reliance on open market operations. Since the 2008 financial crisis, central bank paper and repo obligations have fallen as a share of PBoC liabilities while the share of required reserves has risen. The central bank's most significant innovation post 2008 was the new differential reserve rates system. This has been used mainly as a tool for enforcing credit policy.

At the end of 2011, PBoC chief Zhou Xiaochuan told reporters that the central bank would no longer be relying as much on lending targets.[17] This was not an indication of a more market-oriented approach. It simply reflects the reality that the commercial banks are increasingly offering forms of financing that do not count as loans. The central bank's objective is not to phase out credit policy but rather to make it more effective by including a broader set of banking products in its definition of "credit."

This is not surprising given the state sector's post-2008 advance at the expense of the private sector (see Chapter 2, Section 6). An increased role for the state necessarily precludes the possibility of introducing a more conventional monetary policy regime.

The PBoC is right to focus on improving the effectiveness of its administrative measures. As long as it is unable to control investment by taking away the punch bowl, it will have to keep taking away the ladle instead.

CHAPTER 8

SUPPRESSING "BLIND" INVESTMENT

> Economic construction proceeds in wave-like fashion with its ups and downs, and one wave chasing another. This is to say that there are balance, disruption, and balance restored after disruption.
> —Mao Zedong[1]

BANKRUPTCY PLAYS AN IMPORTANT ROLE IN FREE MARKET ECONOMIES. It is one of the processes of "creative destruction," to use the term that Schumpeter made famous. Shifts in consumption patterns as well as increasing efficiencies in production processes tend to discipline risk-takers betting on past economic trends. In the more extreme cases, bankruptcy becomes a significant enforcer of the mechanisms of the free market.

In China, market discipline is much weaker. With a large share of investment decisions made at the local government level, excess capacity can build up without the restraints imposed on private investors in other economic systems. In such cases there is no creative destruction, no market enforcer to spur a more economically rational use of resources.

This chapter describes Beijing's efforts to restrict new project investment and close down excess capacity by administrative methods that largely replace the forces of creative destruction in a private enterprise economy. It also shows why these efforts frequently fail to serve their intended purpose.

As it attempts to control investment administratively, the central government is always at pains to emphasize the importance of "preserving while suppressing" (*you bao you ya*). "Cutting off everything with one blow" (*yi dao qie*) is to be avoided. Official documents and speeches often call for blocking "blind and redundant" investment while continuing to support projects that make economic sense or serve social goals. Support for agriculture or for developing China's relatively poor western regions are perennial priorities.

"Preserving while suppressing" is more easily said than done. While it is possible to confine austerity measures to particular sectors, there are obvious limits to the central government's ability to weed out inefficient investment on a case-by-case basis. At the same time, powerful local officials are often in a position to protect their own projects regardless of their economic merits. In practice, as the Chinese economists Fan Gang and Zhang Xiaojing noted in their study of the 2003–2004 boom, it is "easy to preserve, hard to suppress."[2]

China now ranks among the world's biggest producers of a variety of industrial products. In 2011, Chinese steel capacity—approximately 800 million tons per annum—exceeded the combined total for Japan, Russia, and the United States, the three next largest producers. Annual cement capacity of over 2 billion tons is almost ten times that of India, the world's second largest producer. Smelting capacity for copper, aluminum, lead, and zinc accounts for 32 percent, 40 percent, 37 percent, and 38 percent of the respective world totals.[3]

Much of this production base is underutilized, however. All of these world-beating Chinese industries, as well as a number of others, are encountering serious excess capacity problems.

At the end of 2005, a report by the National Development and Reform Commission (NDRC, China's top planning body) named eleven sectors suffering from excess capacity. These were iron and steel, aluminum, ferroalloys, coking coal (a raw material used in steel making), calcium carbide (a precursor chemical for plastics manufacturing), auto manufacturing, copper smelting, cement, electric power, coal, and textiles.[4] In 2010, the Ministry of Industry and Information Technology came out with an even longer list. It dropped only two of the original industries—autos and electric power. It added lead and zinc, glass, paper, alcohol, monosodium glutamate, citric acid, leather tanning, printing and dying, and synthetic fibers.[5]

Attempts to reduce investment in luxury housing have also been largely unsuccessful. While demand from ordinary households goes unmet, the supply of empty high-end condominiums and single detached houses has continued to grow. Speculative demand makes upscale residential projects good businesses for developers, who in turn are willing to pay local governments top prices for the land on which to build them. Both naturally chose maximizing revenue over implementing central government directives to build apartments for ordinary families.

Beijing's administrative fixes for excess investment work poorly. They typically meet with strong resistance from the officials responsible for their implementation, who generally prefer expansion to restraint. In some cases, policies intended to slow investment growth even end up stimulating it instead—for example, when new, larger plants are built to replace facilities that have been ordered to close.

Like the banking regulations described in Chapter 6, policies to suppress "blind" investment are seldom carried out in a consistent manner. They have little lasting effect. Once the danger is past, the situation quickly reverts to the status quo ante, though sometimes with new people in change.

While China's enormous fixed capital stock is often seen as a sign of the country's economic strength, it also attests to the difficulty of rationalizing the structure of the economy through administrative means. In many sectors, the country ranks first not only in capacity but also in excess capacity. Neither the invisible hand of the market nor the visible hand of the state has proven strong enough to sweep away an ever growing volume of wasteful and redundant investment.

Many of Beijing's attempts to discipline investors rely on the credit policies described in Chapter 7. This chapter considers alternative, non-monetary, approaches. Sections 1 and 2 cover administrative measures targeting heavy industry and real estate. Section 3 describes the political prerequisites for such policies to be effective. Finally, Section 4 explores the limits of the central government's power to impose efficient outcomes by fiat.

1. Industrial Policy: Beijing's Paper Tiger

Preventing overinvestment and eliminating excess capacity have been central government priorities since the Great Leap Forward. Nonetheless, Beijing's track record in this area has consistently been a poor one. Even a central authority with absolute power would not generally have sufficient information to formulate optimal industrial policies (see Chapter 3, Section 2). In practice, political considerations often make industrial policy goals impossible to implement. Their economic merits become largely moot.

A variety of ministries and commissions as well as the central bank are responsible for the ongoing project of "rationalizing" Chinese industry. Their efforts are typically coordinated by the National Development and Reform Commission (NDRC), which draws up guidelines for particular sectors. Once these provisions are approved by the State Council, the responsibility for coming up with detailed rules for their implementation devolves to central and local government agencies.

Following the 2003–2004 investment boom, for example, the State Council approved a policy designed to "advance the adjustment of the industrial structure" in over 20 industries.[6] This 2005 initiative was accompanied by a detailed list of project types, specifying which were to be "eliminated" (399 project types), "restricted" (190), or "encouraged" (593).[7] This classification scheme was similar to that used in the index accompanying the joint PBoC/CBRC/NDRC 2004 notification on "Strengthening the Coordination of Industrial and Credit Policy" described in Chapter 7, Section 4. Both classified investment on the basis of economies of scale, environmental protection, energy and resource use, product quality, and excess capacity in the sector in question.

The policy prohibited new investment in the "restricted" category. Government departments were instructed not to approve applications for such projects or to provide them with state-owned land. Existing plants meeting the description of restricted project types were allowed to continue operating, however.

In the case of project types to be "eliminated," the regulation also targeted capacity that was already in use. The State Council not only prohibited new investment but also gave existing plants deadlines for shutting down their operations. Local authorities were required to take a variety of actions against those that failed to comply. These included suspending their operating licenses and environmental permits and even cutting off their electricity.

The central government's power to mandate the rationalization of entire industries might at first seem to be one of its strengths. But in practice many of its industrial policies are routinely ignored. Consider the prohibitions on the so-called "fifteen smalls" announced in 1996, as one example.[8] These fifteen categories of small-scale production facilities were banned on the grounds that they wasted resources, damaged the environment, made products of inferior quality, used obsolete technology, and failed to meet safety standards.

Nine years later, the NDRC was still trying to "eliminate" seven of the original fifteen. These repeat offenders could be found in the leather tanning, coking coal, arsenic, mercury, lead/zinc, refined oil products, and electroplating sectors. Some of their descriptions on the 2005 list are copied practically verbatim from the 1996 announcement. The same descriptions also appear, in some cases with minor variations, in the "elimination" section of the updated version of this list released in 2011.

The lead and zinc refining sector, where Chinese 2011 excess capacity was reportedly over 20 percent, provides a number of examples of the types of plants that the NDRC has been unable to close. (As lead and zinc generally occur together in nature, the two metals are usually considered as a single sector.)

Modern zinc smelters typically have capacity for around 400,000 tons per annum and use electrolysis to recover zinc from a zinc sulfate solution. In China, thermal smelting, a method considered obsolete in the rest of the world since the 1970s, is still common. Large plants using this technology produce only 100,000–150,000 tons per annum while yearly production at the smallest producers may be 2,000 tons or less. The latter are extraordinarily primitive. Some use nineteenth-century-style equipment such as horizontal retorts, tube-shaped vessels in which zinc oxide and coal or charcoal are heated to produce a zinc vapor. The metal is collected at the end of the retort farthest from the heat source, where the vapor condenses into a liquid.[9]

Similarly, many small-scale lead producers use early twentieth-century methods for sintering. Sintering is a process that oxidizes lead sulfide ore and fuses the resulting lead oxide particles into a hard, porous substance (known as sinter) from which lead can be reduced in a blast furnace. In modern plants, ore is sintered on a continuous series of moving pallets. These have perforated bottoms through which a draft of air is passed to aid combustion. Heated material is added at one end, sinter offloaded at the other, while hazardous by-products such as sulfur dioxide and lead dust are safely removed from the air.[10]

The sinter pot, a large sphere-shaped metal cauldron, is one of China's "indigenous" alternatives to this technology. As a 1916 textbook on industrial chemistry explains:

> These pots are so built that a blast of air can be blown up through a grating on the bottom on which a coal or wood fire has been made. The ore and lime rock charge is put on top and a light blast is turned on. The sulfur in the ore ignites and, when the blast is increased, most of the charge is sintered together into a large cake.[11]

The resulting pollutants are released directly into the atmosphere, slowly poisoning both the workers at the site and anyone unfortunate enough to live nearby.

Horizontal retorts and sinter pots are just two examples of the wide range of archaic, highly polluting industrial equipment that is still in use in China despite fifteen years of NDRC prohibitions. The continued popularity of such technology is not only evidence of the difficulty of suppressing inefficient investment by administrative means. It also highlights Beijing's inability to deal with issues like environmental protection that even capitalist countries routinely resolve through government intervention.

Beijing has also been unable to rein in excess capacity in the steel industry. This problem was supposed to have been solved in 2006, when the NDRC issued a "black list" of steel plants that had to be shut down by the end of 2007. Yet since then the situation has gotten worse.

Some of the reasons for this failure were exposed by reporters from the Chinese newspaper *Jingji Cankao Bao* (Economics Reference News) who visited a number of blacklisted producers in December 2007. They found that few were likely to meet the NDRC's deadline for dismantling their equipment. One was operating twenty-four hours a day. Others had temporarily halted production until the deadline passed. In only a few cases had any machinery actually been removed.

Local officials and managers had a variety of reasons for not shutting down. In the case of privately owned producers, it was difficult to remove assets without violating China's property rights law. Finding new positions for workers was also a problem. In one case, a 2001 lease for a formerly state-run enterprise required that there be no lay-offs for the following ten years. Some jurisdictions had simply canceled the licenses of the operators in question. Closing them then ceased to be an issue because, as one official explained, they simply "didn't exist."[12]

Paradoxically, the NDRC's attempts to eliminate excess capacity often result in capacity expansions instead. In general, it is desirable to shut the smallest plants. These tend to be the worst polluters and are invariably too small to realize economies of scale. Once it is announced that all producers below a certain size are to be "eliminated," however, many of them will simply replace their old equipment with higher capacity technology that no longer counts as "inefficient."

In 2005, for example, the NDRC required the elimination of steel producers using blast furnaces, electric furnaces, and converters with sizes not exceeding 100 cubic meters, 10 tons, and 15 tons, respectively. Rather than reducing overcapacity, this ruling incentivized a move to larger furnace and converter sizes. At the risk of repeating the same mistake on an even larger scale, the authorities have since raised these cut-off levels. The NDRC's 2011 list shows them as 400 cubic meters for blast furnaces and 30 tons for electric furnaces and converters. (Converters convert pig iron, an intermediate product made by smelting iron ore, into steel.)

Similar unintended consequences resulted from efforts to eliminate inefficient cement production facilities. From 2003 to 2007, Zhejiang Province eliminated all of its shaft kilns, leading to a boom in modern dry-process kiln construction. The new capacity had clear advantages in terms of both pollution abatement and economies of scale. Shaft kilns typically produce only 10–50 tons per day. Their replacements have capacities measured in hundreds or even thousands of tons.

Rationalizing the cement sector required more than just replacing the old plants, however. The number of producers should have decreased in proportion to the increase in the average size of the new kilns. In practice, this did not happen. After several years, the shortage initially created by dismantling the original capacity had turned into a glut. At the same time, much of the new investment was still relatively small scale. Of the eighty-nine dry-process lines operating in the province in 2009, thirty-eight had capacities below 2,000 tons/day, the minimum set by the NDRC's 2005 list of "encouraged" projects.[13]

Since 2005, excess supply problems resulting from plant expansions have led the NDRC to raise its capacity requirements for cement just as it did for steel. In 2005, modern dry process production lines of 1,500 tons or less were "restricted." By 2011, this limit had been raised to 2,000 tons. Similarly, the cut-off diameters for mechanized shaft kilns and dry hollow kilns in the "eliminate" category rose from 2.2 and 2.5 meters, respectively, in 2005 to 3.0 meters for both types in 2011.

Chinese industrial policy has never been an effective way to suppress investment. Sometimes, eliminating existing capacity is impossible for purely practical reasons. For example, local governments may not have sufficient funds to compensate private investors. In other cases, operators of obsolete equipment get around orders for its elimination by the time-honored Chinese practice of "feigned compliance." They may shut down temporarily, then restart their operations once the regulators are satisfied that they no longer exist. Some may even take the step of dismantling their machinery, only to reinstall it again at a later date.

Even those that do follow the NDRC's orders often end up adding to excess capacity. Attempts to manage industry with lists of investments to be "restricted" or "eliminated" can easily have perverse effects in the absence of an effective strategy for industrial consolidation. Efficient outcomes require economies of scale on both a plant-by-plant and a sector-wide basis. It will not necessarily be optimal for any existing plants to be expanded. It may instead be desirable for all of them to be replaced by a small number of new, larger-scale factories built on greenfield sites.

The requirements of industrial policy have proven to be fundamentally at odds with the incentives created by the promotion process for government officials (see Chapter 5). The former require not only the upgrading of inefficient capacity but also the elimination of many of the original producers. The latter generate enthusiastic local government support for capacity expansion but little appetite for eliminating production or curbing new investment. As a result, the central government's attempts to rationalize industry have, for the most part, ranged from ineffectual to completely counterproductive.

2. REAL ESTATE: TREATING THE SYMPTOMS

High-end residential property is another part of the economy where the central government's investment controls have not worked. Like Beijing's restrictions on industrial projects, measures targeting this sector have met with strong local-level resistance. Policies that were supposed to limit overbuilding have proved unworkable due to widespread cheating by both developers and localities.

Despite the fact that China's rapidly growing cities are still short of affordable housing, an excess supply of residential real estate has become a serious problem. Much of what developers are building consists of high-end condominiums and single detached houses (often referred to as "villas") that ordinary Chinese cannot afford. Speculators are among the main buyers of this new supply. As their objective is capital gains rather than rental income, much of what they purchase is left empty.

No one really knows the size of China's stock of vacant housing. Most believe it to be quite large. One estimate from 2010 put the number of empty units at an astonishing 65.4 million, enough to house as much as 14 percent of the entire Chinese population. This number was supposedly based on a survey of electricity meters in 660 cities and towns nationwide. Any dwelling where the power had been off for six consecutive months was counted as unoccupied.

While 65.4 million seems an impossibly high figure, many people took the story seriously, despite an official denial that any such survey had taken place. This is not surprising. China's urban areas are full of buildings where most of lights are never turned on at night. There are even entire "empty cities." Perhaps the most famous of these is Kangbashi New Central District in Ordos, Inner Mongolia, which was designed to accommodate 1 million people but so far has only 50,000 residents. Tianjin is also home to a "new city." According to a 2010 editorial on the website of the Communist Party journal *Qiu Shi* (Seeking Truth), it is overgrown with weeds and practically deserted.[14]

Surprisingly little of this empty space consists of units that developers were unable to sell. From the developers' point of view, high-end residential projects usually work out well regardless of the lack of end-user demand. The paucity of end users does not deter speculative buyers. They are simply betting on a continuation of the long-term upward trend in Chinese housing prices.

Property bubbles are not uncommon in East Asia. Generally they have been associated with excess money creation caused by capital inflows.

In China, the problem is exacerbated by poor internal controls and soft budget constraints at state-owned banks and enterprises, the primary funding sources for speculative real estate. In the case of the banks, this credit may take the form of mortgage lending, project financing, or disguised working capital loans (see Chapter 6). State-owned enterprises are not only active lenders but frequently also set up real estate businesses of their own.

For most of the last ten years the regulators have been trying to reduce investment in obviously wasteful property projects. Among the various measures introduced, one of the most ambitious was the 2006 "90–70" rule, a requirement that 70 percent of new residential construction consist of units with a floor area of 90 square meters (969 square feet) or less. The idea was to force developers to build for ordinary families rather than to satisfy speculative demand. In theory, this should have led to a dramatic increase in the supply of small, affordable apartments and eliminated potential future additions to the stock of vacant high-end space.

At the same time, the Ministry of Land and Resources also announced a new policy on state-owned residential land sales, under which land would no longer necessarily be sold to the highest bidder. Local governments were supposed to allocate sites to developers planning to build flats of 90 square meters or less, or willing to precommit to relatively low selling prices for completed units, even if they did not submit the top bids. As a result, it was hoped that builders would be forced to adopt new business models focusing on low-margin affordable housing projects.

But it was never clear how the 90–70 rule was supposed to be implemented. A few cities interpreted "70 percent" as meaning "70 percent of each project." But most followed the interpretation endorsed by the Ministry of Construction, which said it meant "70 percent of all projects in a given locality."

It soon became clear that neither approach was really feasible. Project-by-project implementation did not make sense because many developers had paid local governments high prices for prime sites that were preapproved for projects with large unit sizes. Converting these into 90–70 buildings would mean that sales revenue would not cover costs. Were the rule to apply only to entire localities, however, there would be no way to be sure of meeting the 70 percent target. There would be no guarantee that for every project with fewer than the requisite number of small units another would be built with more. To make matters worse, there was no guidance on what constituted a locality.

In practice, there were many ways for developers to get around the 90–70 rule, even when it was applied to individual projects. Some sold larger units as two distinct properties, with the buyer receiving a separate title deed for each.[15] Others designed adjacent units—either on the same floor or one above the other—in such a way that they could easily be connected together.[16] As the kitchen might be in one unit, the bedroom in another, both of these would naturally be sold to a single buyer Such practices were not technically in violation of the regulation because it did not specify what was meant by a "unit."

Similarly, the new land auction rules also failed to achieve their intended effect. Local governments naturally weighted their revenues from land sales more heavily than developers' proposed selling prices for finished units. Many localities also sold sites for low-cost housing under an understanding with the winning bidders that they might subsequently be allowed to modify their original plans. The developers could then charge prices higher than those to which they had initially committed.[17]

The 90–70 rule was unofficially abandoned in mid-2009. To judge from the statistics on affordable housing for the two full years when it was in effect, it had no impact at all. In 2007, the affordable housing share of construction starts on new residential floor area fell from 6.8 percent in 2006 to 6.1 percent. In 2008, it fell to 5.2 percent.[18]

It was never likely that the central government could arrest the boom in luxury housing investment through restrictions on the type of space developers could build. The 90–70 rule threatened both local government revenues and developers' margins. It also made little economic sense. China's property bubble is the result of excess credit creation due to capital inflows, inadequate banking supervision, and soft budget constraints. Attempting to control unit sizes was a case of treating the symptom rather than the disease.

3. POLITICAL COMPETITION: A SUBSTITUTE FOR MARKET FORCES

Solving excess capacity problems requires a mechanism for putting investors who put their money in projects of little economic value out of business. In China, neither capital losses nor government policy may be sufficient to accomplish this. In many cases, terminating investment also requires depriving investors of political protection. When the regulators are not as powerful as the individuals they are regulating, prohibiting particular project types or ordering existing capacity to be shut down makes little difference.

The most effective interventions tend to be by-products of leadership changes, either at the central or regional government level. These generate effects that cascade throughout the hierarchy. Once a leader has lost power, his clients at lower levels will be weakened as well. Investors who formally had secure backing for their projects suddenly find themselves at the mercy of "project cleanups" and anticorruption campaigns.

This happened on a large scale following the November 2002 Sixteenth Party Congress, at which Jiang Zemin was replaced by Hu Jintao as Party general secretary. This transition resulted in the ouster of a number of Jiang's protégés and the disruption of their patronage networks. By September 2005, an article in the Ministry of Justice publication *Legal Daily* gave the total number of people investigated since the Congress as "over 30,000," including over 100 at the bureau level or higher.[19] Their offenses involved everything from bribery to approving loans to friends and relatives, which totaled 2.5 billion yuan nationwide. Numerous sensational cases were prosecuted, including those of thirteen people at the ministry level, three of whom received the death penalty.

The best known of these investigations involved the so-called Shanghai faction, which included a number of Shanghai city-government and business leaders. Thanks to their close relationship with Jiang, who had formerly served as Shanghai Party secretary, members of this group were able to violate regulations on land use with all but complete impunity. A 2003 investigation by the Party's Central Commission for Discipline Inspection (CCDI) found that of the 479 parcels of land allocated for real estate projects in Shanghai from July 2001 to March 2003 only fifty-seven had been sold through competitive bidding. The remainder had been transferred via a variety of illicit transactions, sometimes passing through a number of hands before finally being acquired by the developer.[20]

The best known of these was a prime site in the city center called "Dong Ba Kuai" (literally East Eight Pieces), which was acquired by Shanghai businessman Zhou Zhengyi in 2002. Thanks to Zhou's close relationship with then Shanghai Party secretary Chen Liangyu, a powerful Jiang protégé—Zhou was not only able to avoid the required competitive bidding process but also to finance the purchase entirely with loans from state-owned banks. Attempts to block construction by the area's original residents, who faced forced relocation to make room for the project, were unsuccessful. Chen even had the residents' lawyer sentenced to a three-year prison term for providing documents to an NGO. The crime: "illegally providing state secrets to entities outside China."[21]

Hu's purge of the Shanghai faction ultimately claimed Chen himself, however. He was removed from office in 2006. Just a few months later Zhou, now left without a patron, was arrested on bribery and tax evasion charges. He subsequently received a sixteen-year prison term.

Widespread collusion among developers and officials made it unlikely that the central government's efforts to reduce excess capacity through restrictions on land use would be effective. One investigation uncovered 1,083 sites in suburban Shanghai where developers building luxury housing and large-scale industrial parks had violated official land-use policies, including a Ministry of Land and Resources February 2003 "urgent notification" halting the appropriation of land for "villa" projects. As a result of these findings, a joint intervention by the CCDI and the People's Bank of China froze the activities of over twenty developers.[22] This penalty would almost certainly have been impossible to impose while Jiang was still general-secretary.

The problem for a regulator like the Ministry of Land and Resources is that powerful Party leaders are often able to block the implementation of policies that threaten their supporters. In a system dominated by factionalism, the demands of patron–client networks take precedence unless there is a perceived threat to the Party itself.

When high inflation threatens the ordinary person's livelihood, for example, it becomes possible for the State Council to "put on the brakes" for the sake of social order. Then many projects that would ordinarily be able to go ahead without required approvals will be halted, at least temporarily. Some of these will have to be sacrificed for the sake of "killing the chicken to scare the monkeys." Such was the fate of the Tieben Steel Mill. (See Chapter 5, Section 3.)

Similarly, a national embarrassment may result in the downfall of officials for "economic crimes" that might otherwise have gone unpunished. As just one example, former railway minister Liu Zhijin seems to have become the subject of an anticorruption investigation only as a result of the 2011 Wenzhou high-speed rail collision. His use of investment as a vehicle for corruption could perhaps have been tolerated. An incident over which he personally had no control but which damaged the reputation of the Party could not be.

Even well-connected investors can be put out of business under the right circumstances. The process is driven as much by politics as economics. Eliminating excess investment generally requires eliminating the investor's power base. There is no guarantee that this can be accomplished solely because a project is wasteful or unnecessary.

4. THE LIMITS OF DIRECT INTERVENTION

It is often claimed that China has an advantage over countries with democratically elected governments and free markets because it can "get things done." In the absence of "parliamentary cretinism" and the "anarchy of the market," it seems, the Chinese leadership can move rapidly and inexorably toward the accomplishment of any goal it sets for itself.

The history of Beijing's efforts to eliminate excess capacity indicates that this is not entirely true. The central government can easily get things done if lower-level officials want to do them. When central government policy runs counter to local interests, however, regulatory bodies like the NDRC often seem to be practically powerless. Beijing can engineer investment booms in particular sectors without difficulty. Recent overinvestment in wind and solar energy equipment production is a case in point. Eliminating excess capacity is much more difficult.

The advantages of the central government's power to act without legal restraint are not as great as they might appear. Consider the Central Commission for Discipline Inspection, the Party's most powerful tool for keeping officials in line. The CCDI has the power to detain suspects in corruption cases at secret confinement centers for months at a time. Its victims have included top bankers, ministry heads, and even Politburo member Chen Liangyu, who was held for over a year.

The commission's interrogation methods reportedly include burning with cigarettes, sleep deprivation, beatings, and simulated drowning.[23] Arguably its greatest strength, however, is that it can completely cut off a suspect's contact with the outside world. The CCDI is known for snatching officials with little or no warning as they go about their daily routines. Subsequently, the detainees completely disappear. The investigators then have two obvious advantages. The suspect is unable to use his influence to intimidate whistleblowers or to get himself "off the hook." He also has no way to learn what evidence the investigation may have uncovered and what secrets remain hidden.[24]

Yet even so formidable a body as this cannot easily "get things done." In practice, its ability to act is limited by political considerations. It is not so much an impartial enforcer of central government regulations as a weapon to settle factional conflicts. It cannot ensure that economic policies are carried out in a consistent manner. As the case of the Shanghai faction clearly illustrates, policy priorities must line up with the imperatives of intra-Party rivalries before the CCDI can act.

In theory, controlling overinvestment should be easy for an all-powerful central authority. It should be able to forestall any overbuilding at the planning stage. In the unlikely event that excess capacity appeared in the system—left over perhaps from some earlier market-based regime—it could simply be shut down.

Beijing is rarely able to realize these theoretical advantages. When lower-level officials refuse to follow orders, the central government can neither nip excess capacity in the bud nor order production facilities to be closed after the fact. At the same time, soft budget constraints keep market forces from weeding out inefficient producers and allow speculative

bubbles to grow to massive proportions. Excess investment must be eliminated through competition in the political rather than the economic
sphere.

This state of affairs is unlikely to be preferable to the "creative
destruction" that takes place in a private enterprise economy. Political
competition in China is not normally rooted in economic issues. While
power struggles like the one that followed the Sixteenth Party Congress
put many investors out of business, the threat of bankruptcy creates much
stronger incentives to avoid overinvestment. When the CCDI is the disciplining force, staying on the right side in factional struggles will be
more important than optimizing resource use. Investors with the strongest
patrons will not necessarily be those with the best projects from a social
welfare point of view.

To make matters worse, the effects of political competition are often
only temporary. In the short term, particular projects may be put on
hold or canceled. Loans to investors that should not have been made will
be recalled. Soon afterwards, however, many projects will be restarted.
Money will once again start flowing. The "blind investment" genie will
be back out of the bottle.

Direct intervention using administrative methods is one of Beijing's
oldest solutions to the excess capacity problems created by the investment cycle. During the Maoist period, this was the only way to deal
with overinvestment. Projects like the backyard steel mills that became
a prominent feature of the Great Leap Forward did not simply go out of
business. They had to be forced to close. In some cases it was reportedly
even necessary for then-president Liu Shaoqi to intervene personally to
make this happen. (See Chapter 3, Section 4.3.)

Today, over thirty years after the advent of "reform and opening," central government action is still required to eliminate excess capacity in
many cases. Economic reform has failed to produce a system in which
market forces alone are sufficient to suppress "blind and redundant"
investment. Some of the plants the NDRC wants to shut are practically
identical to the "baby plants" that had to be "axed out of existence" in
the early 1960s. Little wonder that so many of today's macroeconomic
policies bear a close resemblance to those of the old command economy.

CHAPTER 9

SCIENTIFIC DEVELOPMENT: MASTER PLAN OR MYTH?

> Only on the basis of intensification and higher effectiveness is it possible to progress toward communism.
> —Gennady Sorokin, Corresponding Member of the USSR Academy of Science[1]

BEIJING PLANS TO ENGINEER A LONG-TERM TRANSITION to a more efficient "mode of growth." Unlike the countercyclical policies described in the previous two chapters, this transition would allow for a permanent reduction in investment volatility. There would be less wasted investment during booms and less need for central government-led busts. Investment would not only become more productive but also account for a smaller share of final demand.

This is obviously the direction in which China needs to move. Many questions remain unanswered, however. How can productivity growth be raised without any change in the socialist character of China's economic system? How are local governments going to be incentivized to pursue more rational policies? How can resistance from powerful interest groups be overcome? Previous attempts to make such changes were unsuccessful. Why should this time be different?

Beijing has spelled out its goals quite clearly but has provided few details on how they are going to be accomplished. A major transformation of the existing system will be required. Yet no significant reforms to China's economic institutions are currently being implemented. Nor have there been any real challenges to the economic power of the local governments that control much of the investment decision-making process.

There is little sign that the central government has any concrete plans to put its rhetoric into practice.

Beijing's new economic desiderata are summed up in General Secretary Hu Jintao's "scientific development concept." As Hu explained the idea in his address to the Seventeenth Party Congress in 2007, scientific development represents a departure from the traditional socialist understanding of development. Historically, development was understood as equivalent to growth in GDP. In contrast, scientific development "puts people first" by improving their standard of living. This may take the form of output increases, fairly divided. It may also include less easily quantifiable advances such as improvements in the natural environment or the enhancement of cultural life. Scientific development, Hu emphasized, is "comprehensive, balanced, and sustainable."[2]

This definition would preclude the sort of "blind and redundant" investment that drives today's investment booms. High levels of excess capacity would be a thing of the past. Productivity growth, rather than local officials' attempts to build their "track records," would be the engine that moves the economy forward.

Productivity-enhancing science and technology breakthroughs are supposed to be a central part of the new growth model. Beijing plans to bring these about by using what are essentially command economy methods. Central government officials will make up the research agenda; scientists will carry it out.

History shows that this is an unlikely paradigm for technological progress. Similar attempts to manage science and technology in the Soviet Union and Japan were unsuccessful. There seems little reason to believe that bureaucratic management of innovation and technological change should work any better in today's China.

To be successful in General Secretary Hu's terms, the transition to scientific development will require more rational incentives for local officials and enterprise managers and a more equitable distribution of national income. Such reforms would face strong opposition from the beneficiaries of the current system. To date, there is no sign that progress is being made on either front. There have been few serious attempts to incentivize better decision making in the state sector. The gap between China's haves and have-nots has continued to widen.

While the scientific development concept is consistently presented as an original contribution to Marxist theory, it is not really a new idea. Every Chinese five-year plan since 1978 has called for increased productivity growth. There are also numerous parallels with the Soviet Union's unsuccessful attempts to engineer an economic transition in the 1980s. Practically all of the key elements of scientific development are described, sometimes in exactly the same words, in documents relating to the final two Soviet five-year plans.

This chapter argues that Beijing is unlikely to be able to restructure the economy in a way that would moderate China's investment booms and busts. Section 1 begins with a description of the scientific development concept. Sections 2 and 3 consider the changes to state sector incentives and the pattern of income distribution that the new mode of growth would require. Section 4 compares Beijing's current goals to those of the Soviet leadership in the 1980s. Section 5 looks at Japan's "fifth generation" computer project as an example of what can go wrong with state-directed attempts to promote indigenous innovation. Section 6 shows why abandoning the "leadership of the Party" might be the best way to make the Chinese economy more efficient. Finally, Section 7 concludes by pointing out that scientific development is an example of what Engels called "utopian" socialism. It has no real theoretical foundation.

1. INDIGENOUS INNOVATION AND INTENSIVE GROWTH

Transitioning to scientific development would logically involve a wide range of mutually complementary changes in the structure of the Chinese economy. There would be changes in how output is produced, what is produced, and how the national income pie is sliced. The factors of production—land, labor, capital, and raw materials—would be used more efficiently, leading to more sustainable growth and reducing the need for investment. Consumption would rise as a percentage of total expenditure. Increased consumption would in turn be encouraged through a more equitable distribution of income.

The starting point for scientific development is supposed to be a transition from extensive growth (using more inputs to produce more output) to intensive growth (getting more output out of the same inputs). The efficiency of investment is the key issue. Sustainability and increased consumption both require that fewer resources be wasted on "blind and redundant" projects. Those projects that go ahead must boost productivity in subsequent periods.

The Chinese leadership tends to think of the switch to intensive growth primarily as an engineering challenge. As General Secretary Hu told the Seventeenth Party Congress, China must become an "innovative nation."[3] This, he said, will be accomplished through increased spending on research and development, which will make possible "breakthroughs in key technologies vital to our economic and social development" (Part V). The "co-innovation" and "re-innovation" of foreign technology are also expected to make important contributions.[4]

The main features of the strategy to spur indigenous innovation are laid out in the "National Medium- and Long-Term Plan for the Development of Science and Technology (2006–2020)," or MLP. This document sets ambitious goals for a wide range of basic and applied research. Chinese researchers are expected to achieve technological breakthroughs that have eluded their international peers in fields including information technology (IT), biosciences, renewable energy, pollution control, and even more esoteric areas such as "the dialogue between the human brain and computers."[5]

Ironically, the MLP sets statistical targets for research in much the same way as traditional campaigns to promote extensive growth set quantitative targets for commodities such as steel and grain. R&D expenditure must increase to 2.5 percent of GDP by 2020. (It was 1.3 percent in 2006.) Reliance on foreign technology, estimated at 60 percent in 2006, must fall to 30 percent. By 2020, China must rank fifth worldwide in terms of number of patent filings.[6]

An obsession with numerical targets for patent filings can also be seen in a recent editorial on the website of the Party journal *Qiu Shi* (Seeking Truth). This noted that Chinese filings for patents in other countries totaled 8,000 in 2010, of which the Shenzhen-based network equipment manufacturer Huawei Technologies accounted for 1,800. Catching up with the United States in science and technology, the author argues, would just be a matter of developing another "30 Huawei's." Together their 54,000 filings would surpass the US 2010 total of 50,000.[7]

This way of thinking substitutes quantity for quality. Just as the targets for steel tonnage during the Great Leap Forward incentivized the production of unusable steel, so quantity targets for patents seem likely to produce many minor design changes, but little real technological innovation.

If the objective is to catch up with the United States, a more productive approach would be to emulate the American model of science and technology research. A 2008 study by the Information Technology and Innovation Foundation (ITIF) found that two-thirds of the top US innovations recognized each year by *R&D Magazine* have been products of government–business partnerships. These collaborations involve private industry, federal laboratories, and federally funded university departments. Government involvement may also take the form of venture capital financing.[8]

The advantage of this system is its decentralized character. The United States, the ITIF study points out, "has no central plan for innovation."[9] A wide variety of agencies and programs are involved. They may even be in competition with one another. The goal is not to pick winners in advance but rather to support a wide variety of promising research efforts in the hopes that some of them will eventually "pan out."[10]

The Chinese system instead focuses on a list of megaprojects with research agendas set by the central government's top leadership, rather than by scientists. China will develop a "new generation" of wireless communications networks, 200-MW high-temperature gas-cooled nuclear reactor power plants, and new genetically modified organisms, for example.[11] While in the United States, government funding is available for practically any proposal that survives peer review, China's state-funded researchers are limited to a predetermined menu of problems imposed by Beijing's political establishment.

2. GETTING THE INCENTIVES WRONG

Scientific development is more than an engineering challenge. The key economic issue is to get the incentives right. In addition to incentivizing innovation, Beijing must also find an alternative to the current practice of evaluating local officials primarily on the basis of GDP growth within their jurisdictions (see Chapter 5). Sustainability and economic efficiency cannot be conjured out of thin air. Decision makers at all levels must be given reasons to focus on these objectives.

The problem for the central government is that scientific development is not an easily quantifiable concept. Setting production targets for basic materials is a straightforward process. "Quality of growth" is harder to measure.

One possible solution would be to base local officials' performance evaluations on "green" GDP, an alternative measure that accounts for environmental degradation in addition to output of goods and services. There is, however, no generally accepted way to calculate green GDP. The problem is that resources such as clean air and water do not have well-established market prices. There is no straightforward way to value them and therefore no unambiguous way to deduct the damage caused by polluting activities from their economic benefits.

In 2004 China's National Bureau of Statistics and the State Environmental Protection Agency began a project to measure green GDP in the expectation that this metric would more fully reflect the central government's new development priorities. Their methodology included estimates of damages due to air, water, and solid waste pollution along with costs associated with natural resource depletion.[12]

While many factors were omitted, the calculation for 2004, released in 2006, generated a 3 percent reduction in measured GDP growth. A more complete account might conceivably have shown zero or even owth. The 2005 figures were never released. They reportedly easurements of environmental losses for each province, something the provincial governments would have been understandably eager to suppress. The green GDP project was formally abandoned in 2009 [13]

It is easy to see why local officials resisted this attempt to measure economic performance in a way that would account for environmental costs. Maximizing green GDP could involve major reductions in employment and local government income. It might well also reduce opportunities to use investment as a vehicle for corruption.

Green GDP is a problematic measure in any case because it is highly sensitive to one's choice of methodology. Changes in the types of environmental damage included and the methods of valuing the associated losses could generate significantly different growth rates for the same jurisdiction. Such changes would also affect the relative rankings of different jurisdictions. It would be difficult to find a formula on which everyone could agree.

The failure of the green GDP experiment reveals two major obstacles to changing the incentives facing Chinese local officials. First, scientific development cannot readily be measured objectively in any straightforward way. Second, there is likely to be little support, particularly among local government officials, for alternative performance indicators that take quality of growth issues into account.

At this point, local and regional officials continue to be judged mainly on the basis of growth in GDP as conventionally measured. As long as this is the case, they will have little reason to be concerned about the real social costs of economic growth. They can instead be expected to continue promoting projects that help to build their own track records or generate bribes and kickbacks. The driving forces behind investment booms remain as strong as ever.

3. INCOME INEQUALITY AND CONSUMPTION

Income redistribution is another essential part of the transition to scientific development. Income is supposed to be redistributed, both from the state to the household sector and from richer to poorer households. Such changes would be desirable not only for the sake of social stability but also as a means of boosting domestic consumption and reducing reliance on investment demand.

Under the current system, state-owned enterprise (SOE) profits do not benefit the households that are their nominal owners. These profits, when they exist, typically remain within the state sector, where they are used primarily to fund investment projects and provide employee perks. The ordinary consumer does not have any meaningful claim to the share of national income attributable to SOEs.

Within the household sector, Chinese income inequality has steadily worsened since 1978. China's Gini coefficient rose from approximately 0.3 in the early 1980s to above 0.4 in the 2000s. Some estimates put it as high as 0.47 in 2007.[14] (A Gini coefficient of zero corresponds to a situation of complete equality, a coefficient of 1.0 to one where a single person receives all of the income.)

The case for reversing this trend is spelled out in a 2007 article in the Chinese academic journal *Economic Research*.[15] Using data from a 2002 survey carried out by the Chinese Academy of Social Sciences, the authors find that the marginal propensity to consume (MPC) is lowest for households at the upper and lower ranges of the income distribution, highest for those in the middle. The poorest households have a strong precautionary savings motive due to the lack of an adequate social safety net. The wealthiest have already satisfied all of their basic needs and may also be concerned with saving for future generations. Income redistribution would raise consumption by moving more consumers into the high MPC section of the curve. (A consumer's MPC is the fraction of a unit increase in her income that she would typically spend on increased consumption.)

In principle, redistributing income could be achieved through fairly straightforward administrative changes. SOE profits and taxes on the wealthy could be used to expand social services, for example. In practice, the political obstacles to any such schemes are likely to be insurmountable. The central government is not powerful enough to compel wealthy households and SOEs to give up part of their share of national income and they cannot be expected to do so voluntarily. Under the current regime, income redistribution seems an obvious nonstarter.

Income redistribution policies may also be incompatible with increasing productivity. Productivity growth tends to be accompanied by greater inequality as entrepreneurs and people with relevant technical skills tend to claim an above average share of productivity-driven output increases. Scientific development would appear to require redistributing income in favor of more productive households rather than lower-income households. This might leave China's Gini coefficient unchanged at the present relatively high level.

4. CHINESE AND SOVIET PRECEDENTS: A HISTORY OF FAILURE

Scientific development is not a new idea. Western governments have been concerned with the social and environmental impacts of economic growth since at least the 1960s. This is also not the first time that a socialist country has focused on these issues. The Chinese leadership has been talking about many of them since the start of "reform and opening" in 1978. In the 1980s, the Soviet Union also had similar policy objectives.

Since 1981 there have been seven Chinese five-year plans. The Sixth Five-Year Plan started in 1981 and ran to 1985. The Twelfth Plan began in 2011. While the eleventh and twelfth were the first to refer to "scientific development," all have stressed economic efficiency and quality of growth as essential for China's future development. The only novel aspects of the current thinking are its emphasis on indigenous innovation and income redistribution.

In his November 1982 address on the Sixth Five-Year Plan to the National People's Congress, then-premier Zhao Ziyang told the delegates that for the remaining three years "the crucial point" was to "make raising economic efficiency the center . . . of all economic work."[16] In September 1985, in describing the main features of the Seventh Five-Year Plan, he told that year's National Party Congress that "we must not one-sidedly pursue excessively high economic growth rates."[17] In the same speech, he cited "high resource consumption" as one of China's "fatal weaknesses."[18]

After the 1989 Tiananmen "incident," Zhao Ziyang was deposed but the rhetoric remained much the same. Li Peng, Zhao's replacement, made similar points in his March 1991 National People's Congress report on the Eighth Plan. "Not only," he said, did the plan have "clear requirements for the speed and quantity of growth," it had "an even greater emphasis on raising the quality of economic growth."[19] He also noted the importance of a "reasonable" income distribution in avoiding "polarization"[20] and, like Zhao, referred to the centrality of efficiency increases in economic work.[21]

Li reiterated these points at the March 1996 National People's Congress in a speech on the Ninth Plan and long range objectives for the following fifteen years. He called for "actively advancing the economic structure and the fundamental transformation of the mode of economic growth." The "key objective" for the fifteen-year period ending in 2010 would be the "transition from an extensive to an intensive mode of growth."[22]

Zhu Rongji, Li's successor as premier, put the case even more emphatically at the March 2001 National People's Congress. During the period of the Tenth Plan, structural adjustment would be the "main line." China had, Zhu said, "already reached a point at which further development would be impossible without adjustment." Continuing with "the existing structure and extensive mode of growth" would only result in an excess supply of products and put an unsupportable strain on resources and the environment.[23] Tenth Plan goals included increasing labor productivity, reducing resource use, and pollution abatement.

Transforming the mode of growth seems to be a bit like the weather—something that everybody talks about but never does anything about. Twelve years after Zhu proclaimed that further development would be impossible without adjustment, the share of investment in GDP continues to rise (see Figure 1.2). Excess capacity continues to grow (see Chapter 8). Resource use and environmental degradation are as unsustainable as ever. While China's leaders continue to claim that they are in the midst of engineering an economic transition, there is little sign that this is happening.

Some of the best historical precedents for the scientific development concept are the now long-forgotten Soviet goals of perestroika (restructuring) and *uskorenie* (acceleration).

The objectives of the Soviet Eleventh and Twelfth Five-Year Plans, covering the period from 1981 to 1990, were surprisingly similar to those of China's two most recent plans, which by coincidence are also the eleventh and twelfth. Like the Chinese leadership today, the Soviets were also confident that their existing system could be "perfected" through a combination of technological progress and better management. Then, as now, a fundamental transformation of the system itself was not "on the table" even as goals supposedly essential for long-term economic progress remained unmet.

At the beginning of the 1980s the Soviet Union was a command economy in a state of stagnation. Growth had begun to fall in the 1960s due to a variety of factors. These included a relaxation in "pressure from above" following Stalin's death in 1953, the gradual depletion of the country's resource endowment, the diversion of resources into arms production, insufficient investment in fixed capital, and a fall in the birthrate.[24] By 1980, the Soviet "golden age" of the 1950s was a distant memory.

The Central Committee hoped to turn this situation around through the "intensification" of the economy. This would make possible an improvement in the "quality of growth," and ultimately raise the standard of living of the ordinary citizen. The key was to "accelerate" productivity growth through economic "restructuring"—to achieve *uskorenie* through perestroika.

In his report to the Twenty-sixth Congress of the Communist Party of the Soviet Union in 1981, N. A. Tikhonov, chairman of the Council of Ministers, stated that "everything . . . must be subordinated to the aim of making the economy more intensive and achieving higher production outputs with smaller inputs and less resources."[25] The Eleventh Five-Year Plan, he claimed, would "take this big stride forward" by "accelerating integrated mechanization and automation in every way, introducing team-based organization of work, perfecting rate setting, and enhancing the incentive role of earnings." There would also be targets for resource conservation, particularly for oil, coal, and metals.[26] In addition, the "switchover to efficiency and quality" would be "linked organically . . . with work to improve production on the basis of modern science and technology." This would include the "universal introduction of fundamentally new machinery and materials and the large-scale use of highly efficient energy-and-material-saving technology."[27]

"Putting people first" was also high on the agenda. General Secretary Leonid Brezhnev told the Twenty-sixth Congress that "intensification and higher intensiveness" would make it possible to "secure the systematic improvement of the working people's living standard."[28] "Concrete concern for concrete people" was to be "the alpha and omega" of the new economic policy.[29] The time had finally come, as Gorbachev economic advisor Abel Aganbegyan wrote in a 1988 article, "to understand that production is for the sake of the people."[30]

For Aganbegyan, as for Hu Jintao, the main requirement for the acceleration of productivity growth was scientific and technical progress. While previously such progress had been "evolutionary"—involving only incremental improvements to existing technology—in the 1980s he asserted that the Soviet Union was "invoking revolutionary changes" to modernize its economy.[31] The key sectors were machine building and research-and-development-intensive industries (e.g., microelectronics and computers). The former would have to grow twice as fast as the overall national economy, the latter four times as fast.[32]

Few revolutionary advances were forthcoming. The revolutionary progress in computers and microelectronics that occurred during the 1980s happened overseas, not in the Soviet Union. As for machine building, enterprises responded to the planners' insistence that they come up with new products by turning out minor variations on existing designs. In 1987, it was reported that of the 3,000 supposedly new machines introduced in the previous year 40 percent represented "no substantial shifts" in technology.[33]

Needless to say, perestroika and *uskorenie* did not save the Soviet Union from collapse. By one estimate, the Soviet economy contracted by 9 percent in 1990 to start the new decade at a level 3 percent below where it had been in 1980, the year before the Twenty-sixth Party Congress.[34]

The scientific development concept includes all of the key features of these failed Soviet policies. It involves a transition from extensive to intensive growth on the basis of science and technology breakthroughs. It calls for overcoming resource constraints by doing more with less. It promises that consumers will be the ultimate beneficiaries of the resulting enhancement in the quality of growth. Most importantly, it aims to reform the system from within. As in the final years of the Soviet Union, transitioning to a fundamentally different politico-economic system is not on the agenda.

5. "Fifth Generation" Computers: A Japanese Precedent

Failures to spur innovation through central government innovation policies have also occurred in capitalist countries. The fate of Japan's "fifth generation" computer project is a case in point. Like China's current approach to generating new path-breaking technologies, it was based on the idea that government ministries should take the lead in determining the most promising directions for scientific research. Despite lavish funding and years of effort by an army of computer scientists, it accomplished little of any value.

The fifth generation initiative was carried out by Japan's Ministry of International Trade and Industry (MITI) during the 1980s. The objective was to develop computers that any ordinary person could use. An essential feature of these machines would be the ability to understand human speech and recognize Japanese characters.[35] Fifth generation computers would not only increase productivity in the service sector[36] but also transform Japan from a follower to a leader in information technology. Some also saw them as a defense against a "sociolinguistic threat" posed by the English language.[37] Technological leadership would guarantee cultural independence.

When MITI launched the project in 1982, massively parallel computing seemed to be the wave of the future. This requires running large numbers of processors simultaneously, all working together and communicating with each other to perform complex tasks. The challenge was to develop not only the necessary hardware but also to write software that could coordinate the assignment of tasks to different parts of the system.

In addition, the new computers were expected to have artificial intelligence capabilities that would allow them to use ordinary language when interacting with users. This would require both software breakthroughs and the compilation of enormous "knowledge bases." The goal, as one fifth generation strategist put it in 1982, was to make it possible for information to be "dissolved into society" in such a way that anyone could utilize it "unconsciously." It would be as readily accessible as the air we breathe.[38]

This vision of a future world of omnipresent information was extraordinarily prescient. But MITI's expectation of how it would be realized turned out to be entirely wrong. Even by the late 1980s, it was already clear that the Ministry's hardware could not compete with much cheaper products like the Sun workstation developed in the United States. By the 1990s advances in chip speeds had made it possible to achieve many of the goals of the fifth generation project using a single processor. The parallel computing approach turned out to be not only unworkable but also unnecessary.

At the same time, simulating human reason and decision making has not turned out to be a prerequisite for creating user-friendly computer applications. This is fortunate because it has never been clear that "strong" artificial intelligence, which would enable machines to think like people, is a realistic possibility. Certainly such machines could never have been built using 1980s vintage hardware and software. In hindsight, it is easy to see that MITI was backing a pipe dream.

MITI's failure to make breakthroughs in IT resulted, at least in part, from the bureaucratic character of its approach to scientific research. Once the Ministry had set the agenda, the researchers had neither the opportunity nor much incentive to change course. For them, keeping the money flowing from the Ministry of Finance became the primary consideration. They became adept at using English buzzwords like "non-von Neumann architecture" or "expert systems" but produced little valuable research. Many of the program's publications were little more than printed versions of presentations by visiting lecturers. Foreign observers described the program as "going over old ground" and "out of touch with current research in the West."[39]

China's MLP appears to be heading down a similar path. Once again central government officials motivated by the desire to boost productivity growth, grandiose visions of world leadership in science and technology, and a fear of foreign cultural domination are mapping a course based (ironically enough) on the latest thinking in Western countries. Researchers will happily sign on to the plan in exchange for funding opportunities. If MITI's experience with fifth generation computers is any guide, they can be expected to make a convincing show of doing real research but make few if any breakthroughs. Eventually they may well lapse into complete irrelevance as they fall hopelessly behind their peers in other countries, many of whom will be emigrants from China.

6. THEORIES OF INTENSIVE GROWTH

While Hu told the Seventeenth Party Congress that the scientific development concept is a "scientific theory," it might be better described as a definition of what constitutes progress. In this respect it is hardly unusual, despite Hu's claim that it constitutes a "concentrated expression of the

Marxist world outlook and methodology with regard to development."[40] All of Hu's main ideas have been around for decades. Even the World Bank and the United Nations share his concern with "pro-poor growth" and sustainability.

For the "scientific development concept" to count as a theory, it would have to explain how "comprehensive, balanced, and sustainable" development can be achieved. This is left unstated. At the same time, a reduction in the role of the state is clearly not part of the plan. "To thoroughly apply the Scientific Outlook on Development," Hu told the Congress, it is necessary to adhere to the "Four Cardinal Principles."[41] These are (1) the socialist road, (2) the dictatorship of the proletariat, (3) the leadership of the Communist Party, and (4) Marxism-Leninism-Mao Zedong Thought.

Evidently, Hu's theory is that a central authority can bring about economic transformations by fiat. The investment decision makers and the "people" will simply adjust their activities to conform to whatever the Party dictates.

Unfortunately there is little reason to think that this will work. Scientific development would require an entirely different set of incentives from those now facing China's officials. Yet there has been no change in the incentive structure, nor is it even clear what sort of change might be necessary.

Under capitalism, transitions to new forms of economic activity are brought about by competitive forces. Nobody has to plan them. Such transitions are, as Schumpeter pointed out in *Capitalism, Socialism, and Democracy,* the result of an evolutionary process that "incessantly revolutionizes the economic structure *from within,* incessantly destroying the old one, incessantly creating a new one" [Schumpeter's italics].[42]

In Schumpeter's view, "development consists primarily in employing existing resources in a different way."[43] Typically this occurs in newly formed firms. "In general," he noted, "it is not the owner of stage-coaches who builds railroads."[44]

It is not clear what advantage new firms have in exploiting new techniques, however. Schumpeter's account also cannot explain why socialist countries have seldom been leaders in innovation. In fact, his reasoning suggests that a central authority should have a clear advantage. It can, Schumpeter wrote, simply "direct the productive resources of the society to new uses exactly as it can direct them to their previous employments."[45] Capitalist start-ups, by contrast, have no guarantee of even getting financing.

Under socialism, revolutionizing the economic structure should be straightforward. Why then did perestroika fail?

The political philosopher Daniel Cloud has answered this question by specifying a mechanism for Schumpeterian evolution.[46] His argument rests on the potential for natural selection to generate outcomes that could not have been anticipated a priori. Where knowledge is diffuse, in the sense that it is not available to everyone, and performative, which makes it hard to transmit, it will be optimal for society to "try out" many different combinations of the knowledge and capital resources of its members. The advantage of private ownership and free contracting is that they facilitate this process. (Performative knowledge is knowledge of how to do something, as opposed to knowledge of facts. See Chapter 3, Section 2.)

In biology, it is obviously the organism that is acted on by natural selection. An explanation of social evolution must begin by identifying analogous units of selection within society. For these to evolve in the same manner as their biological counterparts, Cloud argues that they must satisfy three criteria.

First, they must be indivisible so that parts share a "common selective fate" with the whole. Second, the process that generates new units must be "fair" in the sense that the interests of the individuals involved are all taken into account. This makes it possible for a diverse range of forms to emerge. (This is analogous to the "fairness" exhibited in reproduction, where the genes of both parents are equally represented in the offspring.) Third, this process must be frequently repeated so that there is sufficient opportunity for a large number of variations to be tried.

Privately owned companies meet all three criteria. They are usually indivisible. They are established through negotiation, a process that is supposed to take everyone's interests into account. And they are formed frequently. (The same is true of US government research partnerships with private industry.)

Cloud shows that capital plays a role not unlike that of the genome in facilitating natural selection. Firm formation can be thought of as analogous to reproduction, with proprietors combining money and skills to form new social organisms in much the same way as parent animals combine their genes to form new individuals.

This evolutionary process allows for a wide variety of new ideas to be attempted simultaneously. It is not necessary for anyone to "pick winners" in advance. The winners emerge spontaneously, just as new animal species emerge in nature. Only in hindsight does it become clear why particular alternatives were successful while others failed.

Marx argued that capital simply produces more capital, leading to periodic "crises of accumulation." There is actually a lot more to it than this. More evolutionarily "fit" capital reproduces more successfully than less "fit" capital. As a result, the population of firms that utilize more efficient technology and more effective management strategies grows over time, while firms using aging technologies and outdated management techniques fall by the wayside. The real crisis is that of the planned economy, where state interference stops this whole process in its tracks.

This line of argument suggests that intensive growth is an inherently decentralized process that a central authority could not expect to replicate. Insistence on the "leadership of the Party" may well preclude anything other than an extensive growth model.

7. Unscientific Socialism

A transition to scientific development would make Chinese investment more rational and less volatile. There appears to be little chance of this happening. China is not going to become an innovative country by having the central government dictate the science and technology research agenda. It is also not going to be able to switch from extensive to intensive growth with no change in state sector incentives. Nor is it conceivable that scientific development will result in income being redistributed from the powerful to the powerless.

Scientific development would require an end to excessive local government investment and investment promotion. The most straightforward way to achieve this would be through privatizing the state-owned industrial enterprises and banks as well as state- and collectively owned land. Privatization would eliminate many of the noneconomic motives that now drive investment decision making, remove the influence of state policy on lending decisions, and block the conversion of farms into unproductive industrial zones and vacant high-end residential property.

Reducing the state's economic influence might also help to make China more innovative. Today there is no shortage of Chinese entrepreneurs, but their efforts tend to be directed as much toward improving relationships with local officialdom as with productivity-enhancing innovation. In many cases, as Mises wrote in 1940 of the authoritarian systems of his day, "social competition manifests itself in the endeavors of people to court the favor of those in power"[47] rather than in attempts to build a better mousetrap.

Scientific development would also require that the rule of law replace China's millennia-old tradition of the rule of man. Privatization will only promote efficiency to the extent that private property rights are respected. Effective regulation will also be necessary in cases where the market equilibrium is inefficient. Beijing's environmental protection goals are not going to be met by unregulated private firms.

There is, in fact, nothing scientific about the scientific development concept. It is based on the idea that a country can change its mode of development by administrative fiat without unleashing the creativity of the private sector. This claim is not supported by any theory. It is also contradicted both by China's own experience and that of the Soviet Union.

The appeal of scientific development is easy to understand. It holds out the promise that the inefficiencies resulting from state ownership and Party control can be painlessly solved using science and technology. All that seems to be required is to "direct the productive resources of society to new uses," as Schumpeter put it.

In *Socialism: Utopian and Scientific,* Engels contrasted the utopianism of earlier socialists with what he called "scientific socialism." The socialism he defined as utopian is "the expression of absolute truth, reason, and justice and has only to be discovered to conquer all the world by virtue of its own power."[48] In the real world, any such concept is fanciful because it fails to take into account how the proposed ideal society can be created. "Scientific socialism," on the other hand, proceeds from an analysis of economic history to an understanding of how "active social forces" actually work. This leads to a program of action that must inevitably triumph because it is in accord with the "laws" of social development.

Interestingly enough, by Engels' definition the scientific development concept is not scientific at all. It is intrinsically utopian. Like the ideas of Engels' predecessors, it sets forth a vision of an ideal world but says nothing about how it can be realized. The scientific development concept is actually what Engels called "a mish-mash of such critical statements, economic theories, pictures of future society . . . as excite a minimum of opposition."[49] It is not science but wishful thinking.

CHAPTER 10

CONCLUSION

> What is brought about by history will be done away with by history.
> —Mao Zedong

CHINESE INVESTMENT CYCLES RESULT from a collective action problem facing the Party and its members. On the one hand, overinvestment is undesirable for the Party as a whole because it is economically destabilizing. Individual decision makers, on the other hand, do not take the macroeconomic effects of their actions into account. For local officials, the optimal level of investment may be practically unlimited, particularly when the objective is to advance their own careers or to provide a vehicle for corruption.

This conflict between individual and group interests manifests itself over time as a series of booms and busts. As long as excess demand is not a serious problem, individual opportunism can be allowed free rein. When the economy begins to overheat, regime survival becomes the paramount concern. Investment growth will then be suppressed for as long as is necessary to reduce inflationary pressures and eliminate supply–demand imbalances.

Like booms in market economies, the expansionary phases of this cycle are driven by individuals pursuing their own advantage. In China this is done in the absence of clearly defined property rights, effective regulation, or the rule of law. Investment decisions are not necessarily based on expectations of future revenue streams. They may be made for noneconomic reasons as well, by officials seeking to build their "track records" or to expropriate state- and collectively owned assets.

The same factors warp private investment decisions. Local governments not only control most of the land in their jurisdictions but also have the power to suspend the enforcement of laws and regulations at will. This makes it possible for them to subsidize risk taking by privately owned firms, creating win-win outcomes for officials and investors. The losers are the ordinary people whose lives are destroyed by land grabs and environmental pollution.

1. POLITICS IN COMMAND

Chinese investment booms are particularly wasteful because neither the state nor the market functions in a manner that maximizes social welfare. Asset markets are not social-welfare maximizing because state sector ownership rights are poorly defined. At the same time, the government cannot make up for market failures through regulatory action because regulations are routinely ignored.

Both state and market institutions are compromised by one-party rule, which results in a chronic lack of checks and balances and leads to widespread conflicts of interest. The same individuals can be found bidding on contracts while approving bids, or enforcing environmental regulations while promoting polluting industries. Widespread collusion among bank staff and borrowers undermines the financial sector, disabling both the banks' own internal controls and Beijing's attempts at prudential supervision. At the end of a boom, officials whose promotion prospects depend on GDP growth are put in charge of dismantling inefficient production capacity.

Under these circumstances, investment cannot be controlled using conventional monetary and fiscal policy. When it becomes necessary to "put on the brakes," this must be done using administrative interventions. The central government must order particular types of projects to shut down. Rather than guiding loan growth lower through interest rate hikes, the monetary authorities must limit lending directly. Industrial policy changes and stricter regulation of the banking sector must stand in for the market-based measures that would normally be sufficient to slow investment in private enterprise economies.

The Chinese investment cycle has relatively little to do with market forces because investment is dominated by the state. The cycle is primarily a political phenomenon. Its basic features remain essentially unchanged from the command economy period because the post-1978 economic reforms have not been accompanied by real political reform.

"Reform and opening" has in some ways made things even worse, both by making it possible for individuals to amass personal fortunes and by introducing new varieties of speculative investment. Today soft budget constraints have been extended to anyone with the right political connections while opportunities to receive bribes and kickbacks have added new incentives for local governments to promote unnecessary projects.

Overinvestment now takes the form of empty office towers, redundant airports, and even unvisited theme parks in addition to Great Leap Forward-style small-scale steel and cement plants. While the introduction of the profit motive has created new reasons to overinvest, the restraint normally provided by the threat of bankruptcy remains weak.

Eliminating socialist-style booms and busts would require reining in local governments while at the same time hardening the budget constraints of the system's principal beneficiaries. The first step toward achieving these objectives would be to privatize most of the state-owned enterprises, including the banks, and most of the country's developable land. This would move decision making to firms with hard budget constraints and a clear profit motive. It would also shut off the main sources of financing for speculation. At the same time, localities would lose their most important investment promotion tool—the ability to convert farmland to other uses without adequately compensating the farmers who are its nominal collective owners.

Privatization alone would not be enough to bring about fundamental change, however. Without political reform, the newly privatized firms and banks will be used to support state policy objectives. They would also be likely to get government bailouts when they ran into trouble. Local-level enforcement of laws and regulations on environmental protection would not improve. Farmers would find that their land could still be taken away at any time for the sake of the "public good." The well-connected would continue to privatize profits, socialize losses, and expropriate the property of the powerless.

Exorcising China's socialist animal spirits would require the government to retreat from direct involvement in investment decision making and become an impartial regulator. Democratization would be an obvious starting point. As long as officials are not accountable to the public they will have little trouble blocking attempts to limit their own economic power.

2. DEVELOPMENT WITHOUT FREEDOM

The best proposals for reforming the Chinese economic system are not to be found in the numerous reports on this subject produced by the central government and its associated think tanks. These invariably take the leadership of the Party as a given, thereby trying to solve problems without regard for their underlying causes. It is rather China's dissidents that have identified the best way forward.

Their program is described in *Charter 08,* a manifesto promoted by the Nobel Peace Prize winner Liu Xiaobo in 2008.[1] While the *Charter* is primarily focused on human rights, it is also directly relevant to economic problems. It calls for eliminating government monopolies and the establishment of a "Committee on State-Owned Property," which would be charged with monitoring "the transfer of state-owned enterprises to private ownership in a fair, competitive, and orderly manner." It also advocates a land reform to "promote the private ownership of land."

These changes would be part of a transition to "a system of liberties, democracy, and the rule of law." Public officials and members of legislative bodies would be chosen by direct election. Administrative law would set limits on state power. The judiciary would be independent of the interests of "any particular political party."

Implementing these ideas would make it possible to realize one of the key goals of scientific development—raising investment productivity. Democratic elections would eliminate the incentives to overinvest created by the tournament-based system on which officials' promotion prospects currently depend. Effective administrative law would limit the ability of officials to use investment as a vehicle for corruption—for example, by providing effective deterrents to bid rigging. An independent judiciary would not only protect farmers' land rights but also force investors to take the environmental costs of their projects into account. No longer would expropriating their communities' land and public goods provide a convenient short cut for local leaders seeking to realize their own personal ambitions.

The philosophy of the *Charter 08* promoters is fundamentally at odds with the scientific development concept, however. The "fundamental principles" set forth in the *Charter* include freedom, human rights, democracy, and constitutional rule. These may be contrasted with the "four cardinal principles" on which scientific development is supposed to be based: socialism, proletarian dictatorship, party leadership, and Marxism-Leninism-Mao Zedong Thought.

Charter 08 is consistent with Amartya Sen's view of economic development as "a process of expanding the real freedoms that people enjoy."[2] Basic freedoms are not desirable solely because they promote development, as measured, for example, by GDP growth. For Sen, development is not primarily about being number one in steel production or having the world's fastest trains. It is essentially a matter of making people more free.

Like Sen's idea of "development as freedom," the scientific development concept is also supposed to be a departure from the traditional focus on output growth. The Party's new mantra is "putting people first." Yet if the priority is neither to increase output nor to expand freedom, what does development mean? What purpose does it serve?[3]

Needless to say, little debate on these questions has been allowed. The authorities' reaction to *Charter 08* was to block all references to it on the Internet, harass the signers, and sentence Liu Xiaobo to an eleven-year prison sentence for "inciting the subversion of state power."

This is a crime of which he is clearly not guilty. The reforms described in *Charter 08* would actually strengthen the state by weakening the Party. His real crime was to call for an end to the Party's monopoly on power and to the lawless behavior of its members. *Charter 08* is a call for replacing the rule of man, specifically that of the Party cadre, with the rule of law.

This would include reclaiming the economic ownership rights to state assets now vested in Party-connected elites. The *Charter* is thus a direct threat to those whose fortunes depend on maintaining the status quo. These include, for example, the seventy richest National People's Congress delegates, whose 90 billion US dollar combined net worth in 2011 exceeded a mere 7.5 billion US dollars for the top 660 US officials.[4] They also include the over 5 million party members (out of a total of 80 million) who hold executive positions in state-owned enterprises as well as another 5 million that the political scientist Pei Minxin has estimated occupy "official sinecures" in the central and local governments.[5]

For many of these people, and for many of their friends, relatives, and business partners, freedom means something quite different from what it means to Sen. It has little to do with universal human rights. It is something one enjoys at someone else's expense. Being free means being above the law. And development means expanding the privileges of the ruling class.

Having succeeded in "subjecting society at large to their conditions of appropriation," as Marx and Engels put it in the *Communist Manifesto*, China's elites are no different from any of what the *Manifesto* calls the "preceding classes that got the upper hand." They are not going to dismantle a system that serves their own interests. Indeed some would even strengthen it by expanding the economic role of the state and the power of the party. This was, for example, the program of Chongqing Party Secretary Bo Xilai prior to his removal following a corruption scandal in early 2012.

Political reforms of the kind outlined in *Charter 08* would finally allow China to put the legacy of the Maoist era behind it. But they would not lead to optimal outcomes for the individuals who would be responsible for implementing them. The Party cannot reform itself from within. It is also too powerful to be reformed from without. Until a resolution to this impasse can be found, the animal spirits of the old command economy will continue to be the primary drivers of the Chinese investment cycle.

NOTES

CHAPTER 1

1. Criton M. Zoakos, "In the Grip of China's Bear Hug: Berlin's Big Gamble with Germany's Economic Future." *The International Economy* XXIV, no. 4 (Fall 2010): 47.
2. Note that the official quarterly data series starts from the first quarter of 1992. The quarterly estimates cited for earlier years are from Table 4 in: Jia Yueqing, "A New Look at China's Output Fluctuations: Quarterly GDP Estimation with an Unobserved Components Approach." George Washington University Research Program on Forecasting. Working Paper No. 2011–006, 2011, http://www.gwu.edu/~forcpgm/2011-006.pdf
3. Thomas G. Rawski, "Measuring China's Recent GDP Growth: Where Do We Stand?" August 29, 2002, http://www.pitt.edu/~tgrawski/papers2002/measuring.pdf
4. Chen Wei, ' "Zhongguo Moshi Lun' zhi Fansi" ["A Reassessment of the 'China Model' "]. *Beijing Spring,* January 31, 2011, http://beijingspring.com/bj2/2010/280/2011131221531.htm.

CHAPTER 2

1. Genesis 1:28.
2. John Locke, *Two Treatises of Government* (London: Thomas Tegg, 1823), 118.
3. Locke, 118.
4. Karl A. Wittfogel, *Oriental Despotism: A Comparative Study of Total Power* (New Haven: Yale University Press, 1957).
5. Mark Elvin, *The Retreat of the Elephants: An Environmental History of China* (New Haven: Yale University Press, 2004), 128.
6. Elvin, 117.
7. Wittfogel, 27.
8. Elvin, 176.
9. Robert B. Marks, *Tigers, Rice, Silk, and Silt: Environment and Economy in Late Imperial South China* (Cambridge: Cambridge University Press, 1998), 106.
10. Wittfogel, 27.

11. Marks, 107.
12. X. L. Ding, "The Illicit Asset Stripping of Chinese State Firms." *The China Journal* 43 (January 2000): 2.
13. Armen Alchian. "Property Rights," in *The New Palgrave: A Dictionary of Economics*, ed. John Eatwell, Murray Milgate, and Peter Newman (London: Macmillan Press, 1987), 1032.
14. Yoram Barzel, *Economic Analysis of Property Rights* (Cambridge: Cambridge University Press, 1997), 132–138.
15. Barzel, 138.
16. Robin Dean and Tobias Damm-Luhr, "A Current Review of Chinese Land-Use Law and Policy: A 'Breakthrough' in Rural Reform?" *UCLA Pacific Rim Law and Policy Journal* 19, no 1 (2010): 150–151, http://digital.law.washington.edu/dspace-law/bitstream/handle/1773.1/500/19PacRimL%26PolyJ121%282010%29.pdf?sequence=3.
17. Dean and Damm-Luhr, 152.
18. He Qinglian, " 'Land Enclosure Movement' Feeds Chinese Local Governments." *Epoch Times*, June 19, 2006, http://www.hlrn.org/img/violation/land%20enclosure%20movement,%20china.htm.
19. Gregory M. Stein, "Acquiring Land Use Rights in Today's China: A Snapshot from on the Ground." *UCLA Pacific Basin Law Journal* 24, no 1 (2006): 31, http://ssrn.com/abstract= 942813
20. Freedom House, *Freedom in the World 2011—China*, June 17, 2011, http://www.unhcr.org/refworld/docid/4dfb658533.html.
21. See the illustrations on page of 2 of the June 2010 edition of *Beijing Spring*.
22. He Qinglian, "The Land-Enclosure Movement of the 1990s." *The Chinese Economy* 33, no 3 (2000): 57–88.
23. These statistics are available at http://www.cbrc.gov.cn/chinese/home/docViewPage/110009.html.
24. A complete list is available at http://www.sasac.gov.cn/n1180/n1226/n2425/index.html.
25. National Bureau of Statistics, *Zhongguo TongjiNianjian 2011* [China Statistical Yearbook 2011] (Beijing: China Statistics Press, 2011), Table 5–4.
26. National Bureau of Statistics, 39.
27. Huang Yasheng, *Capitalism with Chinese Characteristics: Entrepreneurship and the State* (Cambridge: Cambridge University Press, 2008), 16–17.
28. Huang, 17.
29. Vladimir I. Lenin, "Five Years of the Russian Revolution and the Prospects of the World Revolution." Report to the Fourth Congress of the Communist International, November 13, 1922. V. I. Lenin Internet Archive 2002, http://www.marxists.org/archive/lenin/works/1922/nov/04b.htm.
30. National Bureau of Statistics, Table 5–14.
31. Wittfogel saw "hydraulic despotism" as a departure from this sequence and as evidence that evolution from one of these Marxian stages to the next is not inevitable.
32. Huang, 39.

33. Unirule Institute of Economics, "Guoyou Qiye de Xingzhi, Biaoxianyu Gaige" [The Nature, Performance, and Reform of the State-owned Enterprises], 2011: 6, http://www.unirule.org.cn/xiazai/2011/20110412.pdf.
34. Unirule Institute of Economics, 86.
35. Unirule Institute of Economics, 89.
36. Unirule Institute of Economics, 88.
37. Unirule Institute of Economics, 5.
38. Unirule Institute of Economics, 5–6.

CHAPTER 3

1. See Chapter 2, Part g in: Nicolai Bukharin, *Historical Materialism: A System of Sociology* (Marxists Internet Archive, 2002), http://www.marxists.org/archive/bukharin/works/1921/histmat/index.htm.
2. See Chapter IV, Part 2 in: Joseph Stalin, *History of the Communist Party of the Soviet Union (Bolsheviks): Short Course* (Marxists Internet Archive, 2008), http://www.marxists.org/reference/archive/stalin/works/1939/x01/index.htm.
3. Bukharin, Chapter 2, Part c.
4. John M. Keynes, *The General Theory of Employment, Interest, and Money* (New York: Prometheus Books, 1997), 161.
5. Keynes, 315.
6. Keynes, 162.
7. Keynes, 320.
8. See Chapter XVII, Part 6 in: Karl Marx, *Theories of Surplus Value* (1863), http://www.marxists.org/archive/marx/works/1863/theories-surplus-value/index.htm.
9. See Chapter 17 in: Rudolf Hilferding, *Finance Capital: A Study of the Latest Phase of Capitalist Development* (London: Routledge & Kegan Paul, 1981), http://www.marxists.org/archive/hilferding/1910/finkap/index.htm.
10. See Chapter 20 in: Ludwig Von Mises, *Human Action: A Treatise on Economics* (Forth Revised Edition) (San Francisco: Fox and Wilkes, 1996),http://mises.org/Books/humanaction.pdf.
11. The earliest of these was the model given in: Paul A. Samuelson, "Interactions between the Multiplier Analysis and the Principle of Acceleration." *Review of Economic Statistics* 21 (1939): 75–78.
12. Robert E. Lucas, "Expectations and the Neutrality of Money." *Journal of Economic Theory* 4 (1972): 103–124.
13. This would also be true in Jevon's sunspot model, where variations in solar radiation affect the economy through changes in crop yields. See: William S. Jevons, "Commercial Crises and Sun-Spots." *Nature* XIX (November 14, 1878): 33–37.
14. Harold Demsetz, "Information and Efficiency: Another Viewpoint." *Journal of Law and Economics* 12 (1969): 1–22.
15. Keynes, 378.

16. Keynes, 378.
17. See Chapter 3, Section 19 in: Nicolai Bukharin and EvgeniiPreobrazhensky, *The ABC of Communism* (Marxists Internet Archive, 2001), http://www.marxists.org/archive/bukharin/works/1920/abc/index.htm.
18. Chapter 3, Section 20.
19. Ludwig Von Mises, *Socialism: An Economic and Sociological Analysis* (New Haven: Yale University Press, 1951), 121.
20. Mises, 122.
21. Bukharin and Preobrazhensky, Chapter 3, Section 19.
22. Mises, *Socialism,* 122.
23. See Part IV in: Friedrich Hayek, "The Use of Knowledge in Society." *American Economic Review* XXXV, no. 4 (1945): 519–530, http://www.econlib.org/library/Essays/hykKnw1.html.
24. Michael Polanyi, *The Tacit Dimension* (Garden City, NY: Doubleday, 1966).
25. James C. Scott, *Seeing Like a State: How Certain Schemes to Improve the Human Condition Have Failed* (New Haven: Yale University Press, 1998).
26. Daniel Cloud, *The Lily: Evolution, Play, and the Power of a Free Society* (Baltimore: Laissez Faire Books, 2011).
27. Scott, 314.
28. Scott, 314.
29. Mises, *Human Action,* 566.
30. Alec Nove, *An Economic History of the USSR* (London: Penguin Books, 1992), 271.
31. Bukharin and Preobrazhensky, Chapter 3, Section 21.
32. Nove, 271.
33. Janos Kornai, *The Socialist System: The Political Economy of Communism* (Princeton, NJ: Princeton University Press, 1992), 187.
34. See Chapter 3 in: Karl Kautsky, *The Dictatorship of the Proletariat* (Marxists Internet Archive), http://www.marxists.org/archive/kautsky/1918/dictprole/ch03.htm. Kolakowksi called Kautsky the "embodiment of Marxist orthodoxy" in the generation following Marx and Engels (Kolakowski, 2005, 379).
35. See Chapter 2 in: Vladimir I. Lenin, *Left Wing Communism: An Infantile Disorder* (Marxists.org 1999), http://www.marxists.org/archive/lenin/works/1920/lwc/index.htm.
36. Vladimir I. Lenin, "Report on the Work of the Council of People's Commissars." Address to the Eighth All-Russia Congress of Soviets, December 29, 1920. V. I. Lenin Internet Archive 2002, http://www.marxists.org/archive/lenin/works/1920/8thcong/ch02.htm.
37. Kornai, 191.
38. Kornai, 192.
39. Kornai, 188.
40. Kornai, 193.
41. Alexander Eckstein, *China's Economic Development: The Interplay of Scarcity and Ideology* (Ann Arbor: University of Michigan Press, 1976), 301–302.

42. Eckstein, 304.
43. Eckstein, 314–319.
44. Liu Shaoqi served as head of state from 1959 to 1968.
45. Barry Naughton, "The Third Front: Defense Industrialization in the Chinese Interior." *The China Quarterly* 115 (September 1988): 353–362.
46. Frank Dikotter, *Mao's Great Famine: The History of China's Most Devastating Catastrophe, 1958–1962* (New York: Walker & Co., 2010).
47. Chen Yun,*Chen Yun Wenxuan: 1956–1985* [Selected Works of Chen Yun: 1956–1985] (Beijing: People's Publishing House, 1986), 78.
48. Jan S. Prybyla, *The Political Economy of Communist China* (Scranton, PA: International Textbook Co., 1970), 387.
49. *People's Daily,* "Quan Guo Yi Pan Qi" [The Whole Country as a Chess Board], February 24, 1959: 1–2.
50. John B. Starr, *Continuing the Revolution: The Political Thought of Mao* (Princeton, NJ: Princeton University Press, 1979), 147.
51. Starr, 148. Note that there is an important difference between Hayek's "decentralized knowledge" and Mao's "scattered and unsystematic" ideas. The former consists of idiosyncratic information about matters such as local production possibilities or supply and demand conditions in some particular market that have little or no relevance outside of their immediate context. This kind of knowledge, which Hayek argued is generally of the greatest economic value, is not amenable to "systematization" or "concentration."
52. Elbert D. Thomas, *Chinese Political Thought: A Study Based upon the Theories of the Principal Thinkers of the Chou Period* (New York: Prentice Hall, 1927), 97.
53. Thomas, 201.
54. Lucian Pye, *The Mandarin and the Cadre: China's Political Cultures* (Ann Arbor: University of Michigan, 1988), 32–33.
55. Robert F. Dernberger, "Radical Ideology and Economic Development in China: The Cultural Revolution and Its Impact on the Economy," in *Comparative Economic Systems: Models and Cases*, ed. Morris Bornstein (Homewood, IL: Richard D. Irwin, 1974), 365.
56. Chris Bramall, *The Industrialization of Rural China* (Oxford: Oxford University Press, 2007), 19–20.
57. Audrey Donnithorne, "China's Cellular Economy: Some Economic Trends since the Cultural Revolution." *China Quarterly* 52 (October/December 1972): 605.
58. Naughton, 368.
59. Song Ning, "Bai Nian Qian de Shengchan Gongyi Women Reng Zai Yong" [We Are Still Using Production Techniques from One Hundred Years Ago]. *Zhongguo Huanjing Bao* [China Environmental Times], October 12, 2009, http://www.ycwb.com/myjjb/2008-04/07/content_1854490.htm.
60. Carl Riskin, "China's Rural Industries: Self-reliant Systems or Independent Kingdoms?" *China Quarterly* 73 (March 1978): 87.
61. Riskin, 80.

62. Roderick MacFarquhar, *The Origins of the Cultural Revolution 2: The Great Leap Forward 1958–1960* (New York: Columbia University Press, 1983), 327.

63. Albert Feuerwerker, *China's Early Industrialization: Sheng Hsuan-Huai (1844–1916) and Mandarin Enterprise* (New York: Antheneum, 1970), 50.

64. Marx took over this view of circulation from Quesnay (see Marx, 1863, Chapter 2), whose (1758) *Economic Table* classified agriculture as "productive," handicraft production and commerce as "sterile" (Newman *et al.*, 1954, 93). Interestingly, Gerlach (2005) argues that Quesnay, known in his day as the "Confucius of Europe," may have derived this idea from Jesuit missionary accounts of the Chinese doctrine of "agricultural fundamentalism" (*nongben*). It seems that Marxism may not have been as foreign to China as is commonly supposed.

65. Donnithorne, 611.

66. I Fan, "Industries in Mainland China in 1969," in *Communist China 1969* (Hong Kong: Union Research Institute, 1970), 275.

67. I, 281.

68. Naughton, 357

69. Bramhall, 20.

70. Donnithorne, 610.

71. Donnithorne, 616.

72. Donnithorne, 611.

73. Donnithorne, 609.

74. Donnithorne, 618–619.

75. Prybyla, 346.

76. Riskin, 97.

77. Prybyla, 369.

78. Prybyla, 373.

79. Riskin, 79

80. Riskin, 82.

81. Prybyla, 371.

82. I Fan, "Industry, Communications and Transportation in Communist China, 1967," in *Communist China 1967*, Part 2 (Hong Kong: Union Research Institute, 1968), 1.

83. I, 1970, 277.

84. Naughton, 363.

85. Wang Haibo, *Zhonghua Renmin Gongheguo Gongye Jingji Shi* [Industrial Economic History of the People's Republic of China] (Taiyuan: Shanxi Economic Publishing House, 1998), 441.

86. Bukharin and Preobrazhensky, Chapter 3, Section 19.

87. Chapter 3, Section 22.

CHAPTER 4

1. Available in: *Zhongguo Maoyi Wujia Tongji Ziliao 1952–1983* [Statistical Materials on Trade and Prices in China 1952–1983] (Beijing: China Statistical Publishing House, 1984).

2. Gary H. Jefferson, Thomas G. Rawski, and Yuxin Zheng, "Chinese Industrial Productivity: Trends, Measurement and Recent Development." *Journal of Comparative Economics* 23 (1996): 146–180.
3. In addition to the consumer price index, which is available in the *China Statistical Yearbook,* other indices can be found in *Zhongguo Maoyi Wujia Tongji Ziliao 1952–1983.*
4. Immanuel C. Y. Hsu, *The Rise of Modern China* (Oxford: Oxford University Press, 2000), 805.
5. Hsu, 803.
6. Hsu, 804, 810.
7. Hang Sheng Cheng, "Great Leap Outward?" *Federal Reserve Bank of San Francisco Weekly Letter,* January 5, 1979: 2, http://www.frbsf.org/publications/economics/letter/1979/el79-01.pdf
8. Zhou Shulian, Tan Kewen, and Lin Senmu, "Jiben Jianshe Zhanxian Guo Chang de Wenti Weisheme Changqi Bu Neng Dedao Jiejue?" [Why Has the Long-Term Problem of the Overextended Basic Construction Front Remained Unresolved?]. *Jingji Yanjiu* [Economic Research] 2 (1979): 2.
9. Janos Kornai, *The Socialist System: The Political Economy of Communism* (Princeton, NJ: Princeton University Press, 1992), 164.
10. Zhou et al., 14–15.
11. Zhou et al., 12.
12. Cheng, 2–3.
13. Gu Yumin, *Dangdai Zhongguo Jingji Fazhan Yanjiu* [A Study of Economic Development in Contemporary China] (Shanghai: Tongji University Press, 1997), 7.
14. Liu Suinian and Wu Qungan, *China's Socialist Economy: An Outline History (1949–1984)* (Beijing: Beijing Review, 1986), 433.
15. Zhou Zhaopeng, "Zhengfu Jingji Tiaojie Zhineng yu Jiaqiang he Gaishan Hongguan Tiaokong" [The Role of Government in Economic Regulation and the Strengthening and Perfection of Macroeconomic Adjustment], in *Zhongguo Hongguan Tiaokong Sanshi Nian* [Thirty Years of Macro-economy Adjustment in China], ed. Wei Kang (Beijing: Economic Science Press, 2008), 2.
16. Liu and Wu, 431.
17. Zhou et al., 15.
18. Liu and Wu, 434.
19. Hsu, 809.
20. Zhou, 3.
21. There were originally several different versions of the system. For a detailed list, see Joseph C. H. Chai, *China: Transition to a Market Economy* (Oxford: Clarendon Press, 1997), 12.
22. Chai, 15.
23. Chai, 11.
24. Gavin Peebles, *Money in the People's Republic of China: A Comparative Perspective* (Sydney: Allen &Unwin, 1991), 35–36.
25. Hsu, 846.
26. Chai, 52.

27. Chai, 33.
28. Meng Jianhua, *Zhongguo Huobi Zhengce de Xuanze yu Fazhan* [China's Monetary Policy Choices and Development] (Beijing: China Finance Press, 2006), 26–27.
29. Peebles, 41.
30. Chai, 173.
31. Zhao Dexin (principal editor), *Zhonghua Renmin Gongheguo Jingji Shi: 1985–1991* [An Economic History of the People's Republic of China: 1985–1991] (Zhengzhou: Henan People's Press, 1999), 78.
32. National Bureau of Statistics, *Zhongguo Jingji Nianjian,1983* [Almanac of the Chinese Economy 1983] (Beijing: Economic Management Publishing House), II-11.
33. National Bureau of Statistics, II-11.
34. Robert Delfs, "Economy: The Long, Long Road Back." *Far Eastern Economic Review*, no. 34, August 23, 1990: 38.
35. Zhao, 79.
36. National Bureau of Statistics, *Zhongguo Jingji Nianjian,1986* [Almanac of the Chinese Economy 1986] (Beijing: Economic Management Publishing House), II-6.
37. Meng, 41. The required reserve rate is a percentage of deposits that commercial banks are required to hold as reserves at the central bank.
38. *Zhongguo Jingji Nianjian,* 1986, II-7.
39. Zhao, 94–96.
40. Zhao, 97.
41. Zhao, 98.
42. Wang Haibo, *Zhonghua Renmin Gongheguo Gongye Jingji Shi* [Industrial Economic History of the People's Republic of China] (Taiyuan: Shanxi Economic Publishing House, 1998), 978.
43. Zhao, 97.
44. Zhao, 177–178, 180.
45. Wang, 856.
46. Wang, 867.
47. Delfs, 38.
48. Michael Taylor, "Chinese Puzzle." *Far Eastern Economic Review*, no. 48, November 29, 1990: 58.
49. He Qinglian, *Xiandaihua de Xianjing: Dangdai Zhongguo de Jingji Shehui Wenti* [Pitfalls of Modernization: Socioeconomic Problems in Contemporary China] (Beijing: Jinri Zhongguo Press, 1998), 52.
50. He, 52.
51. He, 52.
52. Henny Sender, "Cooling Down Growth: Moves to Halt Excessive Investment." *Far Eastern Economic Review*, no. 35, September 2, 1993: 36.
53. Ren Junyin, *Jinrong Gaige Nandian Wenti Yanjiu* [A Study of Problems in Financial Reform] (Beijing: China Finance Press, 1992), 297–298.
54. Cheng Yuk-shing and Tsang Shu-ki, "The Changing Grain Marketing System in China." *The China Quarterly* 140 (1994): 1081.

55. Zhou, 9.
56. Meng, 79–80.
57. Chen Dongqi, "Dui Jin Liang Nian Hongguan Jingji Zhengci Caozuo de Sikao" [Thoughts on the Operation of Macroeconomic Policy During the Last Two Years]. *Jingji Yanjiu* [Economic Research] 12 (1998): 4.
58. Meng, 129, 131.
59. Wang, 808–809.
60. Wang, 926.
61. Fan Gang and Zhang Xiaojing, *Zenme You Guo Re Le? Xin Yilun Jingji Bodong yu Hongguan Tiaokong Fenxi* [Why Is There Overheating Yet Again? The New Round of Economic Fluctuation and an Analysis of Macroeconomic Adjustment] (Nanchang: Jiangxi People's Publishing House, 2004), 33.
62. Meng, 159.
63. Fan and Zhang, 35.
64. Fan and Zhang, 36.
65. Fan and Zhang, 4–6.
66. Fan and Zhang, 44.
67. Fan and Zhang, 45.
68. State Council, "Guanyu Angzhi Bufen Hangye Channeng Guosheng he Chongfu Jianshe Yindao Chanye Jiankang Fazhan Ruogan Yijian de Tong Zhi" [Notification Concerning Recommendations on the Suppression of Excess Capacity and Redundant Construction in Certain Industries to Guide Healthy Industrial Development]. Document No. 38, 2009, http://www.sdpc.gov.cn/zcfb/zcfbqt/2010qt/t20100513_346554.htm.
69. *Epoch Times,* "Jingqiaoqiao de Dongguan he Dalu Jingji Zhuangkuang" [Silent Dongguan and the Mainland Economic Situation], May 25, 2009, http://hk.epochtimes.com/9/5/25/100368g.htm.
70. World Bank, *China Quarterly Update,* March 2009: 18, http://web.world bank.org/WBSITE/EXTERNAL/COUNTRIES/EASTASIAPACIFICEXT/CHINAEXTN/0,,contentMDK:22102737~ pagePK:1497618~ piPK: 217 854~ theSitePK:318950,00.html.
71. Wang Lu, "8% Baowei Zhan: Ciji Zhengci huo Ladong GDP Liangge Baifendian" [The Battle to Maintain 8%: The Stimulus Policy May Pull up GDP by Two Percentage Points], *21st Century Economic Herald,* November 11, 2008, http://www.doc88.com/p-035714823260.html.
72. *Meiri Jingji Xinwen* [Daily Economic News], "Difang Rongzi Pingtai Guanli Banfa Huo Benyuedi Chutai" [Administrative Measures on Local Financing Platforms May Come Out at the End of the Month], March 5, 2010, http://bank.hexun.com/2010-03-05/122864858.html.
73. *Caixin Online,* "Scary View from China's Financing Platforms," February 5, 2010, http://english.caing.com/2010-02-05/100116264.html.
74. Dani Rodrik, "Getting Interventions Right: How South Korea and Taiwan Grew Rich." *Economic Policy* 10, no. 20 (1995): 53–107, http://isites.harvard.edu/fs/docs/icb.topic442978.files/Rodrik%20—%20How%20Korea%20and%20Taiwan%20grew%20rich.pdf

188   Notes

CHAPTER 5

1. Graeme Smith, "Political Machinations in a Rural County." *The China Journal* 62 (July 2009): 59, http://www.slideshare.net/sinocismblog/graeme-smith-bengha-county.
2. Zhang Guoyun, "Bu Heli de Touzi Tizhi Daozhi Chongfen Jianshe" [An Unreasonable Investment System Leads to Redundant Construction]. *Zhongguo Touzi* [China Investment], October 2003, 15.
3. Zhou Li'an, "Jinsheng Boyi Zhong Zhengfu Guanyuan de Jili yu Hezuo" [Cooperation and Government Officials' Incentives in Promotion Competitions]. *Jingji Yanjiu* [Economic Research] 6 (2004): 33–40.
4. Zhou Li'an, "Zhongguo Difang Guanyuan de Jinsheng Jinbiaosai Moshi Yanjiu" [A Tournament Model of Local Government Official Promotions]. *Jingji Yanjiu* [Economic Research] 7 (2007): 36–50.
5. Alec Nove, *An Economic History of the USSR* (London: Penguin Books, 1992), 365.
6. Zhou, "Zhongguo Difang Guanyuan," 40.
7. Chen Guidi and Wu Chuntao, "Target Hitting, Image Projects, and Others." *The Chinese Economy* 38, no. 3 (2005): 18.
8. Chen and Wu, 18.
9. Chen and Wu, 19.
10. Vivian W. Y. Kwok, "Weaknesses in Chinese Wind Power." *Forbes.com,* July 20, 2009, http://www.forbes.com/2009/07/20/china-wind-power-business-energy-china.html.
11. Yang Yue, "Closer Look: Tilting at Unconnected Windmills." *Caixin Online,* April 19, 2011, http://english.caing.com/2011-04-19/100250014.html.
12. Ryan Rutkowski, "China's Wind Power Has Faulty Connection." *Asia Times Online,* June 16, 2010, http://www.atimes.com/atimes/China_Business/LF16Cb03.html.
13. Zhang Jiawei, "Wind Power Factories Called 'Image Projects'." *China Daily.com.cn,* March 10, 2010, http://www.chinadaily.com.cn/china/2010-03/10/content_9567436.htm.
14. Zhou, "Jinsheng Boyi Zhong," 37.
15. Zhou, "Jinsheng Boyi Zhong," 36.
16. Zhou, "Jinsheng Boyi Zhong," 37.
17. Xu Shousong, *Tieben Diaocha: Yige Minjian Gangtie Wangguo de Simang Baogao* [Investigating Tieben: A Report on the Death of a Private-Sector Steel Empire] (Guangzhou: Nanfang Rebao Publishing House, 2005), 6.
18. Ad Ligthart, "The Cement Industry in China." Powerpoint presentation, 2003, http://www.cementdistribution.com/industryinfo/articles/cement_industry_in_china.pdf
19. Zhou, "Jinsheng Boyi Zhong," 38.
20. Tan Haojun, "Ba Cheng Minhang Jichang Kuisun Genyuan Hezai" [Why Eighty Percent of Civilian Airports Are Losing Money]. *Ifeng.com,* February 26, 2011, http://news.ifeng.com/opinion/society/detail_2011_02/26/4867585_0.shtml.

21. Wang Bixue, "Wang Huaibao Gao Xingxiang Gongcheng Gei Shei Kan?" [Who Is Wang Hauibao's Image Project For?]. *Southcn.com,* September 2, 2002, http://www.southcn.com/news/china/gdspcn/200209020215.htm.

22. Tan, "Ba Cheng Minhang.".

23. Jamil Anderlini, "China's Airport Overkill." *FT.com,* February 28, 2011, http://blogs.ft.com/beyond-brics/2011/02/28/chinas-airport-overkill/

24. Wang Xi, Jiang Zhipeng, and Li Jia, "Zhuti Gongyuan Shengsi Zhenxiang" [The Reality Behind the Life and Death of Theme Parks]. *Liaowang Dong-fang Zhoukan* [Oriental Outlook Weekly], September 21, 2009, http://www.news365.com.cn/wxpd/wz/myms/200909/t20090921_2471606.htm.

25. Zhou Fang and Le Yan, "Zhuti Gongyuan: Cong Yi Hong Er Shang Dao Jiti Daobi" [Theme Parks: From Everyone Rushing in Together to Mass Bankruptcy]. *Yifeng.com,* July 23, 2009, C:\Documents and Settings\Mark\My Documents\Book\Local projects\Theme parks IF2009.mht

26. Wang et al., "Zhuti Gongyuan Shengsi Zhenxiang."

27. Hu Yongqi, " 'Landmarks' Smear Image." *China Daily.com.cn,* June 23, 2010, http://www.chinadaily.com.cn/photo/2010-06/23/content_1007 1864.htm.

28. Olivia Chung, "Beijing Calls Halt to Vanity Projects." *Asia Times Online,* March 23, 2011, http://www.atimes.com/atimes/China_Business/ MC23Cb01.html.

29. *Finance.sina.com,* "Xingxiang Gongcheng Keng Le Nongmin!" [Image Projects Defraud Farmers!], November 10, 2000, http://finance.sina.com.cn/2000-11-10/21921.html.

30. Hu, " 'Landmarks' Smear Image."

31. Xu, 25–26.

32. Smith, 52.

33. Smith, 53.

34. Smith, 53.

35. Xu, 104.

36. Tao Ran, Lu Xi, Su Fubing, and Wang Hui, "Diqu Jingzheng Geju Yanbian Xia de Zhongguo Zhuangui: Caizheng Jidong he Fazhan Moshi Fansi" [China's Transition and Development Model Under Evolving Regional Competition Patterns]. *Jingji Yanjiu* [Economic Research] 7 (2009): 26.

37. Xu, 32.

38. Jin Sanlin, "Chengben Ruanyueshu Shi Touzi Guore de Zhongyao Yuanyin" [Soft Budget Constraints Are an Important Cause of Investment Overheating]. *Zhongguo Touzi* [China Investment], June 2004, 37–39.

39. Xu, 80.

40. Janos Kornai, "The Soft Budget Constraint." *Kyklos.* 39, Fasc. 1 (1986): 4–5.

41. Neill Stansbury, "Exposing the Foundations of Corruption in Construction." *Transparency International Global Corruption Report,* 2005: 39–40, http://www.transparency.org/publications/gcr/gcr_2005.

42. Smith, 41.

43. Xie Yanjun, "Henan Jiaotong Ting 'San Chao Yuan Lao' Tong Yan-bai Wai Tao Zhi Mi" [The Mystery of Henan Transportation Department Head

Tong Yan-bai's Flight Abroad]. *Xinhuanet,* February 17, 2004, http://news.xinhuanet.com/legal/2004-02/17/content_1317006.htm.

44. Gong Shengli, "Zhongguo Gaotie de 'Jushi Chuanqi' "[The Myth of China's 'World Beating' High-Speed Rail]. *Beijing Spring,* July 1, 2011, http://beijingspring.com/bj2/2010/140/2011711609041.htm.

45. *The Economist,* "High Speed Rail in China: On the Wrong Track?" February 3, 2011, http://www.economist.com/blogs/gulliver/2011/02/high-speed_rail_china

46. Luo Changping, "City Image Building Lines Official Pockets." *Caijing.com.cn,* October 30, 2008, http://english.caijing.com.cn/2008-10-30/110024617.html.

47. Bloomberg News, "China Cities Value Land at Winnetka Prices with Bonds Seen Toxic." *Bloomberg.com,* July 13, 2011, http://www.bloomberg.com/news/2011-07-13/china-cities-sell-land-at-winnetka-values-with-bonds-seen-toxic.html.

48. Smith, 42.

49. Tao et al., 26.

CHAPTER 6

1. Becky Chiu and Mervyn K. Lewis, *Reforming China's State-Owned Enterprises and Banks* (Cheltenham: Edward Elgar, 2006), 188.

2. Gavin Peebles, *Money in the People's Republic of China: A Comparative Perspective* (Sydney: Allen &Unwin, 1991), 25.

3. Peebles, 43.

4. Peebles, 92.

5. Janos Kornai, *The Socialist System: The Political Economy of Communism* (Princeton, NJ: Princeton University Press, 1992), 133.

6. Peebles, 90.

7. Georg F. Knapp, *The State Theory of Money* (London: Macmillan & Co., 1924), 32, 95.

8. Peebles, 25.

9. Victor C. Shih, *Factions and Finance in China: Elite Conflict and Inflation* (Cambridge: Cambridge University Press, 2008), 107.

10. Peebles, 41.

11. Shih, 41.

12. Shih, 33.

13. Shih, 38.

14. Ren Junyin, *Jinrong Gaige Nandian Wenti Yanjiu* [A Study of Problems in Financial Reform] (Beijing: China Finance Press, 1992), 275.

15. Ren, 199.

16. Shih, 38.

17. Carl E. Walter and Fraser J. T. Howie, *Red Capitalism: The Fragile Financial Foundation of China's Extraordinary Rise* (Singapore: Wiley & Sons, 2012), 58–65.

18. Sebastian Heilmann, "Regulatory Innovation by Leninist Means: Communist Party Supervision in China's Financial Industry." *China Analysis* 38 (June 2004): 17, http://www.chinapolitik.de/studien/china_analysis/no_38.pdf.

19. Shih, 184.

20. Wu Yushan, "Wu Yinhang Shouxin 43 Yi Yuan Tieben Ju E Daikuan de Qian Qian Hou Hou" [Why Five Banks Extended Tieben an Enormous Loan of 4.3 Billion Yuan]. *21st Century Business Herald,* May 8, 2004, http://business.sohu.com/2004/05/08/52/article220045222.shtml.

21. Industrial and Commercial Bank of China, *Global Offering Prospectus.* 2006, 74.

22. Industrial and Commercial Bank of China, 75.

23. Industrial and Commercial Bank of China, 77.

24. Bank of China, *Global Offering Prospectus.* 2006, 167.

25. Bank of China. 2006, 176.

26. Bank of China. 2006, 177.

27. Bank of China. 2006, 177.

28. Industrial and Commercial Bank of China, 92.

29. Bank of China. 2006, 127.

30. China Construction Bank, *Global Offering Prospectus.* 2005, 87.

31. Bank of Communications, *Global Offering Prospectus.* 2006, 105.

32. Bank of China. 2006, 174.

33. National Audit Office, "Quanguo Difang Zhengfuxing Zhaiwu Shenji Jieguo" [Results of the Nationwide Audit of Local Government Debt]. No. 35, 2011.

34. Wen Xiu, Yang Na, Chen Huiying, Zhao Jingting, and Ma Yuan, "How China's Banks Risk Wealth Management Cash." *Caixin Online,* July 21, 2011, http://english.caixin.cn/2011-07-21/100282196.html.

35. Wang Jing, "Auditors Point to Widespread Insolvency in Liaoning Provincial Gov't Assets." *Caixin Online,* September 8, 2011, http://china-wire.org/?p=15605

36. Nie Weizhu and Huang Shixin, " 'Chaidan' Pingtaidai: Yinjianju Xingui Zhengsu Weigui Tudi Diya Daikuan" ['Defusing' Local Platform Loans: CBRC New Rules to Clean Up Illicit Land Mortgages]. *Diyi Caijing Ribao* [First Financial Daily], 23 August 2011, http://finance.eastmoney.com/news/1350,20110823157705979.html.

37. National Audit Office.

38. Industrial and Commercial Bank of China, 75.

39. Industrial and Commercial Bank of China, 76.

40. Zhang Zili, *Houbi Shichang Yunzuo Shiyan Jiaocheng* [A Course on Money Market Operations] (Beijing: China Financial Publishing House, 2006), 77.

41. China Bank Regulatory Commission, "Zhongguo Yinhangye Jiandu Guanli Weiyuanhui Guanyu Piaoju Yewu Fengxian Tishi de Jinji Tongzhi" [China Bank Regulatory Commission Urgent Notification on Risks in the Bills Industry]. Notification No. 10, 2006, http://96.0.18.183/a/fengxiankongzhi/fengxiantishi/2009/1228/726.html.

42. Yu Ning and Li Zhigang, "Yinjianhui Teji Jingshi Piaoju Fengxian" [CBRC Urgently Warns on Bills Risk]. *Sina.com,* May 8, 2006, http://finance.sina.com.cn/bank/plyj/20060508/11432549016.shtml.
43. Diyi Caijing Ribao [First Financial Daily], "Yinhang Xindai You Bao You Yia: Yiyuefen Banyue Toufang Edu Jin 9000 Yi" [Bank Credit to Preserve While Suppressing: 900 Billion Released in First Half of January], January 23, 2009, http://money.163.com/09/0123/07/50B0M1SS0025288B.html.
44. Pingguo Ribao [Apple Daily], "Shi Shei Guafen le 1.53 Wanyi Yuan?" [Who Divided Up the 1.53 Trillion Yuan?] February 17, 2009, http://beijingspring.com/c7/xw/zgbd/20090217191807.htm.
45. Wan Jie and Miao Wenlong, "Guo Nei Wai Shangye Yinhang Caozuo Fengxian Xianzhuang Bijiao ji Chengyin Fenxi" [A Comparison of Current Operational Risk Management Conditions at Domestic and Foreign Banks and an Analysis of the Differences]. *Guoji Jinrong Yanjiu* [International Finance Research] 7 (2005): 10–15.
46. Liu Chengxiang, "1104 Gongcheng Shi Zhongguo Yinhangye Jianguan Fangshi de Gemingxing Gaige" [Project 1104 Is a Revolutionary Reform in Chinese Banking Supervision]. Address to the Seventh China City Commercial Banks Conference, Jinan, Shandong Province, June 3, 2006, http://www.zgjrw.com/News/200663/Scene/135913655700.shtml.
47. Tian Ying and Liao Zhaohui, "Hemou Jili yu Guoyou Shangye Yinhang Gaige" [Collusion and Reform in China's State-Owned Banks]. *Nankai Economic Studies* 2 (2006): 105–120.

CHAPTER 7

1. People's Bank of China, "Zhongguo Renmin Yinhang Huobi Zhengci Weiyuanhui Tiaolie" [People's Bank of China Monetary Policy Committee Regulations], 2010, http://www.pbc.gov.cn/publish/huobizhengceersi/3416/2010/20100914145905843679838/20100914145905843679838_.html.
2. Roubini Global Economics, "China's FX Reserves Break $3 Trillion: That's One Expensive Peg!" April 15, 2011, http://relooney.fatcow.com/SI_FAO-Asia/0_Important_117.pdf.
3. Ba Shusong,and Xing Yujing, "Bianda Man Niu: Ping Yanghang Chabie Cunkuan Zhunbei Jinlu Zhengci" [Flogging a Slow Ox: On the Central Bank's Differential Required Reserve Rate Policy]. *China Finance* 8 (2004): 23–25.
4. Shi Jinfeng, "40 Jia Difang Jinrong Jigou Bei Shishi Chabie Cunzhunlu: Zui Gao Shang Fu 3%" [Differential Required Reserve Rates Applied to 40 Local Financial Institutions: Increases as High as 3%]. *21st Century Business Herald,* February 23, 2011, http://finance.sina.com.cn/roll/20110223/23289422481.shtml.
5. Zhan Xiangyang and Zheng Yanwen, "Chabie Cunkuan Zhunbeijin Lu Zhengci Toushe" [A Perspective on the Differential Reserve Rate Policy]. *China Finance* 5 (2011): 50–51.

6. Industrial and Commercial Bank of China, *Global Offering Prospectus*. 2006, 68.

7. People's Bank of China, "China Monetary Policy Report Quarter Two, 2010," August 5, 2010.

8. Wen Xiu, Yang Na, Chen Huiying, Zhao Jingting, and Ma Yuan, "How China's Banks Risk Wealth Management Cash." *Caixin Online,* July 21, 2011, http://english.caixin.cn/2011-07-21/100282196.html.

9. Liu Dong, "Qita Zichan Fengxian Quanzhong Cong 0% Tizhi 100%" [Risk Weighting for Other Assets Raised from 0% to 100%]. *Diyi Caijing Ribao* [First Financial Daily], August 17, 2011, http://www.21cbh.com/HTML/2011-8-17/xNMzcyXzM1NzkxNg.html.

10. You Xi, "9 Yue Mo 64 Jia Yinhang Rijun Cundai Bi Chaobiao: Liudongxing Fengxian Shangsheng" [Loan-Deposit Ratios at 64 Banks Exceed the Limit at the End of September: Liquidity Risk Rises]. *Diyi Caijing Ribao* [First Financial Daily], December 13, 2011, http://www.21cbh.com/HTML/2011-12-13/4NMzcyXzM4NzY4Nw.html.

11. Shi, "40 Jia Difang Jinrong Jigou."

12. *Shanghai Securities Times,* "Kongzhi Yinhang Bu Liang Zichan: Jiu Da Hangye Xindai Shou Yan Kong" [Controlling Banks' Nonperforming Assets: Strict Controls on Credit to Nine Major Sectors], May 14, 2004, http://business.sohu.com/2004/05/14/01/article220120153.shtml.

13. Wang Lina, "Fangdichan Ye Hongguan Tiaokong Zhengce Tansuo" [An Exploration of the Real Estate Macroeconomic Adjustment Policy]. *China Finance* 15 (2004): 18.

14. He Jiangbin, "Yanghang Ling Shangye Yinhang Mingnian Zhuji Shangbao Xindai Jihua" [Central Bank Orders Commercial Banks to Submit Quarterly Credit Plans Next Year]. *Huaxia Times,* December 10, 2007, http://house.focus.cn/news/2007-12-10/406182.html.

15. *Shanghai Securities Times,* "Xindai Edu Qu Jin: Duo Jia Yinhang Yi Shangtiao Duo Xiang Daikuan Lilu" [Tight Credit Quotas: Many Banks Have Raised Interest Rates on a Variety of Loans], October 19, 2011, http://www.21cbh.com/HTML/2011-10-19/0NMzcxXzM3Mjc0Ng.html.

16. Shi Hongxiu, "Honggaun Tiaokong: Zai Xian You Tizhi Xia Youxiao de Zhengce" [Macroeconomic Adjustment: Effective Policies under the Present System], in *Zhongguo Hongguan Tiaokong Sanshi Nian* [Thirty Years of Macro-economic Adjustment in China], ed. Wei Kang (Beijing: Economic Science Press, 2008), 86.

17. *Huaxia Times,* "Xindai Edu: Zuihou Yi Yue Hai Sheng 6600 Wan" [Credit Quotas: 66 Million Remains in the Final Month], December 18, 2011, http://stock.sohu.com/20111218/n329393181.shtml.

CHAPTER 8

1. This claim was one of Mao's attempts to put a positive "spin" on the failure of the Great Leap Forward. See: Mao Zedong, "Examples of Dialectics," 1959, http://www.marxists.org/reference/archive/mao/selected-works/volume-8/mswv8_48.htm.

2. Fan Gang, and Zhang Xiaojing, *Zenme You Guo Re Le? Xin Yilun Jingji Bodong yu Hongguan Tiaokong Fenxi* [Why Is There Overheating Yet Again? The New Round of Economic Fluctuation and an Analysis of Macroeconomic Adjustment] (Nanchang: Jiangxi People's Publishing House, 2004), 50,

3. Manolo Serapio, "Analysis: China Metals Curbs May End Up Boosting Smelting." *Reuters,* July 12, 2011, http://www.reuters.com/article/2011/07/12/businesspro-us-china-metals-capacity-idUSTRE76B22J20110712

4. Wang Fengjun, "11 Channeng Guosheng Hangye Feng Yu Yu Lai" [Trouble Ahead for 11 Excess Capacity Industries]. *21st Century Business Herald,* December 31, 2005, http://finance.sina.com.cn/g/20051231/08192242742.shtml.

5. Ministry of Industry and Information Technology, "Gongye he Xinxihua Bu Xiang Shehui Gonggau 18 ge Gongye Hangye Taotai Luohou Channeng Qiye Mingdan" [Ministry of Industry and Information Technology Releases List of Enterprises in 18 Industrial Sectors with Obsolete Capacity to be Eliminated], August 8, 2010, http://www.miit.gov.cn/n11293472/n11293832/n13095885/13334343.html.

6. National Development and Reform Commission, "Guowuyuan Guanyu Fabu Shishi 'Cujin Chanye Jiegou Tiaozheng Zhanxing Guiding' de Jueding" [State Council Decision on the Promulgation and Implementation of the 'Provisional Measures for Promoting the Adjustment of the Industrial Structure'], December 2, 2005, http://tzs.ndrc.gov.cn/xkxmql/xkxmyj/t20051222_78940.htm.

7. National Development and Reform Commission, "Chanye Jiegou Tiaozheng Zhidao Mulu (2005 Ben)" [Index for Guiding the Adjustment of the Industrial Structure (2005 Edition)]. Document No. 40, 2005, December 2, 2005, http://www.ndrc.gov.cn/zcfb/zcfbl/zcfbl2005/t20051222_54304.htm.

8. State Council, "Guowuyuan Guanyu Huanjing Baohu Ruogan Wenti de Jueding" [State Council Decision Regarding Various Environmental Protection Issues]. Document No. 31, 1996, August 6, 1996, http://www.zhb.gov.cn/epi-sepa/zcfg/w2/w2.htm.

9. William H. Hunter, "Retort Zinc Production," November 2011, http://www.williamhunter.co.uk/ZINC/retort.htm.

10. Alfredo J. Dammert and Jasbir G. S. Chhabra, "The Lead and Zinc Industries: Long-Term Prospects." World Bank Staff Commodity Working Paper No. 22. (Washington, DC: World Bank, 1990), 46.

11. Frank H. Thorp, *Outlines of Industrial Chemistry* (New York: Macmillan, 1916), 619.

12. Zhang Tao and Cheng Shuangqing, "Taotai Luohou Gangtie Channeng Jing Wan 'Zhangyanfa'" ['Cover Ups' and Game Playing in the Elimination of Obsolete Steel Capacity]. *Jingji Cankao Bao* [Economics Reference News], December 19, 2007, http://jjckb.xinhuanet.com/jcsj/2007-12/19/content_78357.htm.

13. *Zhongguo Huanjing Bao,* "Jilei Bu Zu Fazhan Mangmu Taotai Bu Chedi: Zhongguo Shuini Channeng Guosheng" [Insufficient Accumulation, Blind Development, Incomplete Elimination: Excess Capacity for Chinese Cement], October 12, 2009, http://www.022net.com/2009/10-12/463432 223116367.html.

14. Chen Zhencheng, "Fangwu Gao Kongzhi Qianfu Fangdichan Weiji" [High Housing Vacancies Portend Property Crisis]. *Qiushi Lilun Wang,* August 5, 2010, http://www.qstheory.cn/jj/jjyj/201008/t20100805_41761.htm.

15. *Yangcheng Wanbao* [Yangcheng Evening News], "90/70 Zhengce: Sheng De Aimei, Si De Ganga" [The 90/70 Policy: Dubious Birth, Embarrassing Death], February 23, 2009, http://news.xinhuanet.com/politics/2009-02/23/content_10875727.htm.

16. Yu Bingbing, "Shanghai Nanjing Chengdu Deng Duoge Chengshi 70/90 Zhengce Didiao Tuichu" [70/90 Policy Unofficially Abandoned in Shanghai, Nanjing, Chengdu, and Many Other Cities]. *Shanghai Securities Times,* July 6, 2009, http://bj.house.sina.com.cn/news/2009-07-06/1056318875. html.

17. Gao Lu, "Achievements and Challenges: 30 Years of Housing Reform in the People's Republic of China." ADB Economics Working Paper Series No. 198. Manila: Asian Development Bank, April 2010: 10, http://www.adb.org/Documents/Working-Papers/2010/Economics-WP198.pdf.

18. Gao, 9.

19. Zhong Jiwen, "Shiliu Da Yilai Fanfu Changlian Chengxiao Mingxian: 3 Wan Yu Guanyuan Bei Zhuijiu" [Post Sixteenth Party Congress Anti-corruption Drive Has Evident Accomplishments: Over 30 Thousand Officials Investigated]. *Fazhi Ribao* [Legal Daily], September 29, 2005, http://news.xinhuanet.com/legal/2005-09/29/content_3561252.htm.

20. Zi Ping (ed.), *Gaoceng Fuguan Caise Dangan* [Sex and Wealth Files of Corrupt High Officials] (Hong Kong: Huanqiu Shiye Publishing House, 2005), 324–325.

21. Mark O'Neil, "Zhou Zhengyi Has Lost His Best Friend." *Asia Sentinel,* February 20, 2007, http://www.asiasentinel.com/index.php?option= com_content&task= view&id= 384&Itemid= 31

22. Zi, 326.

23. *Duihua Human Rights Journal,* "Official Fear: Inside a Shuanggui Investigation Facility," July 5, 2011, http://www.duihuahrjournal.org/2011/07/official-fear-inside-shuanggui.html.

24. *Nanfeng Magazine,* "Shenme Shi 'Shuanggui'? Teshu de Zuzhi Cuoshi he Diaocha Shouduan" [What Is 'Shuanggui'? Special Organizational Methods and Interrogation Techniques], October 19, 2003, http://news.sina.com.cn/c/2003-10-19/11251998584.shtml.

CHAPTER 9

1. Gennady Sorokin, "Patterns of Socialist Intensification." *The Soviet Review* XXIV (Winter 1983–84): 47.

2. See Part III of Hu Jintao, "Hold High the Great Banner of Socialism with Chinese Characteristics and Strive for New Victories in Building a Moderately Prosperous Society in All Respects." Report to the Seventeenth National Congress of the Communist Party of China, October 15, 2007, http://www.china.org.cn/english/congress/229611.htm.

3. Hu, Part I.

4. James McGregor, "China's Drive for 'Indigenous Innovation': A Web of Industrial Policies." *US Chamber of Commerce*, July 28, 2010, http://www.uschamber.com/sites/default/files/reports/100728chinareport_0.pdf.

5. McGregor, 14.

6. McGregor, 14–15.

7. *Qiu Shi* [Seeking Truth], "Zheng Xinli: Jingji Fazhan Fangshi Zhong Zai Shixian 'Wu Da Zhuanbian'" [Zheng Xinli: 'Five Great Transformations' Key to Mode of Economic Development], December 1, 2011, http://www.qstheory.cn/jj/201112/t20111201_127134.htm.

8. Fred Block and Mathew R. Keller, "Where Do Innovations Come From? Transformations in the US National Innovation System 1970–2006." *The Information Technology and Innovation Foundation*, July 2008, http://www.itif.org/files/Where_do_innovations_come_from.pdf.

9. Block and Keller, 18.

10. The United States is not free from government attempts to set research and development goals. As in China, programs have been launched to fund "green" initiatives, for example. The difference is one of degree. Most US government-funded research is not carried out at the behest of politicians.

11. McGregor, 40–41.

12. Wu Jianguo and Wu Tong, "Green GDP," in *The Berkshire Encyclopedia of Sustainability, Vol. II–The Business of Sustainability* (Great Barrington: Berkshire Publishing, 2010), 248–250.

13. Jason N. Rauch and Ying F. Chi, "The Plight of Green GDP in China." *Consilience: The Journal of Sustainable Development* 3, no. 1 (2010): 102–116, http://journals.cdrs.columbia.edu/consilience/index.php/consilience/article/view/112/28

14. World Bank and the Development Research Center of the State Council, People's Republic of China, *China 2030: Building a Modern, Harmonious, and Creative High-income Society* (Washington, DC: The World Bank, 2012), 301.

15. Yang Rudai and Zhu, Shi E, "Gongping yu Xiaolu Bu Ke Jian De Ma? Jiyu Jumin Bianji Xiaofei Qingxiang de Yanjiu" [Can Equity and Efficiency Coexist? A Study of the Marginal Propensity to Consume]. *Jingji Yanjiu* [Economic Research] 12 (2007): 46–58.

16. National Bureau of Statistics, *Zhongguo Jingji Nianjian 1983* [Almanac of the Chinese Economy 1983] (Beijing: Economic Management Publishing House, 1983), II-62.

17. National Bureau of Statistics, *Zhongguo Jingji Nianjian 1986* [Almanac of the Chinese Economy 1986] (Beijing: Economic Management Publishing House, 1986), I-20.

18. National Bureau of Statistics, 1986, I-21.
19. National Bureau of Statistics, *Zhongguo Jingji Nianjian 1991* [Almanac of the Chinese Economy 1991] (Beijing: Economic Management Publishing House, 1991), I-9.
20. National Bureau of Statistics, 1991, I-9.
21. National Bureau of Statistics, 1991, I-11.
22. National Bureau of Statistics, *Zhongguo Jingji Nianjian 1996* [Almanac of the Chinese Economy 1996] (Beijing: Economic Management Publishing House, 1996), 5.
23. National Bureau of Statistics, *Zhongguo Jingji Nianjian 2001* [Almanac of the Chinese Economy 2001] (Beijing: Economic Management Publishing House, 2001), 4.
24. Michael Ellman and Vladimir Kontorovich, "Overview," in *The Disintegration of the Soviet Economic System,* ed. Michael Ellman and Vladimir Kontorovich (London: Routledge, 1992), 10–13.
25. Nikolai Tikhonov, A. *Guidelines for the Economic and Social Development of the USSR for 1981–1985 and for the Period Ending in 1990* (Moscow: Novosti Press Agency Publishing House, 1981), 24.
26. Tikhonov, 25–26.
27. Tikhonov, 29–30.
28. Sorokin, 47.
29. Tikhonov, 23.
30. Abel Aganbegyan, "Acceleration and Perestroika," in *The New Stage of Perestroika,* ed. Abel Aganbegyan and Timor Timofeyev (New York: Institute for East-West Security Studies, 1988), 31.
31. Aganbegyan, 38.
32. Aganbegyan, 40.
33. Andrew J. Matosich and Bonnie K. Matosich, "Machine Building: *Perestroika's* Sputtering Engine." *Soviet Economy* 4, no. 2 (1988): 167.
34. Ellman and Kontorovich, 1.
35. J. Marshall Unger, *Fifth Generation Fallacy: Why Japan Is Betting Its Future on Artificial Intelligence* (New York: Oxford University Press, 1987).
36. Unger, 176.
37. Unger, 109.
38. Unger, 173.
39. Unger, 188.
40. Hu, Part III.
41. Hu, Part III.
42. Joseph A. Schumpeter, *Capitalism, Socialism, and Democracy* (New York: Harper & Brothers, 1947), 83.
43. Joseph A. Schumpeter, *Theory of Economic Development* (New Brunswick, NJ: Transaction Publishers, 1983), 68.
44. Schumpeter, 66.
45. Schumpeter, 69.
46. Daniel Cloud, *The Lily: Evolution, Play, and the Power of a Free Society* (Baltimore: Laissez Faire Books, 2011).

47. See Chapter 15, Section 5 in: Ludwig Von Mises, *Human Action: A Treatise on Economics* (Forth Revised Edition) (San Fransisco: Fox and Wilkes, 1996), http://mises.org/Books/humanaction.pdf.

48. See Part I in: Frederick Engels, *Socialism: Utopian and Scientific* (Marx/Engles Internet Archive, 2003), http://www.marxists.org/archive/marx/works/1880/soc-utop/

49. Part I.

CHAPTER 10

1. The *Charter 08* quotations given here are from the translation in: Liu Xiaobo, *No Enemies, No Hatred* (London: Belknap Press, 2012).

2. Amartya Sen, *Development as Freedom* (New York: Anchor Books, 1999), 3.

3. One possible answer to this question is military preparedness. Thus, Liu finds that "the economic program of the Mao era . . . is probably most accurately viewed as dedicated to preparing for war" (67).

4. Bloomberg News, "China's Billionaire People's Congress Makes Capitol Hill Look Like Paupers." *Bloomberg.com,* February 27, 2012, http://www.bloomberg.com/news/2012-02-26/china-s-billionaire-lawmakers-make-u-s-peers-look-like-paupers.html.

5. Pei Minxin, "China's Politics of the Economically Possible." *Project Syndicate,* March 16, 2012, http://www.project-syndicate.org/commentary/china-s-politics-of-the-economically-possible

BIBLIOGRAPHY

Aganbegyan, Abel. "Acceleration and Perestroika," in *The New Stage of Perestroika*, edited by Abel Aganbegyan, and Timor Timofeyev, 25–43. New York: Institute for East-West Security Studies, 1988.

Alchian, Armen. "Property Rights," in *The New Palgrave: A Dictionary of Economics*, edited by John Eatwell, Murray Milgate, and Peter Newman, 1031–1034. London: Macmillan Press, 1987.

Anderlini, Jamil. "China's Airport Overkill." *FT.com*, February 28, 2011, http://blogs.ft.com/beyond-brics/2011/02/28/chinas-airport-overkill/.

Ba, Shusong, and Xing Yujing. "Bianda Man Niu: Ping Yanghang Chabie Cunkuan Zhunbei Jinlu Zhengci" [Flogging a Slow Ox: On the Central Bank's Differential Required Reserve Rate Policy]. *China Finance* 8 (2004): 23–25.

Bank of China. *Global Offering Prospectus*. 2006.

Bank of Communications. *Global Offering Prospectus*. 2006.

Barzel, Yoram. *Economic Analysis of Property Rights*. Cambridge: Cambridge University Press, 1997.

Block, Fred, and Mathew R. Keller. "Where Do Innovations Come From? Transformations in the US National Innovation System 1970–2006." *The Information Technology and Innovation Foundation*, July 2008, http://www.itif.org/files/Where_do_innovations_come_from.pdf.

Bloomberg News. "China Cities Value Land at Winnetka Prices with Bonds Seen Toxic." *Bloomberg.com*, July 13, 2011, http://www.bloomberg.com/news/2011-07-13/china-cities-sell-land-at-winnetka-values-with-bonds-seen-toxic.html.

——"China's Billionaire People's Congress Makes Capitol Hill Look Like Paupers." *Bloomberg.com*, February 27, 2012, http://www.bloomberg.com/news/2012-02-26/china-s-billionaire-lawmakers-make-u-s-peers-look-like-paupers.html.

Bramall, Chris. *The Industrialization of Rural China*. Oxford: Oxford University Press, 2007.

Bukharin, Nicolai. *Historical Materialism: A System of Sociology*. Marxists Internet Archive, 2002, http://www.marxists.org/archive/bukharin/works/1921/histmat/index.htm.

Bukharin, Nicolai, and Evgenii Preobrazhensky. *The ABC of Communism.* Marxists Internet Archive, 2001, http://www.marxists.org/archive/bukharin/works/1920/abc/index.htm.

Caixin Online. "Scary View from China's Financing Platforms," February 5, 2010, http://english.caing.com/2010-02-05/100116264.html.

Chai, Joseph C. H. *China: Transition to a Market Economy.* Oxford: Clarendon Press, 1997.

Chen, Dongqi. "Dui Jin Liang Nian Hongguan Jingji Zhengce Caozuo de Sikao" [Thoughts on the Operation of Macroeconomic Policy During the Last Two Years]. *Jingji Yanjiu* [Economic Research] 12 (1998): 3–12.

Chen, Guidi, and Wu Chuntao. "Target Hitting, Image Projects, and Others." *The Chinese Economy* 38, no. 3 (2005): 9–38.

Chen, Wei. "'Zhongguo Moshi Lun' zhi Fansi" [A Reassessment of the 'China Model']. *Beijing Spring,* January 31, 2011, http://beijingspring.com/bj2/2010/280/2011131221531.htm.

Chen, Yun. *Chen Yun Wenxuan: 1956–1985* [Selected Works of Chen Yun: 1956–1985]. Beijing: People's Publishing House, 1986.

Chen, Zhencheng. "Fangwu Gao Kongzhi Qianfu Fangdichan Weiji" [High Housing Vacancies Portend Property Crisis]. *Qiushi Lilun Wang,* August 5, 2010, http://www.qstheory.cn/jj/jjyj/201008/t20100805_41761.htm.

Cheng, Hang Sheng. "Great Leap Outward?" *Federal Reserve Bank of San Francisco Weekly Letter,* January 5, 1979, 1–3, http://www.frbsf.org/publications/economics/letter/1979/el79-01.pdf.

Cheng, Yuk-shing, and Tsang Shu-ki. "The Changing Grain Marketing System in China." *The China Quarterly* 140 (1994): 1080–1104.

China Bank Regulatory Commission. "Zhongguo Yinhangye Jiandu Guanli Weiyuanhui Guanyu Piaoju Yewu Fengxian Tishi de Jinji Tongzhi" [China Bank Regulatory Commission Urgent Notification on Risks in the Bills Industry]. Notification No. 10, 2006, http://96.0.18.183/a/fengxiankongzhi/fengxiantishi/2009/1228/726.html.

China Construction Bank. *Global Offering Prospectus.* 2005.

Chiu, Becky, and Mervyn K. Lewis. *Reforming China's State-Owned Enterprises and Banks.* Cheltenham: Edward Elgar, 2006.

Chung, Olivia. "Beijing Calls Halt to Vanity Projects." *Asia Times Online,* March 23, 2011, http://www.atimes.com/atimes/China_Business/MC23Cb01.html.

Cloud, Daniel. *The Lily: Evolution, Play, and the Power of a Free Society.* Baltimore: Laissez Faire Books, 2011.

Dammert, Alfredo J., and Chhabra, Jasbir G. S. "The Lead and Zinc Industries: Long-term Prospects." World Bank Staff Commodity Working Paper No. 22. Washington, DC: World Bank, 1990.

Dean, Robin, and Tobias Damm-Luhr. "A Current Review of Chinese Land-Use Law and Policy: A 'Breakthrough' in Rural Reform?" *UCLA Pacific Rim Law and Policy Journal* 19, no 1 (2010): 121–159, http://digital.law.washington.edu/dspace-law/bitstream/handle/1773.1/500/19PacRimL%26PolyJ121%282010%29.pdf?sequence= 3.

Delfs, Robert. "Economy: The Long, Long Road Back." *Far Eastern Economic Review*, no. 34, August 23, 1990, 38.

Demsetz, Harold. "Information and Efficiency: Another Viewpoint." *Journal of Law and Economics* 12 (1969): 1–22.

Dernberger, Robert F. "Radical Ideology and Economic Development in China: The Cultural Revolution and Its Impact on the Economy," in *Comparative Economic Systems: Models and Cases*, edited by Morris Bornstein, 349–366. Homewood, IL: Richard D. Irwin, 1974.

Dikotter, Frank. *Mao's Great Famine: The History of China's Most Devastating Catastrophe, 1958–1962*. New York: Walker & Co., 2010.

Ding, X. L. "The Illicit Asset Stripping of Chinese State Firms." *The China Journal* 43 (January 2000): 1–28.

Diyi Caijing Ribao [First Financial Daily]. "Yinhang Xindai You Bao You Yia: Yiyuefen Banyue Toufang Edu Jin 9000 Yi" [Bank Credit to Preserve While Suppressing: 900 Billion Released in First Half of January], January 23, 2009, http://money.163.com/09/0123/07/50B0M1SS0025288B.html.

Donnithorne, Audrey. "China's Cellular Economy: Some Economic Trends Since the Cultural Revolution." *China Quarterly* 52 (October/December 1972): 605–619.

Duihua Human Rights Journal. "Official Fear: Inside a Shuanggui Investigation Facility," July 5, 2011, http://www.duihuahrjournal.org/2011/07/official-fear-inside-shuanggui.html.

Eckstein, Alexander. *China's Economic Development: The Interplay of Scarcity and Ideology*. Ann Arbor: University of Michigan Press, 1976.

The Economist. "High Speed Rail in China: On the Wrong Track?" February 3, 2011, http://www.economist.com/blogs/gulliver/2011/02/high-speed_rail_china.

Ellman, Michael, and Kontorovich, Vladimir. "Overview," in *The Disintegration of the Soviet Economic System*, edited by Michael Ellman, and Vladimir Kontorovich, 1–39. London: Routledge, 1992.

Elvin, Mark. *The Retreat of the Elephants: An Environmental History of China*. New Haven: Yale University Press, 2004.

Engels, Frederick. *Socialism: Utopian and Scientific*. Marx/Engles Internet Archive, 2003, http://www.marxists.org/archive/marx/works/1880/soc-utop/.

Epoch Times. "Jingqiaoqiao de Dongguan he Dalu Jingji Zhuangkuang" [Silent Dongguan and the Mainland Economic Situation], May 25, 2009, http://hk.epochtimes.com/9/5/25/100368g.htm.

Fan, Gang, and Zhang Xiaojing. *Zenme You Guo Re Le? Xin Yilun Jingji Bodong yu Hongguan Tiaokong Fenxi* [Why Is There Overheating Yet Again? The New Round of Economic Fluctuation and an Analysis of Macroeconomic Adjustment]. Nanchang: Jiangxi People's Publishing House, 2004.

Feuerwerker, Albert. *China's Early Industrialization: Sheng Hsuan-Huai (1844–1916) and Mandarin Enterprise*. New York: Atheneum, 1970.

Finance.sina.com. "Xingxiang Gongcheng Keng Le Nongmin!" [Image Projects Defraud Farmers!], November 10, 2000, http://finance.sina.com.cn/2000-11-10/21921.html.

Freedom House. *Freedom in the World 2011—China,* June 17, 2011, http://www.unhcr.org/refworld/docid/4dfb658533.html.

Gao, Lu. "Achievements and Challenges: 30 Years of Housing Reform in the People's Republic of China." ADB Economics Working Paper Series No. 198. Manila: Asian Development Bank, April 2010, http://www.adb.org/Documents/Working-Papers/2010/Economics-WP198.pdf.

Gerlach, Christian. "Wu-Wei in Europe: A Study of Eurasian Economic Thought." London School of Economics Department of Economic History Working Paper 12/05, December 2005, http://www2.lse.ac.uk/economicHistory/Research/GEHN/GEHNPDF/WorkingPaper12CG.pdf.

Gong, Shengli. "Zhongguo Gaotie de 'Jushi Chuanqi' " [The Myth of China's 'World Beating' High-Speed Rail]. *Beijing Spring,* July 1, 2011, http://beijingspring.com/bj2/2010/140/201171160941.htm.

Gu, Yumin. *Dangdai Zhongguo Jingji Fazhan Yanjiu* [A Study of Economic Development in Contemporary China]. Shanghai: Tongji University Press, 1997.

Hayek, Friedrich. "The Use of Knowledge in Society." *American Economic Review* XXXV, no 4 (1945): 519–530, http://www.econlib.org/library/Essays/hykKnw1.html.

He, Jiangbin. "Yanghang Ling Shangye Yinhang Mingnian Zhuji Shangbao Xindai Jihua" [Central Bank Orders Commercial Banks to Submit Quarterly Credit Plans Next Year]. *Huaxia Times,* December 10, 2007, http://house.focus.cn/news/2007-12-10/406182.html.

He, Qinglian. *Xiandaihua de Xianjing: Dangdai Zhongguo de Jingji Shehui Wenti* [*Pitfalls of Modernization: Socioeconomic Problems in Contemporary China*]. Beijing: Jinri Zhongguo Press, 1998.

——"The Land-Enclosure Movement of the 1990s." *The Chinese Economy* 33, no 3 (2000): 57–88.

——" 'Land Enclosure Movement' Feeds Chinese Local Governments." *Epoch Times,* June 19, 2006, http://www.hlrn.org/img/violation/land%20enclosure%20movement,%20china.htm.

Heilmann, Sebastian. "Regulatory Innovation by Leninist Means: Communist Party Supervision in China's Financial Industry." *China Analysis* 38 (June 2004), 1–24, http://www.chinapolitik.de/studien/china_analysis/no_38.pdf.

Hilferding, Rudolf. *Finance Capital: A Study of the Latest Phase of Capitalist Development.* London: Routledge & Kegan Paul, 1981, http://www.marxists.org/archive/hilferding/1910/finkap/index.htm.

Hsu, Immanuel C. Y. *The Rise of Modern China.* Oxford: Oxford University Press, 2000.

Hu, Jintao. "Hold High the Great Banner of Socialism with Chinese Characteristics and Strive for New Victories in Building a Moderately Prosperous Society in All Respects." Report to the Seventeenth National Congress of the Communist Party of China, October 15, 2007, http://www.china.org.cn/english/congress/229611.htm.

Hu, Yongqi. "'Landmarks' Smear Image." *China Daily.com.cn,* June 23, 2010, http://www.chinadaily.com.cn/photo/2010-06/23/content_10071864.htm.

Huang, Yasheng. *Capitalism with Chinese Characteristics: Entrepreneurship and the State.* Cambridge: Cambridge University Press, 2008.

Huaxia Times. "Xindai Edu: Zuihou Yi Yue Hai Sheng 6600 Wan" [Credit Quotas: 66 Million Remains in the Final Month], December 18, 2011, http://stock.sohu.com/20111218/n329393181.shtml.

Hunter, William H. "Retort Zinc Production." November 2011, http://www.williamhunter.co.uk/ZINC/retort.htm.

I, Fan. "Industry, Communications and Transportation in Communist China, 1967," in *Communist China 1967*, Part 2, 1–47. Hong Kong: Union Research Institute, 1968.

——."Industries in Mainland China in 1969," in *Communist China 1969*, 271–342. Hong Kong: Union Research Institute, 1970.

Industrial and Commercial Bank of China. *Global Offering Prospectus.* 2006.

Jefferson, Gary H., Thomas G. Rawski, and Yuxin Zheng. "Chinese Industrial Productivity: Trends, Measurement and Recent Development." *Journal of Comparative Economics* 23 (1996): 146–180.

Jevons, William S. "Commercial Crises and Sun-Spots." *Nature* XIX (November 14, 1878): 33–37.

Jia, Yueqing. "A New Look at China's Output Fluctuations: Quarterly GDP Estimation with an Unobserved Components Approach." George Washington University Research Program on Forecasting. Working Paper No. 2011-006, 2011, http://www.gwu.edu/~forcpgm/2011–006.pdf.

Jin, Sanlin. "Chengben Ruanyueshu Shi Touzi Guore de Zhongyau Yuanyin" [Soft Budget Constraints Are an Important Cause of Investment Overheating]. *Zhongguo Touzi* [China Investment], June 2004, 37–39.

Kautsky, Karl. *The Dictatorship of the Proletariat.* Marxists Internet Archive, http://www.marxists.org/archive/kautsky/1918/dictprole/ch03.htm.

Keynes, John M. *The General Theory of Employment, Interest, and Money.* New York: Prometheus Books, 1997.

Knapp, Georg F. *The State Theory of Money.* London: Macmillan & Co., 1924.

Kolakowski, Leszek. *Main Currents of Marxism.* New York: W. W. Norton, 2005.

Kornai, Janos. "The Soft Budget Constraint." *Kyklos* 39, Fasc. 1 (1986): 3–30.

——*The Socialist System: The Political Economy of Communism.* Princeton, NJ: Princeton University Press, 1992.

Kwok, Vivian W. Y. "Weaknesses in Chinese Wind Power." *Forbes.com,* July 20, 2009, http://www.forbes.com/2009/07/20/china-wind-power-business-energy-china.html.

Lenin, Vladimir I. *Left Wing Communism: An Infantile Disorder.* Marxists.org, 1999, http://www.marxists.org/archive/lenin/works/1920/lwc/index.htm.

——"Report on the Work of the Council of People's Commissars." Address to the Eighth All-Russia Congress of Soviets, December 29, 1920. V. I. Lenin Internet Archive 2002a, http://www.marxists.org/archive/lenin/works/1920/8thcong/ch02.htm.

——."Five Years of the Russian Revolution and the Prospects of the World Revolution." Report to the Fourth Congress of the Communist International, November 13, 1922. V. I. Lenin Internet Archive 2002b, http://www.marxists.org/archive/lenin/works/1922/nov/04b.htm.

Ligthart, Ad. "The Cement Industry in China." Powerpoint presentation, 2003, http://www.cementdistribution.com/IndustryInfo/articles/cement_Industry_in_china.pdf.

Liu, Chengxiang. "1104 Gongcheng Shi Zhongguo Yinhangye Jianguan Fangshi de Gemingxing Gaige" [Project 1104 Is a Revolutionary Reform in Chinese Banking Supervision]. Address to the Seventh China City Commercial Banks Conference, Jinan, Shandong Province, June 3, 2006, http://www.zgjrw.com/News/200663/Scene/135913655700.shtml.

Liu, Dong. "Qita Zichan Fengxian Quanzhong Cong 0% Tizhi 100%" [Risk Weighting for Other Assets Raised from 0% to 100%]. *Diyi Caijing Ribao* [First Financial Daily], August 17, 2011, http://www.21cbh.com/HTML/2011-8-17/xNMzcyXzM1NzkxNg.html.

Liu, Suinian, and Wu Qungan. *China's Socialist Economy: An Outline History (1949–1984)*. Beijing: Beijing Review, 1986.

Liu, Xiaobo. *No Enemies, No Hatred*. London: Belknap Press, 2012.

Locke, John. *Two Treatises of Government*. London: Thomas Tegg, 1823.

Lucas, Robert E. "Expectations and the Neutrality of Money." *Journal of Economic Theory* 4 (1972): 103–124.

Luo, Changping. "City Image Building Lines Official Pockets." *Caijing.com.cn.*, October 30, 2008, http://english.caijing.com.cn/2008–10–30/110024617.html.

MacFarquhar, Roderick. *The Origins of the Cultural Revolution 2: The Great Leap Forward 1958–1960*. New York: Columbia University Press, 1983.

Mao, Zedong. "Examples of Dialectics." 1959, http://www.marxists.org/reference/archive/mao/selected-works/volume-8/mswv8_48.htm.

Marks, Robert B. *Tigers, Rice, Silk, and Silt: Environment and Economy in Late Imperial South China*. Cambridge: Cambridge University Press, 1998.

Marx, Karl. *Theories of Surplus Value*. 1863, http://www.marxists.org/archive/marx/works/1863/theories-surplus-value/index.htm.

Matosich, Andrew J., and Bonnie K. Matosich. "Machine Building: *Perestroika's* Sputtering Engine." *Soviet Economy* 4, no. 2 (1988): 144–176.

McGregor, James. "China's Drive for 'Indigenous Innovation': A Web of Industrial Policies." *US Chamber of Commerce*, July 28, 2010, http://www.uschamber.com/sites/default/files/reports/100728chinareport_0.pdf.

Meiri Jingji Xinwen [Daily Economic News]. "Difang Rongzi Pingtai Guanli Banfa Huo Benyuedi Chutai" [Administrative Measures on Local Financing Platforms May Come Out at the End of the Month], March 5, 2010, http://bank.hexun.com/2010-03-05/122864858.html.

Meng, Jianhua. *Zhongguo Huobi Zhengce de Xuanze yu Fazhan* [China's Monetary Policy Options and Development]. Beijing: China Finance Press, 2006.

Ministry of Industry and Information Technology. "Gongye he Xinxihua Bu Xiang Shehui Gonggau 18 ge Gongye Hangye Taotai Luohou Channeng Qiye

Mingdan" [Ministry of Industry and Information Technology Releases List of Enterprises in 18 Industrial Sectors with Obsolete Capacity to be Eliminated], August 8, 2010, http://www.miit.gov.cn/n11293472/n11293832/n13095885/13334343.html.

Mises, Ludwig Von. *Human Action: A Treatise on Economics* (Forth Revised Edition). San Francisco: Fox and Wilkes, 1996, http://mises.org/Books/humanaction.pdf.

——*Socialism: An Economic and Sociological Analysis*. New Haven: Yale University Press, 1951.

Nanfeng Magazine. "Shenme Shi 'Shuanggui'? Teshu de Zuzhi Cuoshi he Diaocha Shouduan" [What Is 'Shuanggui'? Special Organizational Methods and Interrogation Techniques], October 19, 2003, http://news.sina.com.cn/c/2003-10-19/11251998584.shtml.

National Audit Office. "Quanguo Difang Zhengfuxing Zhaiwu Shenji Jieguo" [Results of the Nationwide Audit of Local Government Debt]. No. 35, 2011.

National Bureau of Statistics. *Zhongguo Tongji Nianjian 1983* [China Statistical Yearbook 1983]. Hong Kong: Hong Kong Economic Weekly Publishing House, 1983.

——.*Zhongguo Maoyi Wujia Tongji Ziliao 1952–1983* [Statistical Materials on Trade and Prices in China 1952–1983]. Beijing: China Statistical Publishing House, 1984.

——.*Zhongguo Jingji Nianjian 1986* [Almanac of China's Economy 1986]. Beijing: Economic Management Publishing House, 1986.

——.*Zhongguo Tongji Nianjian 2011* [China Statistical Yearbook 2011]. Beijing: China Statistics Press, 2011.

National Development and Reform Commission. "Guowuyuan Guanyu Fabu Shishi 'Cujin Chanye Jiegou Tiaozheng Zhanxing Guiding' de Jueding" [State Council Decision on the Promulgation and Implementation of the 'Provisional Measures for Promoting the Adjustment of the Industrial Structure']. December 2, 2005a, http://tzs.ndrc.gov.cn/xkxmql/xkxmyj/t20051222_78940.htm.

——."Chanye Jiegou Tiaozheng Zhidao Mulu (2005 Ben)" [Index for Guiding the Adjustment of the Industrial Structure (2005 Edition)]. Document No. 40, December 2, 2005b, http://www.ndrc.gov.cn/zcfb/zcfbl/zcfbl2005/t20051222_54304.htm.

Naughton, Barry. "The Third Front: Defense Industrialization in the Chinese Interior." *The China Quarterly* 115 (September 1988): 351–386.

Newman, Philip C., Arthur D. Gayer, and Milton H. Spencer (editors). *Source Readings in Economic Thought*. New York: W. W. Norton, 1954.

Nie, Weizhu, and Huang Shixin. " 'Chaidan' Pingtaidai: Yinjianju Xingui Zhengsu Weigui Tudi Diya Daikuan" ['Defusing' Local Platform Loans: CBRC New Rules to Clean Up Illicit Land Mortgages]. *Diyi Caijing Ribao* [First Financial Daily], August 23, 2011, http://finance.eastmoney.com/news/1350,20110823157705979.html.

Nove, Alec. *An Economic History of the USSR*. London: Penguin Books, 1992.

O'Neil, Mark. "Zhou Zhengyi Has Lost His Best Friend." *Asia Sentinel,* February 20, 2007, http://www.asiasentinel.com/index.php?option= com_content&task=view&id= 384&Itemid= 31.

Peebles, Gavin. *Money in the People's Republic of China: A Comparative Perspective.* Sydney: Allen & Unwin, 1991.

Pei, Minxin. "China's Politics of the Economically Possible." *Project Syndicate,* March 16, 2012, http://www.project-syndicate.org/commentary/chinas-politics-of-the-economically-possible.

People's Bank of China. "Zhongguo Renmin Yinhang Huobi Zhengci Weiyuanhui Tiaolie" [People's Bank of China Monetary Policy Committee Regulations]. 2010a, http://www.pbc.gov.cn/publish/huobizhengceersi/3416/2010/20100914145905843679838/20100914145905843679838_.html.

———"China Monetary Policy Report Quarter Two, 2010." August 5, 2010b, http://www.pbc.gov.cn/image_public/UserFiles/english/upload/File/China%20Monetary%20Policy%20Report%20Quarter%20Two,%20 2010%20.pdf

People's Daily. "Quan Guo Yi Pan Qi" [The Whole Country as a Chess Board], February 24, 1959: 1–2.

Pingguo Ribao [Apple Daily]. "Shi Shei Guafen le 1.53 Wanyi Yuan?" [Who Divided Up the 1.53 Trillion Yuan?], February 17, 2009, http://beijingspring.com/c7/xw/zgbd/20090217191807.htm.

Polanyi, Michael. *The Tacit Dimension.* Garden City, NY: Doubleday, 1966.

Prybyla, Jan S. *The Political Economy of Communist China.* Scranton, PA: International Textbook Co., 1970.

Pye, Lucian. *The Mandarin and the Cadre: China's Political Cultures.* Ann Arbor: University of Michigan, 1988.

Qiu Shi [Seeking Truth]. "Zheng Xin-li: Jingji Fazhan Fangshi Zhong Zai Shixian 'Wu Da Zhuanbian' " [Zheng Xin-li: 'Five Great Transformations' Key to Mode of Economic Development], December 1, 2011, http://www.qstheory.cn/jj/201112/t20111201_127134.htm.

Rauch, Jason N., and Ying F. Chi. "The Plight of Green GDP in China." *Consilience: The Journal of Sustainable Development* 3, no. 1 (2010): 102–116, http://journals.cdrs.columbia.edu/consilience/index.php/consilience/article/view/112/28.

Rawski, Thomas G. "Measuring China's Recent GDP Growth: Where Do We Stand?" August 29, 2002, http://www.pitt.edu/~tgrawski/papers2002/measuring.pdf.

Ren, Junyin. *Jinrong Gaige Nandian Wenti Yanjiu* [A Study of Problems in Financial Reform]. Beijing: China Finance Press, 1992.

Riskin, Carl. "China's Rural Industries: Self-reliant Systems or Independent Kingdoms?" *China Quarterly* 73 (March 1978): 77–98.

Rodrik, Dani. "Getting Interventions Right: How South Korea and Taiwan Grew Rich." *Economic Policy* 10, no. 20 (1995): 53–107, http://isites.harvard.edu/fs/docs/icb.topic442978.files/Rodrik%20–%20How%20Korea%20and%20Taiwan%20grew%20rich.pdf.

Roubini Global Economics. "China's FX Reserves Break $3 Trillion: That's One Expensive Peg!" April 15, 2011, http://relooney.fatcow.com/SI_FAO-Asia/0_Important_117.pdf.

Rutkowski, Ryan. "China's Wind Power Has Faulty Connection." *Asia Times Online,* June 16, 2010, http://www.atimes.com/atimes/China_Business/LF16Cb03.html.

Samuelson, Paul A. "Interactions Between the Multiplier Analysis and the Principle of Acceleration." *Review of Economic Statistics* 21 (1939): 75–78.

Schumpeter, Joseph A. *Capitalism, Socialism, and Democracy.* New York: Harper & Brothers, 1947.

———. *Theory of Economic Development.* New Brunswick, NJ: Transaction Publishers, 1983.

Scott, James C. *Seeing Like a State: How Certain Schemes to Improve the Human Condition Have Failed.* New Haven: Yale University Press, 1998.

Sen, Amartya. *Development as Freedom.* New York: Anchor Books, 1999.

Sender, Henny. "Cooling Down Growth: Moves to Halt Excessive Investment." *Far Eastern Economic Review*, no. 35 (September 2, 1993), 36.

Serapio, Manolo. "Analysis: China Metals Curbs May End Up Boosting Smelting." *Reuters,* July 12, 2011, http://www.reuters.com/article/2011/07/12/businesspro-us-china-metals-capacity-idUSTRE76B22J20110712.

Shanghai Securities Times. "Kongzhi Yinhang Bu Liang Zichan: Jiu Da Hangye Xindai Shou Yan Kong" [Controlling Banks' Nonperforming Assets: Strict Controls on Credit to Nine Major Sectors], May 14, 2004, http://business.sohu.com/2004/05/14/01/article220120153.shtml.

———"Xindai Edu Qu Jin: Duo Jia Yinhang Yi Shangtiao Duo Xiang Daikuan Lilu" [Tight Credit Quotas: Many Banks Have Raised Interest Rates on a Variety of Loans], October 19, 2011, http://www.21cbh.com/HTML/2011-10-19/0NMzcxXzM3Mjc0Ng.html.

Shi, Hongxiu. "Honggaun Tiaokong: Zai Xian You Tizhi Xia Youxiao de Zhengce" [Macroeconomic Adjustment: Effective Policies Under the Present System], in *Zhongguo Hongguan Tiaokong Sanshi Nian* [Thirty Years of Macroeconomic Adjustment in China], edited by Wei Kang, 84–88. Beijing: Economic Science Press, 2008.

Shi, Jinfeng. "40 Jia Difang Jinrong Jigou Bei Shishi Chabie Cunzhunlu: Zui Gao Shang Fu 3%" [Differential Required Reserve Rates Applied to 40 Local Financial Institutions: Increases as High as 3%]. *21st Century Business Herald,* February 23, 2011, http://finance.sina.com.cn/roll/20110223/23289422481.shtml.

Shih, Victor C. *Factions and Finance in China: Elite Conflict and Inflation.* Cambridge: Cambridge University Press, 2008.

Smith, Graeme. "Political Machinations in a Rural County." *The China Journal* 62 (July 2009): 29–59, http://www.slideshare.net/sinocismblog/graeme-smith-bengha-county.

Song, Ning. "Bai Nian Qian de Shengchan Gongyi Women Reng Zai Yong" [We are Still Using Production Techniques from One Hundred Years Ago].

Zhongguo Huanjing Bao [China Environmental Times], October 12, 2009, http://www.ycwb.com/myjjb/2008-04/07/content_1854490.htm.

Sorokin, Gennady. "Patterns of Socialist Intensification." *The Soviet Review* XXIV (Winter 1983–84): 46–64.

Stalin, Joseph. *History of the Communist Party of the Soviet Union (Bolsheviks)*: *Short Course*. Marxists Internet Archive, 2008, http://www.marxists.org/reference/archive/stalin/works/1939/x01/index.htm.

Stansbury, Neill. "Exposing the Foundations of Corruption in Construction." *Transparency International Global Corruption Report*, 2005: 36–50, http://www.transparency.org/publications/gcr/gcr_2005.

Starr, John B. *Continuing the Revolution: The Political Thought of Mao*. Princeton, NJ: Princeton University of Press, 1979.

State Council. "Guowuyuan Guanyu Huanjing Baohu Ruogan Wenti de Jueding" [State Council Decision Regarding Various Environmental Protection Issues]. Document No. 31, August 6, 1996, http://www.zhb.gov.cn/epi-sepa/zcfg/w2/w2.htm.

———."Guanyu Angzhi Bufen Hangye Channeng Guosheng he Chongfu Jianshe Yindao Chanye Jiankang Fazhan Ruogan Yijian de Tongzhi" [Notification Concerning Recommendations on the Suppression of Excess Capacity and Redundant Construction in Certain Industries to Guide Healthy Industrial Development]. Document No. 38, 2009, http://www.sdpc.gov.cn/zcfb/zcfbqt/2010qt/t20100513_346554.htm.

Stein, Gregory M. "Acquiring Land Use Rights in Today's China: A Snapshot from on the Ground." *UCLA Pacific Basin Law Journal* 24, no 1 (2006): 1–50, http://ssrn.com/abstract= 942813.

Tan, Haojun. "Ba Cheng Minhang Jichang Kuisun Genyuan Hezai" [Why Eighty Percent of Civilian Airports Are Losing Money]. *Ifeng.com,* February 26, 2011, http://news.ifeng.com/opinion/society/detail_2011_02/26/4867585_0.shtml.

Tao, Ran, Lu Xi, Su Fu-bing, and Wang Hui. "Diqu Jingzheng Geju Yanbian Xia de Zhongguo Zhuangui: Caizheng Jidong he Fazhan Moshi Fansi" [China's Transition and Development Model Under Evolving Regional Competition Patterns]. *Jingji Yanjiu* [Economic Research] 7 (2009): 21–33.

Taylor, Michael. "Chinese Puzzle." *Far Eastern Economic Review*, no. 48 (November 29, 1990): 58.

Thomas, Elbert D. *Chinese Political Thought: A Study Based upon the Theories of the Principal Thinkers of the Chou Period*. New York: Prentice Hall, 1927.

Thorp, Frank H. *Outlines of Industrial Chemistry*. New York: Macmillan, 1916.

Tian, Ying, and Liao Zhaohui. "Hemou Jili yu Guoyou Shangye Yinhang Gaige" [Collusion and Reform in China's State-Owned Banks]. *Nankai Economic Studies* 2 (2006): 105–120.

Tikhonov, Nikolai. A. *Guidelines for the Economic and Social Development of the USSR for 1981–1985 and for the Period Ending in 1990*. Moscow: Novosti Press Agency Publishing House, 1981.

Unger, J. Marshall. *Fifth Generation Fallacy: Why Japan Is Betting Its Future on Artificial Intelligence*. New York: Oxford University Press, 1987.

Unirule Institute of Economics. "Guoyou Qiye de Xingzhi, Biaoxian yu Gaige" [The Nature, Performance, and Reform of the State-Owned Enterprises], 2011, http://www.unirule.org.cn/xiazai/2011/20110412.pdf.

Walter, Carl E., and Fraser J. T. Howie. *Red Capitalism: The Fragile Financial Foundation of China's Extraordinary Rise*. Singapore: Wiley & Sons, 2012.

Wan, Jie, and Miao Wenlong. "Guo Nei Wai Shangye Yinhang Caozuo Fengxian Xianzhuang Bijiao ji Chengyin Fenxi" [An Comparison of Current Operational Risk Management Conditions at Domestic and Foreign Banks and an Analysis of the Differences]. *Guoji Jinrong Yanjiu* [International Finance Research], 7 (2005): 10–15.

Wang, Bixue. "Wang Huai-bao Gao Xingxiang Gongcheng Gei Shei Kan?" [Who Is Wang Haui-bao's Image Project For?]. *Southcn.com*, September 2, 2002, http://www.southcn.com/news/china/gdspcn/200209020215.htm.

Wang, Fengjun. "11 Channeng Guosheng Hangye Feng Yu Yu Lai" [Trouble Ahead for 11 Excess Capacity Industries], *21st Century Business Herald*, December 31, 2005, http://finance.sina.com.cn/g/20051231/08192242742.shtml.

Wang, Haibo. *Zhonghua Renmin Gongheguo Gongye Jingji Shi* [Industrial Economic History of the People's Republic of China]. Taiyuan: Shanxi Economic Publishing House, 1998.

Wang, Jing. "Auditors Point to Widespread Insolvency in Liaoning Provincial Gov't Assets." *Caixin Online*, September 8, 2011, http://china-wire.org/?p=15605.

Wang, Lina. "Fangdichan Ye Hongguan Tiaokong Zhengce Tansuo" [An Exploration of the Real Estate Macroeconomic Adjustment Policy]. *China Finance* 15 (2004), 17–19.

Wang, Lu. "8% Baowei Zhan: Ciji Zhengci huo Ladong GDP Liangge Baifendian" [The Battle to Maintain 8%: The Stimulus Policy May Pull Up GDP by Two Percentage Points]. *21st Century Economic Herald*, November 11, 2008, http://www.doc88.com/p-035714823260.html.

Wang, Xi, Jiang Zhipeng, and Li Jia. "Zhuti Gongyuan Shengsi Zhenxiang" [The Reality Behind the Life and Death of Theme Parks]. *Liaowang Dongfang Zhoukan* [Oriental Outlook Weekly], September 21, 2009, http://www.news365.com.cn/wxpd/wz/myms/200909/t20090921_2471606.htm.

Wen, Xiu, Yang Na, Chen Huiying, Zhao Jingting, and Ma Yuan. "How China's Banks Risk Wealth Management Cash." *Caixin Online*, July 21, 2011, http://english.caixin.cn/2011-07-21/100282196.html.

Wen, Xiu, Zhang Yuzhe, Yu Ning, and Zheng Fei. "Trouble on the Highway." *Caixin Online*, June 29, 2011, http://english.caixin.cn/2011-06-29/100274315.html.

Wittfogel, Karl A. *Oriental Despotism: A Comparative Study of Total Power*. New Haven: Yale University Press, 1957.

World Bank. *China Quarterly Update,* March 2009, http://web.worldbank. org/WBSITE/EXTERNAL/COUNTRIES/EASTASIAPACIFICEXT/ CHINAEXTN/0,,contentMDK:22102737~pagePK:1497618~piPK:217 854~ theSitePK:318950,00.html.

World Bank and the Development Research Center of the State Council, People's Republic of China. *China 2030: Building a Modern, Harmonious, and Creative High-income Society.* Washington, DC: The World Bank, 2012.

Wu, Jianguo, and Wu Tong. "Green GDP," in *The Berkshire Encyclopedia of Sustainability, Vol. II–The Business of Sustainability,* 248–250. Great Barrington: Berkshire Publishing, 2010.

Wu, Yushan. "Wu Yinhang Shouxin 43 Yi Yuan Tieben Ju E Daikuan de Qian Qian Hou Hou" [Why Five Banks Extended Tieben an Enormous Loan of 4.3 Billion Yuan]. *21st Century Business Herald,* May 8, 2004, http://business. sohu.com/2004/05/08/52/article220045222.shtml.

Xie, Yanjun. "Henan Jiaotong Ting 'San Chao Yuan Lao' Tong Yanbai Wai Tao Zhi Mi" [The Mystery of Henan Transportation Department Head Tong Yanbai's Flight Abroad]. *Xinhuanet,* February 17, 2004, http://news. xinhuanet.com/legal/2004-02/17/content_1317006.htm.

Xu, Shousong. *Tieben Diaocha: Yige Minjian Gangtie Wangguo de Simang Baogao* [Investigating Tieben: A Report on the Death of a Private-Sector Steel Empire]. Guangzhou: Nanfang Rebao Publishing House, 2005.

Yang, Rudai, and Zhu, Shi E. "Gongping yu Xiaolu Bu Ke Jian De Ma? Jiyu Jumin Bianji Xiaofei Qingxiang de Yanjiu" [Can Equity and Efficiency Coexist? A Study of the Marginal Propensity to Consume]. *Jingji Yanjiu* [Economic Research] 12 (2007): 46–58.

Yang, Yue. "Closer Look: Tilting at Unconnected Windmills." *Caixin Online,* April 19, 2011, http://english.caing.com/2011-04-19/100250014.html.

Yangcheng Wanbao [Yangcheng Evening News]. "90/70 Zhengce: Sheng De Aimei, Si De Ganga" [The 90/70 Policy: Dubious Birth, Embarrassing Death], February 23, 2009, http://news.xinhuanet.com/politics/2009-02/23/ content_10875727.htm.

You, Xi. "9 Yue Mo 64 Jia Yinhang Rijun Cundai Bi Chaobiao: Liudongxing Fengxian Shangsheng" [Loan-deposit Ratios at 64 Banks Exceed the Limit at the End of September: Liquidity Risk Rises]. *Diyi Caijing Ribao* [First Financial Daily], December 13, 2011, http://www.21cbh.com/HTML/2011-12-13/4NMzcyXzM4NzY4Nw.html.

Yu, Bingbing. "Shanghai Nanjing Chengdu Deng Duoge Chengshi 70/90 Zhengce Didiao Tuichu" [70/90 Policy Unofficially Abandoned in Shanghai, Nanjing, Chengdu, and Many Other Cities]. *Shanghai Securities Times,* July 6, 2009, http://bj.house.sina.com.cn/news/2009-07-06/1056318875.html.

Yu, Ning, and Li, Zhigang. "Yinjianhui Teji Jingshi Piaoju Fengxian" [CBRC Urgently Warns on Bills Risk]. *Sina.com,* May 8, 2006, http://finance.sina. com.cn/bank/plyj/20060508/11432549016.shtml.

Zhan, Xiangyang, and Zheng Yanwen. "Chabie Cunkuan Zhunbeijin Lu Zhengci Toushe" [A Perspective on the Differential Reserve Rate Policy]. *China Finance* 5 (2011): 50–51.

Zhang, Guoyun. "Bu Heli de Touzi Tizhi Daozhi Chongfun Jianshe" [An Unreasonable Investment System Leads to Redundant Construction]. *Zhongguo Touzi* [*China Investment*], October 2003, 15.

Zhang, Jiawei. "Wind Power Factories Called 'Image Projects.'" *China Daily.com.cn,* March 10, 2010, http://www.chinadaily.com.cn/china/2010-03/10/content_9567436.htm.

Zhang, Tao, and Cheng Shuangqing. "Taotai Luohou Gangtie Channeng Jing Wan 'Zhangyanfa'" ['Cover Ups' and Game Playing in the Elimination of Obsolete Steel Capacity]. *Jingji Cankao Bao* [Economics Reference], December 19, 2007, http://jjckb.xinhuanet.com/jcsj/2007-12/19/content_78357.htm.

Zhang, Zili. *Houbi Shichang Yunzuo Shiyian Jiaocheng* [A Course on Money Market Operations]. Beijing: China Financial Publishing House, 2006.

Zhao, Dexin (Principal editor). *Zhonghua Renmin Gongheguo Jingji Shi: 1985–1991* [An Economic History of the People's Republic of China: 1985–1991]. Zhengzhou: Henan People's Press, 1999.

Zhong, Jiwen. "Shiliu Da Yilai Fanfu Changlian Chengxiao Mingxian: 3 Wan Yu Guanyuan Bei Zhuijiu" [Post Sixteenth Party Congress Anti-corruption Drive Has Evident Accomplishments: Over 30 Thousand Officials Investigated]. *Fazhi Ribao* [Legal Daily], September 29, 2005, http://news.xinhuanet.com/legal/2005-09/29/content_3561252.htm.

Zhongguo Huanjing Bao. "Jilei Bu Zu Fazhan Mangmu Taotai Bu Chedi: Zhongguo Shuini Channeng Guosheng" [Insufficient Accumulation, Blind Development, Incomplete Elimination: Excess Capacity for Chinese Cement], October 12, 2009, http://www.022net.com/2009/10-12/463432223116367.html.

Zhongguo Jingji Nianjian 1983 [Almanac of the Chinese Economy 1983]. Beijing: Economic Management Publishing House.

Zhongguo Jingji Nianjian 1986, 1991, 1996, 2001. Beijing: Economic Management Publishing House.

Zhou, Fang, and Le Yan. "Zhuti Gongyuan: Cong Yi Hong Er Shang Dao Jiti Daobi" [Theme Parks: From Everyone Rushing in Together to Mass Bankruptcy]. *Yifeng.com,* July 23, 2009, C:\Documents and Settings\Mark\My Documents\Book\Local projects\Theme parks IF2009.mht

Zhou, Li'an. "Jinsheng Boyi Zhong Zhengfu Guanyuan de Jili yu Hezuo" [Cooperation and Government Officials' Incentives in Promotion Competitions]. *Jingji Yanjiu* [Economic Research] 6 (2004): 33–40.

——."Zhongguo Difang Guanyuan de Jinsheng Jinbiaosai Moshi Yanjiu" [A Tournament Model of Local Government Official Promotions]. *Jingji Yanjiu* [Economic Research] 7 (2007): 36–50.

Zhou, Shulian, Tan Kewen, and Lin Senmu. "Jiben Jianshe Zhanxian Guo Chang de Wenti Weisheme Changqi Bu Neng Dedao Jiejue?" [Why Has the Long-Term Problem of the Overextended Basic Construction Front Remained Unresolved?] *Jingji Yanjiu* [Economic Research] 2 (1979): 12–18.

Zhou, Zhaopeng. "Zhengfu Jingji Tiaojie Zhineng yu Jiaqiang he Gaishan Hongguan Tiaokong" [The Role of Government in Economic Regulation and the Strengthening and Perfection of Macroeconomic Adjustment], in *Zhongguo Hongguan Tiaokong Sanshi Nian* [*Thirty Years of Macro-Economy Adjustment in China*], edited by Wei Kang, 1–15. Beijing: Economic Science Press, 2008.

Zi, Ping (ed). *Gaoceng Fuguan Caise Dangan* [Sex and Wealth Files of Corrupt High Officials]. Hong Kong: Huanqiu Shiye Publishing House, 2005.

Zoakos, Criton M. "In the Grip of China's Bear Hug: Berlin's Big Gamble with Germany's Economic Future." *The International Economy* XXIV, no. 4 (Fall 2010): 46–47.

INDEX

Printed and bound in Great Britain by
CPI Antony Rowe, Chippenham and Eastbourne

moot